WOMEN AS SINGLE PARENTS

WOMEN AS SINGLE PARENTS

Confronting Institutional Barriers in the Courts, the Workplace, and the Housing Market

Edited by

ELIZABETH A. MULROY
Boston University

Auburn House Publishing Company
Dover, Massachusetts

Library of Congress Cataloging in Publication Data

Women As Single Parents: confronting institutional barriers
in the courts, the workplace, and the housing market/edited
by Elizabeth Mulroy.
    p. cm.
  Bibliography: p.
  Includes index.
  ISBN 0-86569-176-2
  1. Single-parent family—United States. 2. Single mothers—United
States. 3. Family policy—United States. I. Mulroy, Elizabeth.
HQ759.915.S53 1988
306.8'56—dc19   88-11920
                                                       CIP

CONTENTS

Experiencing Single Parenthood

CHAPTER 3

Gender Bias in the Courts
Lynn Hecht Schafran

CHAPTER 4

Restructuring Family Life
Frances Smalls Caple

PART III

A Call for Federal and State Action   165

CHAPTER 7

The Role of the Courts in Welfare Reform   167
Barbara Sard

CHAPTER 8

Federal Policy-making and Family Issues   203
Anne L. Radigan

PREFACE

Current trends suggest that the single-parent family is not a transitory phase between marriages but is a family form here to stay. The lowered socioeconomic status of women who are single parents is raising serious equity questions concerning the distribution of goods and services to women and children in America. This new dilemma is challenging fundamental assumptions and values concerning the role of the state in determining, and then in meeting, levels of basic human need for the most vulnerable among us.

Most books written about families and children assume a nuclear family structure. Single-parent families are rarely discussed in depth, reflecting the research findings and conventional wisdom of the mid-1970s that the female-headed family was a transitional, deviant state. Books about poverty most often concentrate only on the public welfare system and view women as Aid to Families with Dependent Children (AFDC) recipients. This book approaches the subject of women as single parents in the context of their social environment. The authors investigate how single mothers try to access several sources of income such as child support, wages, in-kind housing benefits, and public welfare benefits, and they analyze the meaning of their experiences for shelter options and social policy.

This book evolved out of my own research over the past three years on single mothers and their housing needs. Some of the findings demonstrated that single mothers were vulnerable on many fronts, not just in terms of their housing. Their serious efforts to shelter their children were thwarted by low income, by personal constraints, and by institutional barriers that extended far beyond supply and demand factors in the private housing market.

Affordable shelter is a first line of defense against the forces pushing people toward poverty. But affordable shelter for families at the margins has become increasingly scarce. The growing numbers of single mothers and children who are now living among the homeless in our cities and towns point to a poverty-housing crisis in an era of perceived economic prosperity. Homelessness among families headed by single mothers is a tip-of-the-iceberg warning of a poverty-housing crisis which exists for most single mothers whose incomes have plummeted after marital dissolution. A 75 percent cutback in federal housing programs in the past eight years, the reduced supply of rental units in the private market, and low income from meager or no child support payments, low wages, and very low AFDC benefits have all contributed to the poverty-shelter nexus for single mothers. We have attempted to call attention to the interrelationship of these factors and to the need for a comprehensive, interdisciplinary analysis of possible solutions.

The literature on women and poverty is growing. Most studies rely on quantitative data derived from large data sets. What is now needed is qualitative research that will flesh out the statistics and will seek to explain the perspective of single mothers themselves. This perspective needs to be heard. *Women As Single Parents* has taken up that challenge. The contributing authors have conducted scholarly research and have spent many years in direct professional practice with groups or agencies that serve the poor; they also have first-hand knowledge of the administrative structures with which single mothers interact. Using these dual vantage points, they present their research findings in a manner that will help to bridge the gap between theory and practice. We hope that these efforts will provide a beneficial and stimulating resource for our intended readers—students, practitioners, and policymakers.

Boston   ELIZABETH A. MULROY
August 1988

ACKNOWLEDGMENTS

A debt of gratitude is owed to the single mothers who were interviewed by the various contributors and whose lives this book is about. Despite our intrusion into their daily struggles, they responded with dignity. They have our deepest respect and admiration.

This book was made possible by the sustained help of colleagues, family, and many friends. I thank our authors for sharing their fresh ideas, their research, and their wealth of practice-based experience. Their cooperation in making suggested revisions is appreciated, as we worked to develop a conceptual cohesiveness to the book. Bill Baer and Jon Pynoos of the University of Southern California School of Urban and Regional Planning have been consistently supportive of the project from the beginning and have generously shared their time and thoughts to critique manuscript revisions. Richard Bolan and Eugenie Ladner Birch were immensely helpful in the early stages of framing the research and sharpening the focus. Assistance in conducting Section 8 housing research in the field was ably provided by Alan Feldman, Steve Dubuque, Chris Harrison Spaulding, Bill Riley, and Bill Heggerty.

I owe an intellectual debt to the late John W. Dyckman. His untimely death was not only a major loss to the planning profession but a personal loss of my mentor, colleague, and friend.

This book could not have been completed during this past year without the support of many colleagues at Boston University School of Social Work. Dean Hubie Jones not only provided the necessary institutional support but, by his own example, challenged us all to question traditional social welfare policies and the institutions in American culture which reinforce them. Many colleagues have been generous with their time, encouragement, and exchange of ideas, especially Carolyn Dillon, Judith Gonyea, Rob Hudson, Brad Googins, Melvin Delgado, Lee Staples, and Don Oellerich. Ric Plaisance graciously typed countless versions of the manuscript and ably assisted in tying up administrative loose ends.

I am grateful to John Harney, at Auburn House, for his initial interest and enthusiasm for this project, and for his and Eugene Bailey's patience and encouragement throughout the process of bringing it to completion. I owe a special debt to Margaret Kearney for the confidence she expressed in the project all along and for her numerous constructive editorial suggestions on substance and style which made the final manuscript more cohesive.

Finally, I am grateful for the contributions and sacrifices made by my family, who provided an environment of love, understanding, and support. I especially thank my mother, Dorothy, who read every page of the manuscript with interest and attention to detail; my son, Andy, who provided technical wizardry with the recalcitrant word processor; and my daughter, Adrienne, who provided constant moral support.

ELIZABETH A. MULROY

ABOUT THE EDITOR

Elizabeth A. Mulroy, a social worker and urban planner, teaches social policy, planning, and management at Boston University School of Social Work, where she is also Director of the Human Services Management Program. A graduate of Simmons College, she holds M.S.W. and Ph.D. degrees from the University of Southern California. Her most recent research is on single mothers and housing, management of social programs, and organizational change. She has served as administrative assistant to former U.S. Congresswoman Margaret Heckler (R-Mass.), has lectured extensively on urban planning and the changing family, and has served as a consultant in housing management, planning, and human services for families and children.

ABOUT THE CONTRIBUTORS

Teresa Amott, who holds a Ph.D. in Economics from Boston College, specializes in labor economics and social policy affecting the poor. She is currently a professor at the University of Massachusetts at Boston, has published several articles on women and the economy, and is a member of the editorial collective of *Dollars and Sense* magazine. For the past 10 years she has worked with a variety of women's groups, labor unions, and grassroots organizations to develop strategies for achieving economic justice. During the 1988 presidential campaign, she served as advisor on family policy to Democratic candidate Jesse Jackson.

Frances Smalls Caple teaches Human Behavior in the Social Environment and Family Practice in the School of Social Work at the University of Southern California. She is also a licensed clinical social worker engaged in direct practice with families and children; in teaching practitioners how to work with families and children; and in staff training and development for public schools, mental health clinics, and Head Start programs. She received her M.S.W. and Ph.D. degrees from the University of Southern California. Her current research interests are in black children and school failure, and the relationships between families, schools, and communities.

Anne L. Radigan served as Director of the Congressional Caucus for Women's Issues during the 98th and 99th Congressional sessions. She organized and coordinated introduction of the 22-point Economic Equity Act of 1985 and the national parental leave bill introduced by United States Congresswoman Patricia Schroeder (D-Colo.), Olympia J. Snowe (R-Maine), and numerous Congressional co-sponsors. A graduate of the University of Connecticut, she previously served as legislative assistant to United States Representative Toby Moffett (D-Ct.). She is currently a freelance writer specializing in women's issues.

Barbara Sard, a graduate of Radcliffe College and Harvard Law School, is Managing Attorney of the Income Maintenance Unit at Greater Boston Legal Services. She has been a welfare lawyer for more than 10 years, and is also a Lecturer at Harvard Law School where she teaches a course entitled "Welfare Law: Perspectives from Practice." She is lead counsel in the recently victorious *Massachusetts Coalition for the Homeless vs. Secretary of Human Services* case, in which the Massachusetts Supreme Judicial Court declared that Massachusetts executive officials have the duty to pay AFDC benefits sufficient to keep families in their own homes.

Lynn Hecht Schafran is an attorney and Director of the National Judicial Education Program to Promote Equality for Women and Men in the Courts, a project of the NOW Legal Defense and Education Fund in cooperation with the National Association of Women Judges. A graduate of Smith College and Columbia Law School, she is a member of the New Jersey Supreme Court Task Force on Women in the Courts and more than a dozen other task forces on gender bias in the courts now in operation throughout the country. Ms. Schafran is Special Counsel to the New York City Commission on the Status of Women, a member of the American Bar Association Commission on Women in the Profession, and immediate past chair of the Committee on Sex and Law of the Association of the Bar of the City of New York.

Frank I. Smizik has been a legal services attorney for more than 15 years. He is currently a housing lawyer at the Massachusetts

Law Reform Institute. A graduate of the University of Pittsburgh and Duquesne Law School, he has written articles on condominium conversion law and tenants' rights and inclusionary zoning and public/private displacement. He also chairs the Board of Commissioners of the Brookline (Mass.) Housing Authority.

Michael E. Stone is a professor of community planning and social policy at the University of Massachusetts at Boston and is a specialist on progressive housing policy. He graduated from UCLA and holds a Ph.D. from Princeton. Professor Stone's research interests include housing affordability and housing finance, preservation of subsidized housing, anti-displacement strategies, and arson prevention—topics on which he has written extensively. He frequently provides research and expert testimony in major law suits. He authored "Housing & the Dynamics of U.S. Capitalism" in *Critical Perspectives on Housing*, which is widely cited in the debate over federal housing policy. For nearly two decades he has provided technical assistance to community-based and advocacy groups concerned with housing affordability.

Part I

BACKGROUND

Chapter 1

INTRODUCTION

Elizabeth A. Mulroy

Interest in family life and public and private efforts to preserve "traditional" American family values are currently among the nation's most controversial issues. The debate is fueled by diversity in family form, including the increase in formation of single-parent families, one of the most dramatic changes in family composition during the last 25 years. Consider these statistics:

- There were a record 8.9 million single-parent families in 1986—26 percent of the 33.9 million families with children under age 18 at home.
- By 1986, 14.8 million children under age 18, or 24 percent, lived with only one parent, compared with 9 percent in 1960 and 12 percent in 1970.
- Between 1960 and 1982 the fraction of black children under the age of 3 who were not living with both parents rose from 30 to 60 percent.
- Nine out of 10 children in single-parent families reside in households headed by their mother.[1]

The single-parent family phenomenon, then, is primarily about households headed by single mothers with minor children. In *The New American Poverty*, Michael Harrington observed that poverty in the 1980s is more intransigent than the old, and that low-income single mothers and their children are a part of it. Persons in female-headed households, usually children, comprise the highest percentage of persons living below the poverty level in the United States. Moreover, they are twice as likely as other households in

3

the United States to have a housing problem. Single mothers are the most problem-ridden group among those living in substandard shelter in the United States.[2] Moreover, homelessness among families in affluent America in the 1980s has become a national disgrace. While definitions and precise measurement of homelessness are difficult to determine, a national 29-city survey conducted by the U.S. Conference of Mayors in 1987 found that two-thirds of all homeless families in America were headed by single parents.[3]

Myths about Single Mothers

Over the past decade, myths about single mothers have emerged, built on an ideology and historical theme of poverty as a moral issue. First, many assume that a low-income, separated, or divorced woman raising children alone is single by choice, discounting a man's decision to leave a household with unsupported children.

Second, many believe that mothers can pull themselves up out of poverty if only they would accept gainful employment in the market economy and work hard. Those excused from the work ethic are the elderly, the disabled, and children who comprise clearly identifiable categories of the "worthy" poor, deserving of social welfare benefits and society's largesse. The assumption is that single mothers with minor children are able-bodied adults who can make a rational, conscious decision to work or not to work outside the home, that they willingly choose not to work, and that their circumstances remain static over time. Therefore, mothers who turn to public welfare for their source of income are presumed to be lazy, living off the public trough, and in effect "unworthy." In addition, single mothers who receive public assistance but have never been married are branded "immoral."

Third, many argue that opportunity is endless and freedom of choice abounds for everyone in American society—not only employment opportunities but also decisions about where families will live. Therefore, the fact that poor minority families are often clustered in deteriorating central city neighborhoods is interpreted to mean that they remain there by choice, primarily for the low rent and to be near "their own kind."

These stereotypes are sweeping generalizations that ignore the diversity within the single-parent family population and the complexity of the forces that bear on the decision making in these families. In sum, these stereotypes ignore the realities experienced by single-parent families.

Myths as Recurring Images

Such myths are often reinforced through recurring images of single mothers in the media. One image is that of "Supermom" who is doing it all: She is usually portrayed as working in an attractive white-collar job, earning a good income that supports home-based child care or a live-in housekeeper. Invariably she is white, lives in a well-appointed, well-maintained suburban single-family home, and has time for quality parenting in the evening and an active social life.

An alternative image is that of the poor single mother, usually a woman of color, who may leave her children without adult super-vised child care while she works (often a night shift), or is on a brief errand. Should an accident or injury occur when she is away, her image is that of the neglectful parent. Yet across America when applications are made to establish neighborhood child care centers to meet the need, community resistance frequently emerges to deny these permits based on technical rationale: increased traffic, noise, or zoning restrictions. When the single mother then stays home to provide full-time supervision of her children and needs to rely on public assistance in order to do it, she is branded as unmotivated.

Images of the white single mother of means and the stereotypical low-income single mother of color both perpetuate injurious myths about single motherhood in that they cause observers to make superficial judgments: Any single mother can be a successful American consumer and "make it" on her own if she is in the work force; or, if she is at home and on AFDC, she is not a good mother. An underlying issue is the extent to which both images challenge the ideal of American domesticity. For example, there is deviance from widely held images of family life which include the idealized model of a breadwinner father and a housewife mother who follow prescribed and understandable roles. Even though the single-parent family in the first image is perceived to be economically secure, neither family form has a male head of household, making the concept of single parenthood itself threatening in a patriarchal society. Therefore, not only do these recurring stereotypical im-ages create a false impression of who single mothers are and what single motherhood is like, but they have subliminal power to cloud the debate over what families headed by single mothers really need.

Diversity in Family Form: What Is a Family?

As the 1980s wane and America turns the corner of a new decade, the nuclear family form has not lost its role in nurturing and strengthening its individual family members. Rather, we need to recognize that a diversity of family forms has emerged in what now is a postnuclear family age.

For example, advances in biotechnology have created reproductive alternatives such as artificial insemination, which, when combined with the legal arrangements of surrogate parenthood, are challenging fundamental assumptions about how a family should be defined. Is surrogate motherhood a humane solution to family formation for infertile couples, or is it rent-a-womb exploitation of a class of women who have been victims of sexual exploitation for centuries? Could the surrogate "natural" mother, and "her" child comprise a family? Or should the family be formed only by the "natural" father, his wife, and "his" child? Moreover, scientific and technical innovations in genetic engineering and organ transplantation are stretching the realm of what is "natural" to new levels of complexity.

During the past two decades, alternative households have formed as women and men lived together as couples, brought children into the world and raised them, yet never married. Also, gays and lesbians are more openly expressing their sexual orientation. When two homosexuals in a loving relationship live together in a household unit that may include children from a previous heterosexual marriage, is a family formed?

The scope of all these departures from traditional family form is creating profound family policy issues for the 1990s. Such changes are pushing on the boundaries of our moral and ethical guidance systems, leaving extraordinary legal and public policy dilemmas with which society must struggle. The household headed by a single mother, then, is not the only form to depart from the traditional model. The main point is that the family headed by a single mother is a viable family form that also has the potential for nurturing and strengthening individual family members if there are supportive—not antagonistic—public and private institutional structures through which it can meet its basic human needs.

Debate Over Social Programs

Some important social policy issues on federal and state legislative agendas that affect the well-being of single-parent families headed by mothers with minor children are welfare reform, child support, pay equity, child care, health care, social services, affordable housing, and family/workplace issues such as parental leave. In a policy-making climate that is trying to reduce the federal deficit by cutting domestic social programs, important decisions are being made with little knowledge about the needs of low-income single-parent families or the interactive effects of program cuts on family life.

Decisions will be made about the nature of social welfare programs, about their level of funding, and about how they will be implemented locally. As in the past, the goals established for social welfare programs reflect societal values and attitudes as to who is needy and who is not. They also reflect a piecemeal, fragmented approach that has resulted in the absence of a national goal in support of a coherent family policy. Axinn and Levin point out that "the family is the basic organizing device of modern society and that all social policy decisions impinge on family well-being. In this sense, then, social policy and family policy are essentially one."[4]

Critics on the right argue that government has already spent too much on social programs since the 1960s. They argue that availability of social programs themselves is what increases welfare dependency by stifling personal responsibility and initiative. Murray proposes "scrapping the entire federal welfare and income support structure for working-aged persons, including AFDC, Medicaid, Food Stamps, Unemployment Insurance, Workers' Compensation, subsidized housing, disability insurance, and the rest. It would leave the working-aged person with no recourse whatsoever except the job market, family members, friends, and public or private locally funded services."[5] Critics on the left contend that such arguments ignore large-scale economic dislocations and divergent class interests of capitalism: "What has been momentarily forgotten in the disarray created by the conservative attack, is that the welfare state is the only defense many people have against the vicissitudes of the market economy."[6]

Perceptions of the family and theories about causation of their poverty are at the center of these political debates. This book will investigate the realities of family life among single mothers with minor children so that more informed policy decisions that profoundly affect them can be made.

Focus of the Book: Reality of Single-Parent Families' Lives

The purpose of this book is to refute the myths surrounding single mothers and to inject *reality* into the social policy debate. It will provide a window on single parenthood by examining how single mothers perceive their world and how they organize their lives.

Women with minor children who become heads of household absorb dual gender roles. They are responsible for providing (1) household income and shelter and (2) housekeeping, child raising, and caregiving. Assumption of dual gender roles creates changes and stresses both in the internal family system and in its relationship with institutions in the external environment.

The household undergoing changes in family composition, particularly the loss of the spouse/father, is vulnerable to economic insecurity and bouts of short-term, if not long-term, poverty and residential mobility. Simultaneously, the family experiences changing relationships with public and private institutions in the external environment, including schools, employers, public welfare agencies, the courts, and landlords. More specifically, this book is about the impact of *all* these interactions on the lives of single-parent families. Implications will be drawn for social welfare policy, and implementation strategies will be recommended to bring about progressive social change.

Others have examined theories of poverty and have critiqued the effects of public welfare policies on women and children.[7] In addition to public welfare policies, well-being of single parent families is also influenced by judicial decisions in family courts, economic policies, employment practices, housing policies and rental practices. Therefore, this volume approaches the single-parent family phenomenon from an interdisciplinary perspective, drawing on the expertise of academics and practitioners in fields of law, social work, urban planning, housing, economics, and public policy.

Guide to the Book

The book is divided into three parts. In Part I, Background, Elizabeth Mulroy introduces in Chapter 1 the contemporary dilemma of the single-parent phenomenon. In Chapter 2, Mulroy examines the changes in American family life that have contributed to the single-parent phenomenon and the impacts of changing family form on the well-being of single mothers in three areas: their economic status, their "packaging" of income supports from a variety of sources, and their housing needs. This approach draws implications for the spatial distribution of single mothers in the marketplace in terms of their urban/suburban location, housing costs and quality, and their levels and sources of income—themes on which subsequent chapters are based.

Part II, Experiencing Single Parenthood, contains four chapters that explore the single-parent phenomenon and illuminate a diverse range of experiences single mothers have with the court system, with restructuring their family life, with the labor market, and with their search for affordable housing. Chapter 3 addresses a topic about which very little was previously known—gender bias in the courts. Lynn Hecht Schafran depicts a court system that is difficult and expensive to navigate. She argues that gender bias creates problems for women in the courts, particularly single mothers. Gender bias encompasses stereotyped thinking about the nature of roles of women and men, society's perception of the value of women and men and what is perceived as women's and men's work, and myths and misconceptions about the economic and social realities of women's and men's lives. She describes how gender bias in the courts impacts those areas of the law that affect women in their status as single mothers: divorce, including access to the courts, property division, and alimony; child support; domestic violence; and custody.

In Chapter 4, Frances Caple analyzes single-parent family life as a social system. She examines theoretical constructs pertaining to family processes in all family types, including the two-parent family. Caple postulates that the family system is not an independent unit but is part of a dependent, interactive system with others in its external environment. Therefore, attempts at internal family restructuring, adaptation, and strengthening after separation and divorce, for example, are dependent not only on internal family resources, but also on availability and access to supportive services in neighborhood and community-based institutions where single-parent families live.

In Chapter 5, Teresa Amott challenges the assumption of current social policy that paid employment will end poor women's need for government support. Through a careful analysis of statistical data, Amott identifies barriers to labor force participation for single mothers that prevent attainment of a "family wage": occupational segregation; existence of a dual labor market; high child care costs; and part-time, part-year work. She then analyzes some of the new social policy initiatives, including child support collection, welfare-to-work programs, and impacts of the Omnibus Budget Reconciliation Act. Amott concludes that neither labor market income nor public assistance at current levels can adequately support single mothers and their children. She recommends social policy changes that will expand their opportunities to attain a "family wage."

Chapter 6 addresses a problem of basic concern to nearly all low- and moderate-income households, and to single mothers in particular—finding affordable housing. Elizabeth Mulroy presents findings from her study of single mothers who tried to find affordable housing in the tight Massachusetts private rental market using the Section 8/Existing Rental Assistance Program. This federal rent subsidy approach is considered to be one of the more valuable housing resources available to low-income households. Mulroy's study of housing search and housing choice identifies how single mothers organize and carry out their search; how they negotiate discriminatory landlord barriers; and what personal, environmental, and regulatory factors help and hinder their participation in the rent subsidy program. She concludes that social factors, in addition to cost, motivate single mothers to seek Section 8 Rental Assistance as a broad-based housing resource. Therefore, in the sample studied, the program had trouble meeting the housing needs of many minority low-income single mothers because their housing problems were set in larger systems of discrimination and poverty which the Section 8 program does not address.

Part III, A Call for Federal and State Action, focuses on three different strategies for institutional change that can be instrumental in improving the well-being of single-mother households: welfare reform through litigation, congressional policy-making, and state right-to-housing amendments. Since the late 1960s and the welfare rights movement, successful affirmative litigation efforts have expanded welfare benefits through court action. In Chapter 7, Barbara Sard addresses the role of the courts in welfare reform. First she analyzes historical precedents and legal issues which set the stage for welfare litigation; then she outlines how state courts and state laws can be utilized to help achieve adequate welfare benefits. To explain how this can be accomplished, Sard presents events leading up to the 1987 landmark decision of the Massachusetts Supreme Judicial Court declaring the right under state law of needy families to receive a level of welfare benefits or other assistance sufficient to enable them to live in permanent housing. Using the *Massachusetts Coalition for the Homeless* v. *Secretary of Human Services* as a case study, Sard details how judicial decision-making can accomplish social change in combination with social movements or political coalitions.

Chapter 8 examines how the congressional policy-making process responds to the documented need for family/workplace programs. Anne Radigan uses the Child Support Enforcement Amendments of 1984, which became law, and the Federal Equitable Pay Practices Act, which failed to become law, as case studies that delineate how interests of concern to single-parent families do and do not become public policy. She argues that because of its broad-based agenda and cumbersome process, Congress will continue to make decisions in a fragmented, sporadic way, with only incremental gains achieved. She concludes that social change will come only from formation of a broad political agenda for "family issues," supported by bipartisan political coalitions.

In Chapter 9 Frank Smizik and Michael Stone address the affordable housing crisis by recommending a right-to-housing amendment to a state constitution. First, they argue that housing is a basic need, which should be a constitutional right. Then, using the Massachusetts Right to Housing Project as an example, Smizik and Stone demonstrate how "right to housing" can increase housing opportunities through state and local action and expand housing choices for single-parent households.

In Chapter 10, the final chapter, Elizabeth Mulroy draws some conclusions from the lively and provocative themes presented by the contributors. She argues that single mothers are role-burdened by a multiplicity of responsibilities of solo-parenthood, which are exacerbated by unresponsive institutions with which single parent families interact. She calls for increased economic and social opportunities for single-parent families, especially for people of color; for an improved policy-making process; and for greater attention to equitable implementation plans and practices within administrative structures.

Endnotes

1. Statistics drawn from U.S. Bureau of the Census, "Household and Family Characteristics: March 1986," *Current Population Reports*, ser. P-20, no. 419 (Washington, D.C.: U.S. Government Printing Office, 1987), Table F; U.S. Bureau of the Census, "Marital Status and Living Arrangements: March 1985," *Current Population Reports*, ser. P-20, no. 410 (Washington, D.C.: U.S. Government Printing Office, 1986); Mary Jo Bane and David Ellwood, "Single Mothers and Their Living Arrangements," Harvard University study prepared for the Department of Health and Human Services, Cambridge, Mass., 1984.

2. Eugenie Birch, "The Unsheltered Woman: Definitions and Needs," in *The Unsheltered Woman: Women and Housing in the 1980's*, ed. Eugenie Birch (New Brunswick, N.J.: Center for Urban Policy Research, 1985), p. 35.

3. *A Status Report on Homeless Families in America's Cities* (Washington, D.C.: U.S. Conference of Mayors, May 1987).

4. June Axinn and Herman Levin, *Social Welfare: A History of the American Response to Need* (White Plains, N.Y.: Longman, 1982), p. 2.

5. Charles Murray, *Losing Ground* (New York: Basic Books, 1984), pp. 227–28.

6. Fred Block, Richard Cloward, Barbara Ehrenreich, Frances Fox Piven, *The Mean Season: The Attack on the Welfare State* (New York: Pantheon Books 1987), p. ix.

7. See, for example, Sheldon Danziger and Daniel Weinberg (eds.), *Fighting Poverty: What Works and What Doesn't* (Cambridge: Harvard University Press, 1986); Mimi Abrahamovitz, *Regulating the Lives of Women* (Edison, N.J.: South End Press, 1988); Ruth Sidel, *Women and Children Last* (New York: Viking-Penguin, 1986); Irwin Garfinkel and Sara McLanahan, *Single Mothers and Their Children* (Washington, D.C.: Urban Institute Press, 1986); Michael Harrington, *The New American Poverty* (New York: Penguin, 1984).

Chapter 2

WHO ARE SINGLE-PARENT FAMILIES AND WHERE DO THEY LIVE?

Elizabeth A. Mulroy

Like most American households, single-parent families are a diverse population in terms of the ages of household head, the level of household income, and the location of their residence. However, the prevalence of single mothers who are poor within this demographic group and the problems poverty brings to children in particular raise serious questions about why family form is changing, the conditions under which single-parent mothers are living, and what can be done about it.

This chapter focuses on three themes: (1) the growth in female headship, (2) the impact of single motherhood on economic and social well-being, and (3) housing conditions and shelter needs. Further reference to single-parent families in this chapter will mean households headed by single mothers with minor children.

> **Example 1:** Deborah and her two young children have an uncertain financial future. Deborah is 29 years old, and her children are ages 8 and 4. They live in a small town in the Northeast. She married at 20, and within a year gave birth to the couple's first child. For the next several years she was employed, in addition to taking care of her growing family. Both she and her husband worked, yet their combined household income was $9,300. Three years ago they divorced. Deborah did not receive child support because her husband was not making much money. She turned to

public welfare and received $491 per month through the Aid to Families with Dependent Children (AFDC) program.

Within a year Deborah's ex-husband got a good union job, and Deborah thought he should pay child support. He refused to do so voluntarily, so Deborah went to court. It took two years, but eventually the judge ordered the children's father to pay $440 per month in child support directly to Deborah.

Deborah applied for several jobs. When she first went on welfare, she also applied for federal housing assistance through the Section 8 rent subsidy program. Her waiting list number came up for subsidized housing, she got the housing certificate, and she found a two-bedroom apartment to rent with the subsidy that she thought would meet Section 8 housing code standards. Good fortune struck again. She got one of the jobs she had applied for, and it paid about $190 per week after taxes. When combined with child support, she anticipated receiving a total monthly household income of about $1,200. This income level gave her and the children the economic independence they needed. She had succeeded in working her way off welfare.

Deborah's rent and utilities totaled $640.00, or 53 percent of her monthly income. She felt she was stretching the budget too tight, but the rent was moderate for the market and there were very few vacancies from which to choose. Deborah's annual income for a family of three still qualified her for the Section 8 rent subsidy. However, because her income level had risen since she had applied for rental assistance, she believed that taking responsibility for housing her family on her own without government help was the right thing to do. She signed the lease and moved into the apartment without benefit of housing assistance.

Six months later she got a layoff notice at work. Simultaneously, her ex-husband, who by now had been paying his full child support obligation for six months, threatened to pay a lesser amount. Knowing how difficult it was to get a child support order in the first place, she believed he would make good on his threats. All of the family's sources of income unraveled at once. Deborah feared that she would be evicted from her apartment because she could no longer pay the rent, had no savings, and could not get her housing subsidy back. When she gave up the certificate six months before, she had forfeited her chances. She would have to reapply for subsidized housing, go to the bottom of the waiting list, and wait for at least three years. She went looking for another job but did not get one.

Deborah's period of relative economic independence was short-lived. She is very worried about her insecure financial future and the impact it will have on her two young children.[1]

Deborah's situation is not an uncommon one among the burgeoning population of single-parent families in America. Her experience illustrates the interdependence of the decisions she made, as well as those made by persons and institutions outside her personal sphere of control—decisions that seriously affect her and her children's well-being. The father's actions and the court's decisions regarding child support, a firm's labor market decisions, public welfare benefit levels, subsidized housing regulations, and landlord actions in the private housing market all involve a tangled web of public and private issues that had an effect on her swings in and out of poverty.

In 1983, the median income of single mothers was $9,540, only 37 percent as much as married couple families. Moreover, the younger the ages of children in the home, the lower the household income. When Deborah was married, she and her husband's combined income still did not lift them out of poverty. The relationship between household income and marital dissolution is not clearly known. But marital dissolution, the reason for Deborah's change in marital status, has been determined to be the main cause in formation of single-parent families among both whites and blacks (see Figure 2–1).

Changes in American Family Life

The Growth in Female Headship

Trends toward "singleness" and living independently are growing among all strata in society. Trends toward "singleness" derive from a postponement of first marriage, a growing proportion of never-married persons, and an increase in divorce and separation. These changes in marital status have resulted in an assortment of different living arrangements, including more persons who live alone, more adults who live in unmarried couple households, more young adults who live with their parents, and more children who live in single-parent families.

Analysis by race shows that in 1985, 54 percent of black children were living with one parent; 29 percent of children of Spanish origin and 18 percent of white children were also in these living arrangements (see Figure 2–2). Ellwood and Bane estimate that in 10 years, about 45 percent of white and 87 percent of black

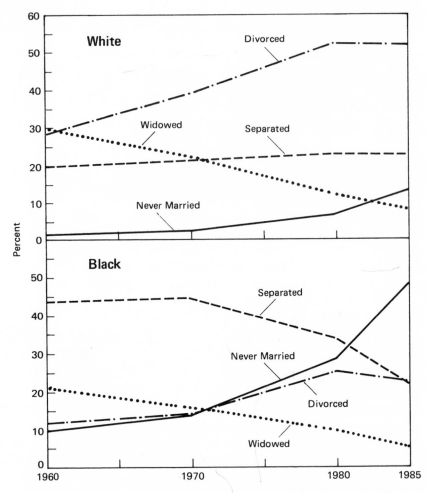

Figure 2-1 **Children under 18 Years Living with One Parent, by Marital Status of Parent: 1985, 1980, 1970, and 1960.** Source: U.S. Bureau of the Census, "Marital Status and Living Arrangements: March 1985," *Current Population Reports, Series P-20,* no. 410 (Washington, D.C.: U.S. Government Printing Office, 1986).

children 17 years old will have spent some part of their lives not living with both parents.[2]

The Increase in Marital Breakup

In the past 25 years some clear trends in changing marital status can be observed. These trends point to marital breakup as the main cause of formation of single-parent families among both

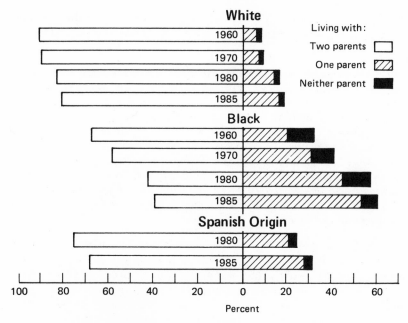

Figure 2-2 **Living Arrangements of Children under 18 Years: 1985, 1980, 1970, and 1960.** Source: U.S. Bureau of the Census, "Marital Status and Living Arrangements: March 1985," *Current Population Reports, Series P-20,* no. 410 (Washington, D.C.: U.S. Government Printing Office, 1986).

blacks and whites (see Figure 2–1). Since 1960, the divorced proportion among whites has risen from 28 to 52 percent, the separated from 20 to 23 percent; the widowed proportion has dropped from 30 to only 8 percent. The proportion of children who lived with a never-married parent increased from 2 to 13 percent, and from 7 to 13 percent in the five-year period from 1980 to 1985. Further, 85 percent of all white single mothers were once married, but are now separated, divorced, and to a lesser extent widowed.[3] The picture for whites points to divorce and separation as a straightforward reason for the increase in formation of single-parent families. The picture for blacks is less clear-cut.

Figure 2–1 shows that changes in marital status among black single-parent heads of households display a sharp decline in separated status, dropping from 44 percent in 1960 to 22 percent by 1985, accompanied by a rise from 12 to 23 percent among the divorced. The percentage of black children in a household with a never-married parent increased from 28 to 48 percent in the five-year period from 1980 to 1985 alone. However, Bane and Ellwood point out that contrary to common assumptions, it is a dramatic decline in marriage rather than an increase in fertility among unmarried women which is the major cause of a jump in single mothers among blacks:

> *In 1970, 27 percent of all black women between the ages of 18 and 44 had never been married. By 1982, 44 percent had never married. (By contrast, 20 percent of whites had not been married in 1970, and 26 percent in 1982.) The fraction of never married women who had children rose somewhat over this period. But mainly because marriage had dropped so precipitously, never married mothers as a fraction of the population jumped dramatically—from 11 percent of 18–44-year-old black women in 1970 to 21 percent in 1982. A dramatic decline in marriage rather than an increase in fertility among unmarried women was a major cause of the jump in single mothers among blacks.*[4]

Among both whites and blacks, then, increased marital breakup appears to be a major reason for changing family structures. Among blacks, declines in marriage, an increase in divorce, and to a lesser degree increase in births to unmarried women were even more important contributors.

Living Arrangements of Single Mothers

The increase in numbers of single-parent families can also be traced to the trend among households in general to live independently. That is, in the past, a single mother and her child often remained in the home of her parents or relatives, creating a subfamily within the primary family unit. According to 1983 census data, 1,631,000 single mothers continue to do so. But recent trends show that single mothers utilize earnings, AFDC benefits, and public or subsidized housing benefits to establish their own independent family units, often trying to escape overcrowded conditions.

The nature of living arrangements themselves and the methods used by the Census Bureau to determine household status have caused difficulties in collecting data on single-parent families, particularly on subfamily units. For example, until 1983 a single mother living in her parents' home with her child was coded by her relationship to the parent head of household. She was coded as a child, and her own child was coded as other relative of the head with no parent present. When the Census Bureau refined its methods to identify the single mother as head of a subfamily, the number of single-parent families it reported approximately doubled.[5] In 1986, the Census Bureau reported approximately 8.9 million single-mother households when the number of single mother heads of households and single-mother heads of subfamily units were combined.[6]

Age and Household Composition of Single-Parent Families

Single-parent families are predominantly small in size, and the ages of family members are getting younger. Nearly three-quarters of all female-headed households are composed of a mother and her one or two children. From 1970 to 1979, the number of single-parent families with children under the age of 6 doubled. By the end of the decade there were 2.4 million single-parent families with school-aged children ages 6 to 17, reflecting also a lower median age of the female head, which has been steadily declining.[7]

All of these changes in American family life have had a profound effect on the economic and social well-being of women and their children. The chapter will now turn to a discussion of these issues.

Economic Vulnerability of Single-Parent Families

The impoverishment of children in America is a serious national problem and a topic of public policy debate. The level of material resources available to children—that is, the degree to which their needs for food, clothing, and shelter are satisfied—is important to their physical and psychological well-being. Deprivation resulting from low family income during childhood has immediate and long-term consequences for a child's social development and level of educational attainment.[8]

Public attention is drawn to the "feminization" of poverty because families headed by women are six times more likely than two-parent families to have incomes below the poverty line. This section will examine some impacts of marital dissolution that create a lowered income status for single-parent families, and discuss methods of income packaging that single mothers turn to in order to support themselves and their children.

Lowered Economic Status after Marital Breakup

Marital breakup, found to be the primary determinant in the formation of single-parent families, produces a precipitous decline in women's household incomes. The percentage of the drop is a function of the income level during marriage. For example, in a recent study Weiss compared income sources for married and for single-parent families for five years after marital breakup. He found

that the previous male head of household provided 80 percent of
the family's income, while the wife or other family members
contributed 20 percent. Following the marital break, incomes of
the newly formed single-mother households were reduced in every
income category—lower, middle, and higher—the reduction being
the greatest where the marital income had been the largest. In the
upper-income level, separation and divorce reduced the income of
single-parent households to about one-half of what it had been in
the last married year; in the middle-income level, income was
reduced to about two-thirds; and in the lower-income level, income
was reduced to about three-fourths of its previous level.[9] These
declines persisted for as long as the family was headed by a female.
Once down, the income remained down in spite of a combination
of the new female head's employment and receipt of either private
transfer payments such as child support or public transfer payments such as Aid to Families with Dependent Children (AFDC).
Conversely, the average income of the married couple increased
steadily. When the incomes of the separated and divorced five
years after the year of marital disruption are compared with the
incomes of the married five years after the index year, it is seen in
every income category that the incomes of the separated and
divorced are about half of those of the married.[10] Two examples of
a severe drop in income are the experiences of Elizabeth P. and
Gertrude B.

   Example 2:   Elizabeth P. is a white, 35-year-old single mother
   of a 12-year-old son. During her marriage her husband earned
   $40,000 annually, and she was a full-time housewife. In their
   divorce settlement the court ordered the father to pay $400 each
   month in child support, which he never paid. Elizabeth went on
   AFDC; her annual income dropped to $4,128, which was aug-
   mented by in-kind benefits of food stamps, Medicaid, and subsidized housing. In addition to raising her child, Elizabeth returned
   to school and is now a full-time student at a local community
   college. In the meantime, the state's child support enforcement
   program has managed to collect $100 per month in child support
   from the father, which is paid directly to the court.

   Example 3:   When times were good, Gertrude B, her husband,
   and the four youngest of their eight children lived in their own
   home in an affluent suburban community about 35 miles from
   Boston. Her husband earned around $30,000 a year. She reports
   that he had a good job and was a good provider. He was also an
   alcoholic. As his alcoholism progressed, he started to spend the

family savings. They finally divorced. He was ordered by the court to pay $500 per month in child support for the four remaining children in the home. He paid his child support not directly to Gertrude but for household expenses like the mortgage and groceries. Gertrude herself never saw any cash. He paid the full $500 per month for two years; then, as his addiction increased, his earnings declined and he paid only $160 per month.

Gertrude and the children finally couldn't afford to keep the house. Then her husband died. Gertrude had a ninth grade education, had never worked outside the home, and had no resources. There were delinquent property taxes due which she could not pay, so the town took the house for back taxes. She and the children were forced to move. They found an apartment in an old manufacturing city about 20 miles away. This would be the first of many moves they would make over a three-year period. The most frequent reason for moving was reported to be sale of the building in which they were living, followed by new owners raising the rent to levels Gertrude could not afford, and ending in eviction. This pattern repeated itself until Gertrude and her youngest child, now 14, ended up doubling up in the apartment of one of her older children. Now, at age 55, she is virtually homeless and on AFDC.

The decline in economic status is also harsh for those families on the edge of poverty during marriage. The drop in income pushes them over into poverty without benefit of private transfer payments such as child support, which is received more often by those whose marital incomes were in the upper- and middle-income levels.[11] The experience of Teresa P. illustrates this problem.

Example 4: Teresa P. is a 34-year-old single mother of a 15-year-old son, a 9-year-old daughter, and a 4-year-old son. Both she and her husband worked during their marriage, and their combined annual income was about $9,600. He had addiction problems with both alcohol and drugs and was frequently abusive to her and the children. When they separated, Teresa went on AFDC. Welfare workers and the courts requested identifying information about the father so he could be contacted to pay child support. She refused to give it because she feared he would disrupt her and the children's lives and harm them with his abusiveness. A few years later she met a new man with whom she developed a relationship, and she became pregnant. After she told him of the pregnancy, he disappeared and she never saw nor heard from him again. She gave birth to the child and is raising all three children on AFDC, without ever receiving any child support.

To cope with her economically vulnerable position, the single mother tries to assemble a "resource" package consisting of (1) mothers' earnings, (2) private transfer payments such as child support and help from relatives or friends, and (3) means-tested public transfers such as welfare benefits and food stamps. Her family's economic and social well-being is determined by access to these resources, their amounts, and their reliability.

Development of Income Support Packages after Marital Breakup

The preponderance of single mothers are working mothers whose main source of income is their own wages. In 1985, over two-thirds of women heading households with children under age 18 were in the labor force. More were working full-time than part-time, yet their median annual income was $13,000.[12] This income level makes single mothers vulnerable to two critical factors in their transition to solo headship. The first factor is the amount of income they receive plus the source of that income, be it earnings or transfer payments. For example, is it a steady, regular income stream, or is it irregular and unpredictable?[13] The steadier the source of income, the more stability the family can count on in a transition period characterized by turmoil and uncertainty.

Frequent residential mobility among single-parent families makes receipt of reliable and regular income from any source a very important factor. Marital breakup itself exerts changes in family composition, with someone moving out, usually the father. However, studies show that marital dissolution creates family disruption and patterns of frequent residential mobility not only for fathers but for mothers and their children as well.[14]

The second factor is the manner in which the total family financial package is put together. Is there free or low-cost housing, such as doubling up with parents or relatives; receipt of the family home as part of the divorce settlement; in-kind contributions of free child care or a car from relatives or a friend? For example, in her study of divorced mothers and fathers, Anderson-Khlief found that women with the same earned income levels after divorce were living in extremely different socioeconomic circumstances, depending on how the rest of the income package was put together. The most important items were found to be earned income, steadiness of child support, availability of free child care, and the nature of the housing settlement.[15] Consider the experience of Alice C.

Example 5:   Alice C. is a 28-year-old black mother of two children ages 6 and 5. During her marriage she and her husband both worked, and their combined income was $18,000, mostly from his earnings. When they divorced, the court ordered Alice's husband to pay $240 a month in child support for two children. He paid it for two months; then the amount declined, and payment became intermittent. He now pays about $60 per month directly to Alice, and it is irregular. Alice couldn't afford to pay the rent. To make ends meet, Alice wanted to work full-time, but the only way she could do that was to have good, affordable child care. Alice's mother agreed to let Alice and the children move in with her, and also agreed to provide child care so Alice could work. Alice and the two children are living in a one-bedroom apartment they converted in the basement of her mother's house. Access to these resources enabled Alice not only to take a full-time job but also a part-time job. Her sources of income combined now total $13,680 a year. She pays her mother rent and utilities, which amount to 29 percent of her monthly income.

Since Alice was not a homeowner in marriage, there was no housing settlement in her resource package. The inconsistency of child support made her all the more dependent on reliable child care; provision of reliable child care by her mother was the pivotal factor in enabling Alice to work full-time. The family is getting by through income packaging of earnings, child care, and affordable housing, made possible by resources from a familial support system.

Role of Marital Wealth.   Differences in income packaging vary with the income level and housing arrangements of the family prior to marital dissolution. Families suffer a severe reduction in income across all income levels, but women in the higher-income levels during marriage rely on their own earnings—accounting for 87 percent of their income—and on child support after divorce. These two resources combined still result in a 50 percent decline in total family income. Middle-income marital households exhibit a mix of patterns—earnings as 68 percent of income, some child support, some reliance on public assistance. Gradually, they move toward upper-income-level patterns. When marital household income has been in the middle level, there is short-term reliance on public transfers, followed by increased labor force participation and increased earnings.[16]

Not only does marital dissolution have a profound impact on decreasing incomes of single-parent families; it also severs the social status and shelter patterns established during marriage, as demonstrated in the case studies. Housing tenure, which refers to one's status as a homeowner or renter, has been shown to play an important part in postmarital income packaging. For homeowners, the housing settlement in the divorce decree is a significant factor in determining living arrangements, consumption patterns, and mobility decisions of the single-parent family after divorce.

For example, in interviews with 50 divorced women, 60 percent of whom were homeowners, Anderson-Khlief found that 38 percent of the women got the house in the settlement, and 12 percent retained joint ownership with mother and children allowed to reside in it.[17] Of all the women in the study, the only ones who were able to stay put after marital dissolution were those who had access to living in the family home and to regular child support payments. Middle-income women who had been homeowners and received less or irregular child support ultimately became "house poor." As in the case study of Gertrude B., they could not keep up mortgage payments, maintenance expenses, and taxes and were forced to relinquish the family home. Most of these families became renters and moved to what they considered to be undesirable neighborhoods.

In a study by Rein it was found that only widows and fathers with custody of their children are likely to remain in the same home three years after their change in marital status. Groups, then, likely to stay in the marital home represent only a small proportion of single-parent families.[18]

The lower-income mothers in Anderson-Khlief's study were renters during marriage and had no housing settlement in their resource package, as were nearly all the mothers cited in case histories here. After divorce, their mobility increased as they moved from apartment to apartment; they had the greatest need for stable housing opportunities and for private transfers such as child support, but received little or none.

Single mothers, then, are slipping further away from the American dream—ownership of a single-family house. Those who were homeowners during marriage and could not afford to keep the family home have lost significant financial and social benefits provided by homeownership. Equity in a home brings tax advantages, facilitates obtaining credit, and provides access to other resources such as social position and community power. The lowered economic status of single mothers prevents their reentry into the mortgage market. In 1981, tenure patterns showed that 65 percent of all householders owned their own homes. By contrast, only 48 percent of all female-headed households were homeowners. Today, female-headed households constitute 40 percent of all renters; four years ago they comprised only 32 percent.[19]

Role of Paternal Employment. Some recent studies have pointed to the declining employment opportunities for young men, particularly among blacks, which may influence formation of female headship by decisions to marry, to separate, or to divorce.[20] For those who are separated or divorced, the employment pattern of the father during marriage influences the resources available to the single-parent family after dissolution. It is not just the amount of income the father received that matters but the nature of the formal linkages to organizations that provide fringe benefits as well. Men with unstable income patterns lack an affiliation with some large, formal (work) organization, which cuts them and their families off from organizational protections that provide income supports after the marriage ends. For example, fathers who have an unstable work history, an on off on welfare pattern, and never seem to be able to hold a job are not in a position to collect unemployment, disability benefits, health coverage, paid vacations, and so on. Divorced women whose ex-husbands have such job patterns are "high risk" welfare candidates who find child support to be an unreliable, undependable component of their income packages; nor do these women have access to private health coverage or other necessary family protections.[21]

The Child Care Dilemma. Affordable child care is a vital, in-kind benefit to a single mother's resource package. The lack of affordable, reliable, and quality child care is a problem for all working mothers, but it is an acute problem for single mothers raising children alone. Single mothers often report waitressing or domestic jobs as part of some welfare/work income package. These jobs can provide the needed degree of flexible hours required by single mothers. First, the single mother may have to work around child care arrangements determined by the personal schedule of the provider, who may be a relative or a friend. Second, children's school attendance schedules need to be accommodated. Hourly wage jobs can provide this flexibility. However, they do not provide the organizationally based income supports that are part of the nonwelfare scene. The lack of child care pushes mothers into jobs that also lack fringe benefits and job security—those associated with part-time or even full-time work with hourly wage pay: secretarial, clerical, waitressing, domestic. These interrelated factors produce tentative employment patterns which are welfare-prone.[22] The availability of affordable, reliable, and quality child care is a pivotal factor on which single mothers' entry into higher-paying jobs with organizationally based fringe benefits and job security depend.

Role of Income Transfers. According to the Survey of Income and Program Participation conducted by the Census Bureau in the period from July 1983 to September 1983, on a monthly average, about 30 percent of the U.S. population participated in one or more government programs. Approximately 13.5 million nonfarm households, about 16 percent of the U.S. total, received some form of "means-tested" (income eligible) benefits. These benefits were either in the form of cash assistance or a noncash benefit. The major programs providing cash benefits included AFDC and other cash assistance (3.8 million recipient households), and SSI (Supplementary Security Income) (2.8 million recipient households). Major programs providing means-tested noncash benefits were Medicaid (7.5 million), food stamps (6.3 million), and public or subsidized housing (3.5 million).

The two programs affecting the largest number of households were not means-tested. About 20 million households had one or more persons covered by Medicare, and 22.7 million households contained one or more persons receiving Social Security or Railroad Retirement benefits.

The household group most likely to receive means-tested transfer payments is single mothers with minor children. About 55 percent of these households received at least one transfer payment, compared to about 10 percent of married couple households. It should be noted, however, that because of their predominance, married couple families still represent the largest single household group receiving means-tested benefits. For example, of the 13.5 million households receiving means-tested benefits, about 5 million were married couple families, 3.2 were single-mother with minor children families, 1.1 million were male nonfamily householders, and 2.7 million were female nonfamily householders.

More single mother households were recipients of noncash, in-kind benefits—specifically Medicaid (2.2 million)—than of cash assistance (1.9 million). Public and subsidized housing is also an in-kind benefit. During the Reagan era affordable housing programs sustained a 75 percent cutback in public investment.[23] In the United States, 3.5 million households are living in either public or subsidized units. Yet, in 1983, fewer than one in five single mothers received in-kind benefits of public or subsidized housing in their income packages.[24]

Whereas most of AFDC recipient households were headed by single mothers with minor children in the third quarter of 1983, this group represented only about one-third of all single mother households.[25] Of all the factors involved in the changing numbers of AFDC caseloads, it has been shown that the number of families dependent on AFDC is most sensitive to swings in the divorce rate. Lower-income families who have no other reliable means of support after the marital break turn to AFDC and food stamps, which are steady and reliable sources of income. These public transfer payments are significant sources of long-term income almost solely for those separated and divorced mothers who had been in the lower-income category when married.

Bane and Ellwood point out that contrary to viewing public transfers as a "last resort," which is a prevailing attitude toward income maintenance policies, they are, in fact, the only and perhaps the "best" option for a single mother who has no other regular or reliable source of income in her resource package. They point out that 75 percent of women who go on AFDC do so because of a change in household composition that involves the departure of a spouse/father who leaves unsupported children.[26]

Residential Location and Housing Problems of Single-Parent Families

The nature of housing problems for single-parent families is tied to their location of residence. Indices of a housing problem generally include two factors: housing quality and tenure status. The Department of Housing and Urban Development (HUD) measures housing quality in terms of (1) the physical adequacy of each dwelling (it surveys the plumbing, heating, and electrical systems and the kitchen and bathroom facilities), (2) the presence of overcrowding (viewed as more than one person per room), and (3) excessive costs (considered to be 30 percent of income for rent or 40 percent of income for mortgage and maintenance). By these standards, data from the 1981 Annual Housing Survey show that about 33 percent of all dwellings in the United States are problem-ridden. Female heads of households (including elderly and younger women living alone) occupy over 40 percent of these problem-ridden dwellings. Moreover, among all female heads of household, mothers with minor children have the most difficulty with their housing (see Table 2–1).

An analysis of housing quality among female heads of households who rent reveals that female-headed families with minor children are the most problem-ridden group among those living in substandard shelter in the United States (see Table 2–2).[27]

Census data show that female-headed families are somewhat more urban than the general population, and are more concentrated in central cities (see Table 2–3). Yet, nearly one-half of

Table 2–1 Housing Quality of the Female-Headed Family and the Elderly Female
(in thousands)

	Total Number	Percent	Female-Headed Households with Children under 18 Number	Percent	Elderly Female-Headed Households Number	Percent
Occupied Units	13,169		5,856	44.4	7,313	55.3
Total with a housing problem	5,973	45.4	3,162	53.9	2,811	38.4
Physically Inadequate	1,647	12.5	861	14.7	786	10.8
Crowded	380	0.3	365	6.2	15	0.2
Cost-burden	3,946	29.9	1,936	33.1	2,010	27.5

Source: Special tabulations based on 1981 National Housing Survey, U.S. Department of Housing and Urban Development, Washington, D.C. In Birch, E., *The Unsheltered Woman: Women and Housing in the 1980's* (1985) (New Brunswick, N.J.: Center for Urban Policy Research, 1985).

Table 2–2   Housing Quality of Impacted Female Heads of Household Who Rent, 1981 (in thousands)

	Total Impacted Households	Female-headed Families with Children Under 18 (Renters)	Elderly Female-Headed Households (Renters)
Occupied units	6,304	3,639	2,665
Total with a			
housing problem	4,010	2,464	1,546
percent	63.6	67.7	58.0
Physically inadequate	992	669	323
percent	15.7	18.4	12.1
Crowded	288	285	3
percent	4.6	7.8	0.1
Cost-burdened	2,730	1,510	1,220
percent	43.3	41.5	45.8

Source: Special tabulations based on 1981 National Housing Survey, U.S. Department of Housing and Urban Development, Washington, D.C. In Eugenie Birch, *The Unsheltered Woman* (New Brunswick, N.J.: Center for Urban Policy Research, 1985).

female-headed families live in the suburbs, and that figure continues to grow. From 1970 to 1979, the number of households headed by women who lived in central cities grew by 41 percent, while the number of households headed by women who lived in the suburbs increased by 71 percent.[28] Some housing problems—specifically, housing costs and mobility—can be seen in both urban and suburban locations.

Central City Renters and Housing Quality

Within a region, rental units tend to be concentrated in urbanized areas and specifically in central cities. Since single mothers are primarily renter households, they also are concentrated in urban areas, and specifically in central cities. As demonstrated in Table 2–1, they are beset by problems of substandard conditions, overcrowding, and of cost. High rents in urban areas pose serious problems. Studies on single mothers and their housing needs concur that their primary housing problem is cost, and that the high cost of housing on their severely reduced incomes explains their high levels of residential mobility.[29]

Rein and his colleagues found that postmarital break rent burdens (the relationship of housing expenses to income) had increased by 53 percent for those low-income single mothers who were divorced, and by 70 percent for those who were separated.

Table 2–3 Location of Female Householders in the United States, 1980 (in thousands)

	Total U.S. Households	Total in SMSAs		Urban		Rural	
				Inside Central Cities	Outside Central Cities		
		Number	%	% of SMSA	% of SMSA	Number	%
All female householders	21,723	16,336	72.6	52.4	47.6	5,886	24.8
All U.S. householders	83,527	57,869	68.2	46.2	54.0	27,789	30.8
Female-headed families	9,403	6,833	72.6	52.8	47.2	2,750	27.3
All U.S. families	61,019	40,612	66.6	39.1	60.9	20,407	33.4
Female non-family households	12,320	9,503	77.1	52.1	47.9	2,817	22.9
All U.S. non-family households	23,913	17,257	72.7	49.5	50.5	6,656	27.8

Source: U.S. Department of Commerce, Bureau of the Census. Money Income of Households, Families and Persons in the United States, 1981; General Population, U.S. Summary, 1980. Washington, D.C.: U.S. Government Printing Office, 1981.

While they had moved to reduce their rent burden, and usually were able to reduce the housing cost, the decline in income was even greater, resulting in an increased rent burden. In effect, single mothers are forced movers. Moreover, their high rent burdens mean less money for other things, and result in a continuing reduced standard of living for the family.

The pressure for more affordable housing can result in residential moves from standard quality rental housing in safe central city neighborhoods to substandard housing in deteriorated central city neighborhoods. Such moves can reduce housing costs, but in the process push families into unsafe housing and neighborhood conditions. Mobility can also end by families deciding to double up with relatives or friends, and while reducing housing costs, this creates overcrowded conditions. Low-income single-parent families are then entangled in a multiplicity of central city housing problems which become very difficult to escape. New housing construction built to accommodate demand is likely to be owner-occupied single-family housing. Nationwide from 1970 to 1980 the stock of owned units increased by 30 percent, and rented units increased by only 21 percent. This disparity represents one barrier to single-parent families' mobility out of central cities.[30]

The "Nouveau Poor" and Suburban Displacement

The suburbs and small towns house the "nouveau poor." These are single mothers who were homeowners during marriage, and who have since experienced a dramatic shift from middle- to low-income status. They are left house-poor in suburbia. Frequently, the "nouveau poor" are forced to move through the phenomenon of suburban displacement.

Displacement is caused when a household is forced to move because of circumstances beyond its control. It has long been a serious problem in central city neighborhoods where poor renters have been displaced for decades. It began with landlord abandonment and with urban renewal programs of the 1950s and 1960s. It continues in the 1980s with condominium conversion, gentrification (where young urban professionals return to the city to live near their office sector jobs, forcing out lower-income households), and urban revitalization projects.[31]

Displacement is a housing problem because it establishes a pattern of forced residential mobility and insecurity. Like urban displacement of renters, suburban displacement also involves considerable hardship. It can be caused by two factors. The first is by court orders which enforce sale of the family home as part of divorce settlements. The second is by restrictive zoning regulations that prevent re-use of single-family homes.

For example, mothers and children remain in the family home in order to give children residential stability and educational continuity, and to maintain networks of community support after marital breakup. High cost burdens cause many single mothers to attempt alternative living and working arrangements. Their purpose is to maximize limited resources while continuing their primary responsibility for raising children and supervising children's daily activities. Some try renting out a portion of their homes as accessory apartments, or house sharing with another family. Divorced and separated mothers who house share have higher total family incomes and less participation in subsidized or public housing programs than those who head independent family units.[32] Others try to establish at-home employment activities. Some examples include a mail-order arts and crafts business, a secretarial service, or day care as a licensed day care mother, using the home to babysit for children of other working parents.

However, there are barriers to doubling up and to working out of one's house. These housing arrangements in suburbia are usually thwarted by rigid community zoning restrictions designed to preserve traditional single-family residential neighborhoods intended for the idealized nuclear family. Moreover, land use regulations reflect community values and attitudes that convey permissibility for women with children to work at home as long as it is unpaid housework. A conflict develops between the "postnuclear" family's right to live as it chooses to bring its housing to its highest and best use, and the community's right to regulate the use of land. A community's land use regulations that restrict neighborhoods to single-family zones, exclude multi-family development, and erect barriers to the construction of affordable housing opportunities for both homeownership and renting are likely to result in the exclusion of the "nouveau poor."[33] In the end, these land use regulations force the "nouveau poor" to move out and in effect, create suburban displacement. Patterns of residential mobility and family instability are set in motion.

Conclusion

Chapter 2 has presented background on single-parent families which depicts their situations to be tenuous, at times fragile, and vulnerable to forces, trends, and policies in American society. Despite the great diversity among personal experiences of single-parent families, most of these families have already experienced some of life's catastrophic events: divorce and separation, relocation, unemployment. In addition, though not reported here, such households have not been immune to serious illnesses of children and adults.[34] Part II of this volume, Experiencing Single Parenthood, will now analyze problems single-parent families face in the courts, in restructuring family life, in the labor market, and in the housing market.

Endnotes

1. The case of Deborah S. and all case studies reported in this chapter are drawn from research on single-parent mothers conducted by the author in a larger study, "The Housing Plight of Low-Income Single-Parent Mothers: A Study of Housing Search and Housing Choice in the Section 8 Rental Assistance Program" (Ph.D. diss., University of Southern California, 1986). All names of respondents have been changed.
2. David Ellwood and Mary Jo Bane, "Family Structure and Living Arrangements Research," Harvard University study prepared for the Department of Health and Human Services, Cambridge, Mass., 1984, p. 4.
3. Mary Jo Bane and Robert Weiss, "Alone Together: The World of Single-Parent Families," *American Demographics* (May 1980).
4. Ellwood and Bane, "Family Structure," p. 6.
5. Mary Jo Bane and David Ellwood, "Single Mothers and Their Living Arrangements," Harvard University study prepared for the Department of Health and Human Services, Cambridge, Mass., 1984, p. 3.
6. U.S. Bureau of the Census, "Household and Family Characteristics: 1985," *Current Population Reports,* ser. P-20, no. 419 (Washington, D.C.: U.S. Government Printing Office, 1987), Table F.
7. U.S. Bureau of the Census, "Families Maintained by Female Householders 1970–79," *Current Population Reports,* ser. P-23, no. 107 (Washington, D.C.: U.S. Government Printing Office, 1983).
8. Martha Hill, "Female Household Headship and the Poverty of Children," in *Five Thousand American Families—Patterns of Economic Progress,* vol. X (Ann Arbor: Institute for Social Research, University of Michigan, 1983), p. 325.
9. Robert Weiss, "The Impact of Marital Dissolution on Income and Consumption in Single-Parent Households," *Journal of Marriage and the Family* (February 1984): 117.
10. In addition to Weiss's study, see also Bane and Weiss, "Alone Together," p. 12; Greg Duncan and James Morgan, "Persistence and Change in Economic Status and the Role of Changing Family Composition," in *Five Thousand American Families—Patterns of Economic Progress,* Vol. X; Hill, "Female Household Headship and the Poverty of Children."
11. Weiss, "The Impact of Marital Dissolution," p. 121.

12. For a full discussion refer to Teresa Amott, "Working for Less: Single Mothers in the Workplace," Chapter 5 in this volume.

13. George Masnick and Mary Jo Bane, *The Nation's Families: 1960–1980* (Dover, Mass: Auburn House, 1980).

14. For example, see Martin Rein et al., "The Impact of Family Change on Housing Careers." Unpublished report prepared for the U.S. Department of Housing and Urban Development by the Joint Center for Urban Studies, Cambridge, Mass., 1980; Susan Bartlett, "Residential Mobility and Housing Choices of Single-Parent Mothers," unpublished paper, Joint Center for Urban Studies, Cambridge, Mass., 1980; and Bane and Weiss, "Alone Together."

15. Susan Anderson-Khlief, *Divorced But Not Disastrous* (Englewood Cliffs, N.J.: Prentice-Hall, 1982).

16. Weiss, "The Impact of Marital Dissolution on Income and Consumption in Single-Parent Households," p. 121.

17. Susan Anderson-Khlief, "Housing Needs of Single Parent Mothers," in *Building for Women*, ed. Suzanne Keller (Lexington, Mass: Lexington Books, 1981).

18. See Rein et al., "The Impact of Family Change," pp. 2–8.

19. Eugenie Birch, "The Unsheltered Woman: Definitions and Needs," in *The Unsheltered Woman: Women and Housing in the 1980s,* ed. Eugenie Birch (New Brunswick, N.J.: Center for Urban Policy Research, 1985), p. 39.

20. See, for example, Irwin Garfinkel and Sara S. McLanahan, *Single Mothers and Their Children* (Washington, D.C.: Urban Institute Press, 1986), Chapter 3; Bane and Ellwood, "Single Mothers and Their Living Arrangements," p. 35.

21. Susan Anderson-Khlief, "Income Packaging and Life Style in Welfare Families," Joint Center for Urban Studies, Cambridge, Mass., 1978, p. 14.

22. Ibid., p. 16.

23. See Peter Dreier, "Community-Based Housing: A Progressive Approach to a New Federal Policy," *Social Policy* 18, no. 2 (Fall 1987): 19.

24. U.S. Bureau of the Census, "Economic Characteristics of Households in the United States: Third Quarter 1983," Table 8. Refer to Elizabeth Mulroy, "The Search for Affordable Housing," Chapter 6 of this volume, for an analysis of how low-income single mothers try to access a federal rent subsidy program in the wake of federal housing program cuts and diminished supply.

25. U.S. Bureau of the Census, "Economic Characteristics of Households in the United States: Third Quarter 1983," *Current Population Reports*, series P-70, no. 1 (Washington, D.C.: U.S. Government Printing Office, 1984), Table F.

26. Bane and Ellwood, "Single Mothers and Their Living Arrangements," p. 33.

27. Birch, "The Unsheltered Woman," p. 35.

28. U.S. Bureau of the Census, "Families Maintained by Female Householders, 1970–79," *Current Population Reports,* series P-70, no. 1 (Washington, D.C.: U.S. Department of Commerce, 1983).

29. See Rein et al., "The Impact of Family Change"; Bartlett, "Residential Mobility and Housing Choices of Single Parent Mothers"; Anderson-Khlief,

Divorced But Not Disastrous; and Weiss, "The Impact of Marital Dissolution on Income and Consumption in Single-Parent Households."

30. Birch, "The Unsheltered Woman," p. 42.
31. For a historical perspective on displacement, see, for example, Herbert Gans, *The Urban Villagers* (New York: Free Press, 1962); for a contemporary analysis, see John Yinger, "State Housing Policy and the Poor," in *The State of the Poor in the 1980s,* ed. Manuel Carballo and Mary Jo Bane (Dover, Mass: Auburn House, 1984).
32. U.S. Bureau of the Census, "Population Profile of the United States," *Current Population Reports,* ser. P-23, no. 130 (Washington, D.C.: U.S. Government Printing Office, 1983).
33. For an excellent discussion of zoning barriers to single-mother householders in the suburbs and the public policy implications, see Edith Netter and Ruth Price, "Zoning and the Nouveau Poor," *Journal of the American Planning Association* (Spring 1983): 171–81.
34. See, for example, Esther Rothblum and Violet Franks, "Custom-Fitted Straightjackets: Perspectives on Women's Mental Health" in *The Trapped Woman,* ed. Josefina Figueira-McDonough and Rosemary Sarri (Newbury Park, Calif: Sage, 1987); and Ruth Sidel, *Women and Children Last* (New York: Viking Penguin, 1986), ch. 7.

Part II

EXPERIENCING SINGLE PARENTHOOD

Chapter 3

GENDER BIAS IN THE COURTS

Lynn Hecht Schafran

Despite massive evidence to the contrary, the myth of the carefree divorcee dies hard. Millions of Americans fall asleep listening to Johnny Carson and his sidekicks bemoan their alimony payments. Tabloids trumpet million-dollar awards to wives in newsworthy divorces. Comedians joke about husbands driven to the poorhouse by onerous demands for child support. Yet for every divorce in which a wife is enriched and a husband impoverished, there are thousands upon thousands in which the reality is exactly the opposite. Although divorce involves financial dislocation for both women and men, it is women who are the most seriously disadvantaged in both the near and long term, and it is the courts which play a significant role in women's impoverishment. Whether the single mother is a married woman seeking a divorce or a never-married woman seeking to enforce child support, she comes to court with three strikes against her: she is a woman, she lacks the resources to retain adequate counsel, and her issues are those with which the legal system would prefer not to deal.

This chapter describes how gender bias in the courts impacts those areas of the law that affect women in their status as single mothers: divorce, including access to the courts, property division and alimony; child support; domestic violence; and custody. It concludes with a discussion of the efforts being made to eliminate gender bias in the courts through judicial, legal and law school education, legislation, and judicial screening and discipline.

Women and the Legal System

The battle to secure legal rights for women has been long and arduous and is far from over. Women were not accorded rights under the U.S. Constitution because in the Founding Fathers' political context women did not exist as actors in civil life. Not until 1971 did the United States Supreme Court use the equal protection clause of the Fourteenth Amendment to strike down a statute as being discriminatory on the basis of sex. During most of the 19th century women could not enter into a contract or own property. Custody was almost always awarded to fathers, who were seen as having a property right in their children. Wives were the property of their husbands. Until well into the 20th century women could not vote or serve on juries, but they could be denied jobs solely because they were women, be paid less than men for doing the same work, and be fired when they became pregnant. Women were denied credit and equal access to education. Abortion and in some states even contraception were illegal. Wives who failed to follow their husbands anywhere they wished to go could be divorced for abandonment. Husbands were awarded almost all family property at divorce. Rape victims were cross-examined on their entire sexual histories. Domestic violence and sexual harassment were concepts that did not even exist.

Despite the great progress made over the last 20 years in reforming the laws that particularly affect women, in the courts today women must still contend with problems ranging from demeaning behavior on the part of judges, lawyers, and court personnel to outright judicial unwillingness to apply and enforce the new laws so as to effectuate their remedial intent. Minority group women may bear the double burden of sex and race discrimination, or they may find themselves denied effective access to the courts for want of a skilled interpreter.

The court system is difficult to navigate on one's own, but lawyers are expensive. Women as a group are poorer than men, and even women who are apparently well off are usually poorer than their husbands if not totally dependent on them for their economic status. In a contest for support enforcement or a change of custody, the man's deeper pockets place the woman at a significant disadvantage. Single mothers are also often denied meaningful access to the courts because of the Reagan administration's sustained attack on funding for the Legal Services Corporation. Two-third of Legal Services' clients are poor women seeking legal assistance for matters such as welfare, housing, domestic violence, divorce, child support, and social security—a fact not often recognized in discussions of women's issues. The legal services first cut were those for family law matters, because scarce funds had to be dedicated to criminal defense work.

The issues that bring a single mother to court are usually family law issues such as child and spousal support, custody, or domestic violence. These issues are disfavored by the legal system, which prefers to focus on enhancing commerce, an area in which it is easier to maintain the fiction that law is pure, rational, objective, abstract, and principled. Although family law cases are a significant, if not the major, category of cases on every state's civil docket, every law school requires students to take courses in contracts, real property, and torts (civil wrongs); only one, however, requires family law. Some judges go to great lengths to avoid being assigned to hear matrimonial cases. In some states the family courts receive small shares of the judicial system's budget, despite the enormity of their caseloads, and family law is seen as not "real law" but the area in which to dump less competent lawyers who yearn to be judges and to whom political favors are owed. The judicial system's effort to move family law cases out of the courts and into alternative dispute resolution is also of concern to women's rights advocates. After decades of struggling to have the law and the courts deal seriously with these issues, these advocates are not pleased to see them being reprivatized, decided in a forum in which there is no record made for a possible appeal and thus no accountability.

Women in the Courts Today

"[G]ender bias against women litigants, attorneys and court employees is a pervasive problem with grave consequences. Women are often denied equal justice, equal treatment and equal opportunity." Such was the finding of the New York Task Force on Women in the Courts, a blue-ribbon panel which reported to that state's chief judge in 1986 about the myriad obstacles to equity for women in the New York court system.[1] In 1984, the New Jersey Supreme Court Task Force on Women in the Courts made a similar finding:[2]

> *Although the law as written is for the most part gender neutral, stereotyped myths, beliefs and biases were found to sometimes affect decision making in the areas investigated: damages, domestic violence, juvenile justice, matrimonial and sentencing. In addition, there is strong evidence that women and men are sometimes treated differently in courtrooms, chambers and at professional gatherings.*

Gender bias is an age-old, multifaceted problem. It encompasses stereotyped thinking about the nature and roles of women and men, society's perception of the value of women and men and what is perceived as women's and men's work, and myths and misconceptions about the economic and social realities of women's and men's lives. Each aspect of gender bias creates problems for women in the courts, particularly for single mothers. A judge's stereotyped belief that a good mother is at home full-time may cost the mother in the paid work force custody of her children. Devaluation of women as individuals is revealed in judicial indifference to domestic violence and the enforcement of support awards. Devaluation of women's unpaid work as homemakers and mothers is reflected in divisions of marital property at divorce in which the wife is awarded a much smaller share than the husband. Myths and misconceptions about women's access to well-paying jobs and the costs of child raising result in minimal child support awards that impoverish women and their children.

The existence of these and other problems for women in the courts has been documented repeatedly throughout the country. Reported opinions, news articles, anecdotal materials; studies by academic, community, government, women's rights and legal organizations; and most recently, studies by supreme court task forces in several states have shown that gender bias is often a factor in both case outcome and the treatment of women in the courtroom environment.[3] Studies of judicial attitudes toward women's roles reveal a strong preference among some judges for the traditional family of breadwinner father/homemaker mother. Decisions and judges' comments in employment discrimination cases show that some judges are uncomfortable with women wanting employment in the better-paying jobs previously reserved to men, or are disbelieving about the level and kinds of gender-based discrimination that still confront women in the paid work force.

Despite rape shield laws limiting cross-examination, stereotypes dating to the Bible and reinforced by biased legal texts cause rape victims to be treated as seductive temptresses who provoked their attackers. Sometimes the ordeal of sexual assault is treated as a joke. As one judge said in dismissing an attempted rape charge, "You can't blame a man for trying." Judicial mistrust of women's sexuality also distorts juvenile justice, where girls brought to court for status offenses such as truancy and staying out late are seen as promiscuous and treated far more harshly than similarly situated boys. Among adult criminal offenders, women who commit violent crimes are seen by some judges as violating women's presumably passive nature and again treated more harshly than similarly situated men.

Domestic violence victims are often asked what they did to provoke their batterers and told to go home and make up with them. In personal injury cases, homemaker women receive small awards because their unpaid work is devalued. In divorce cases women are often awarded small shares of marital property, little or no alimony, and totally insufficient child support. Enforcing any award can be a nightmare. Some judges openly express the view that women need only small financial settlements because they will soon remarry and have another man to take care of them. Women seeking custody may be punished for life-styles and social arrangements that are acceptable for men.

Any female witness or litigant may encounter a courtroom environment in which judges, lawyers and court personnel address her familiarly (e.g., first names, "sweetheart," "little girl"), comment on her clothing and physical attributes, make sexist jokes and remarks, and on occasion even subject her to verbal or physical sexual advances. The female attorney may have to contend with similar mistreatment and yet say nothing about it lest she anger the judge and disadvantage her client.

The following discussion of the areas of substantive law that affect women as single mothers demonstrates how these attitudes lead to case outcomes and a courtroom environment in which women are made second-class litigants in our courts.

Divorce in the Courts

The termination of a marriage with minor children has several legal aspects: division of marital property, custody, spousal and child support, and the enforcement of those awards. Although most divorces are resolved through negotiated settlements rather than trials, these settlements reflect what lawyers believe they would obtain at trial, based on those cases which are fully litigated. Law reform efforts by women's rights and family law advocates over the last 15 years have created a gender-neutral statutory framework for divorce which, when applied with concern for the actual personal and economic circumstances of the parties and their children, can be equitable. In practice however, the findings of the New Jersey Supreme Court Task Force on Women in the Courts mirror those in every state:

> [D]espite the objectives of [New Jersey's equitable distribution stat-
> ute] and our case law to achieve gender equity in distributing

*property and apportioning the economic burden of divorce, we may
in fact be falling far short of that goal. . . . New Jersey women of all
ages may be the victims of a gender-based maldistribution of earnings and resources at and after divorce.*

This maldistribution of earnings and resources affects women's
ability to litigate their cases, to gain and retain custody of their
children, to obtain and enforce support awards, and to enjoy a
decent standard of living after divorce.

Access to the Courts

The woman who becomes a single mother by virtue of divorce
effectively assumes that status from the moment the decision to
divorce is made by either party. Because the costs of litigation are
enormous, the question of how the divorce itself will be paid for is
critical. Although the laws in most states provide that the court is
to award the nonmonied spouse counsel and expert fees sufficient
to permit the effective litigation of the issues, this rarely happens.
As an attorney from upstate New York wrote to the New York Task
Force on Women in the Courts:

> *The greatest area of discrimination in Monroe County involves court
> awards of counsel fees to women. The courts are excessively stingy
> and inconsistent in cases where the wife has no identifiable assets
> and [the] husband is able to pay. As a result, members of the private
> bar will not accept this type of matrimonial case, and deserving
> women go unrepresented.*

For many single mothers, who are almost always poorer than
their husbands, the entire divorce process is shaped by the inability to afford proper representation. Extremely few sources for free
or low-cost legal assistance are available in divorce litigation. The
lawyer a woman retains must often curtail activities such as pressing the husband for full disclosure of his financial assets—something that many men hide with great success during divorce
litigation—because the woman cannot pay for the hours necessary
to develop that information. If the family has any assets such as a
business or investments, a properly conducted case requires ap-
praisal by accountants and other financial experts. This, too, the
woman finds difficult to afford. Knowing that women can rarely
afford lengthy divorce litigation, some fathers engage in what is
called "custody blackmail"—that is, they threaten to sue for custody, which they do not want, as a way to force the woman to
reduce or abandon her claims for child and spousal support. Even
when they can afford counsel, many women report extreme dissat-

isfaction with their attorneys' attitudes and the quality of representation. New York State's chapter of NOW (National Organization for Women) reports that half the thousands of calls it receives on its hotline each year relate to divorce, and that half those calls relate to poor representation by lawyers. For example, patronizing attitudes, failure to respond to phone calls, failure to explain the woman's rights or what to expect, and sexual harassment.

Although mediation is presented as a less expensive, less emotionally damaging way to conduct a divorce, it, too, has drawbacks for women. Mediation works best between parties of equivalent power. When the female party is less worldly, poorer, truly afraid of losing custody, and perhaps intimidated by a spouse's psychological or physical cruelty, as is often the case for women, she is far more likely to compromise in order to satisfy the mediator, even though the "compromise" is in fact a one-sided bargain. Divorce mediation that is effective for women requires mediators aware of and skilled in overcoming these gender-based power imbalances, not to mention their own gender-based biases. The sex of the mediator, like the sex of the judge, is no guarantor of sensitivity to these issues.

Division of Marital Property

Marital property generally means all property—homes, cars, clothing, furnishings, businesses, savings, investments—that the couple has acquired during the marriage. Nine states are community property states and by law must divide all marital property in half. The other states divide property according to "equitable distribution"—a legal construct that gives the judge power to determine what percentage of the property and debts should be awarded to each partner, regardless of whose name is on the deed, bank book, loan form or other indicia of ownership. Some states require judges to divide the property equally unless there are important reasons for an unequal division. Most states have a list of factors that the court is to take into account in dividing the property, such as the duration of the marriage; the age, health and income of the parties; and the contributions made by one party as a spouse, parent, wage earner and homemaker to the career or career potential of the other. Some states simply require the judge to divide the property "equitably." In all equitable distribution states, judges have great discretion in dividing the property, and there is substantial evidence that women are often shortchanged.

Many judges do not see the unpaid work a woman performs as homemaker and mother as having contributed significantly to the acquisition of marital assets and as being equal in value and importance to a husband's paid work outside the home. There is insufficient recognition of how women contribute to their husband's earning capacity—often the only true asset of the marriage—by keeping the family's emotional motor running and making it possible for him to focus on his job, career, or business without worrying about how his children are getting to the doctor or whether he will have a clean shirt to wear. (Although men are increasing their participation in homemaking and child care, repeated studies show that women still bear the majority of these responsibilities.) The fact that most women today work full- or part-time outside the home and thus hold down two jobs, as wage earner and homemaker, also often goes unrecognized. Even when husband and wife do the same work, the wife's effort may go unrewarded. Farm wives find that some judges disregard the fact that the wife has labored right alongside her husband to make their farm viable.

The New Jersey Supreme Court Task Force on Women in the Courts reported an unwritten rule that women would receive no more than 35 to 45 percent of the marital assets. The New York Task Force on Women in the Courts reported that an analysis of the 70 cases reported since enactment of the equitable distribution law in 1980 showed women awarded less than a 50 percent share of marital property overall and *de minimis* shares of businesses and professional practices. The Task Force also reported on judges accepting husbands' "expert valuations" of businesses and property in the face of clear evidence that the property was being undervalued.

Another factor disadvantaging women in property division is that often the court finds a way to keep the husband's business intact but has no qualms about ordering the sale of the home—in effect the wife's business—whether immediately or as soon as the children are 18. An interesting variant on this theme was pointed out in a 1986 Vermont study, which showed that men who had built their family houses themselves got to keep them.[4] Although it would appear that requiring a 50–50 split is the way to eliminate inequities in property division, because women are usually poorer and have less earning potential than men, and because alimony and child support are difficult to secure and enforce, fairness will often dictate that a significant majority of the assets be awarded the wife. A 50–50 presumption in the law is preferable to a rigid standard.

The important reality is that in most marriages there is minimal accumulation of assets. According to the U.S. Census Bureau, of the 16.5 million ever-divorced women in the country as of spring 1986, only 36 percent were awarded a property settlement.[5] The most significant asset in most marriages, even those in which there is substantial property, is the husband's earning capacity, to which the wife contributed through her work as a homemaker, and often by foregoing her own education to put her husband through school. Thus, the question of whether, how much, and for how long alimony will be awarded is far more crucial to women's postdivorce economic status than the division of property.

Alimony

There is a widespread myth that the award of alimony (also known as maintenance and spousal support) to a wife at divorce is the norm. This is not true now and never was. Census Bureau data reveal that only 19 percent of women divorced before 1970 had an agreement or award to receive alimony. In 1985, the most recent year for which data are available, only 14.6 percent of the 19 million ever-divorced or currently separated women in the country had an agreement or award to receive alimony. For women divorced since 1980, the figure is 13 percent.

Moreover, the percentages alone present too rosy a picture for women because they cover three possibilities: (1) an award of one dollar a year which allows the court to retain jurisdiction of the case so that application for meaningful alimony can be made in subsequent years if circumstances reduce the economically dependent spouse to penury; (2) permanent alimony payable until the economically dependent spouse remarries or the payer dies; and (3) rehabilitative or short-term alimony, which is alimony paid for a few years, usually one to three, to enable the dependent spouse to obtain education or training that will make her economically self-sufficient. (The statutes are gender-neutral and alimony may be, and on occasion is, awarded to men.)

Examination of the amount of these awards and compliance with them further darken the picture for the single mother. The Census Bureau reports that of the 840,000 women due to receive alimony payments in 1985, half received the full amount due, one-quarter received partial payment, and one-quarter received nothing. The mean amount received was $3,733 which, after adjusting for inflation, represented a decrease of more than 25 percent in purchasing power from the mean amount received in 1978, when the Census Bureau first began collecting these data.

Why are so few women awarded alimony and why are the awards so low and so poorly enforced? Judges have always had a horror of what is called the "alimony drone"—the woman who lives a life of leisured luxury while her former husband struggles to support her. In 1967, a New York judge wrote in a leading family law journal:[6]

> *Alimony was never intended to assure a perpetual state of secured indolence. It should not be suffered to convert a host of physically and mentally competent young women into an army of alimony drones, who neither toil nor spin, and become a drain on society and a menace to themselves.*

When increasing numbers of women began to enter the paid work force in the late 1960s, the stage was set for judges to act on their reluctance to award permanent alimony. A Florida appellate court in 1972 refused to extend a middle-aged woman's short-term alimony award, stating: "In this era of women's liberation movements and enlightened thinking . . . the woman is as fully equipped as the man to earn a living and provide for her essential needs."[7] Although in this case the court's motivation was a good faith though mistaken belief that women's access to well-paid employment had become the norm, subsequent alimony decisions from all parts of the country reveal that judicial protectionism of men's income and living standard and indifference to a stark postdivorce economic inequity between husband and wife are motivating factors in these cases. As a New Jersey appellate court judge told his colleagues at a 1984 New Jersey judicial college program called "Economic Aspects of Homemaking in Damages and Divorce":

> *I took strong exception to something I saw developing when I was a matrimonial judge. The woman's equality was somehow warped when it passed through the minds of the judges of our state.*
>
> *A couple is splitting up. The husband is making in the range of $35,000–$40,000. The wife has not worked in a few years. She gets a job and she's an entry level teacher, an entry level nurse. The judge says, "Now she's self-supporting. She doesn't need alimony." To say that the husband can keep his whole $40,000 when the wife gets up to $12,000 is just completely unfair. . . . There's something very wrong in the way men view what is sufficient for women to have.*

Otis v. *Otis*[8] was a 1980 Minnesota case dealing with a 49-year-old woman married for 25 years who had not worked outside the home since the birth of her child. Her business executive husband earned $125,000 per year plus bonuses. The Minnesota Supreme Court awarded her three years of rehabilitative alimony, stating that she could return to her former work as a secretary and earn between $12,000 and $18,000 per year. The court held that all the law required was that the woman be able to meet her "reasonable needs" without reference to her marital standard of living.

In *Holston* v. *Holston*,[9] a 1984 Maryland case, the trial court awarded three years of $150 per week rehabilitative alimony to a woman with five minor children married to a dentist earning $85,000 per year. She had put him through school at the expense of her own education by working as a secretary, and as in *Otis*, the trial court suggested she return to that job. In overruling this award, the appeals court noted that if she could obtain such a job, she would earn $13,000 per year at the local rate, which would give her earnings less than 15 percent of her husband's and therefore their respective standards of living would be "unconscionably disparate."

The Wisconsin Supreme Court dealt with a similar case in 1987. In *LaRoque* v. *LaRoque*,[10] the wife raised five children and toiled ceaselessly in the political vineyards to help her husband achieve his ambitions, first as a district attorney, later as a judge. At the time of divorce, he was an appellate judge earning $60,000. She had been a part-time teacher in the early years of the marriage but had not worked in a paid job for 20 years. The trial court awarded her short-term alimony of $1,500 per month for 5 months, and $1,000 per month for 12 months. The court suggested she could again work as a teacher, a job paying $12,000 a year to start, for which she was not certified, and as she had told the court, did not want. She had asked for rehabilitative alimony sufficient to enable her to secure training in psychology. The appellate court upheld all aspects of the decision, which also included a skewed property division, except that it extended the $1,000 per month alimony until such time as she could earn $1,000 monthly herself. The supreme court reversed, holding that the trial court had failed to carry out either the support or fairness objectives of the Wisconsin maintenance statute: "A court must not reduce the recipient spouse to subsistence level while the payor spouse preserves the predivorce standard of living."

The fact that these latter two cases were reversed on appeal is singular not only because they were reversed, but because it is rare that a woman is able to appeal. As discussed above, the financial ability to litigate is a major barrier to single mothers' access to the courts. What is entailed in an appeal can be seen in the *LaRoque* case. The trial court decision was rendered in 1984; the court of appeals ruled in 1985. In 1987 the supreme court sent the case back to the trial court for a new determination of the amount and duration of alimony in accordance with the high court's directive.

Short-term alimony does have its place. It is not wrong for the courts to encourage women to become self-supporting, both for their own self-interest and self-esteem and to eliminate repeated litigation about the modification and enforcement of awards. Studies have shown that women provided with sufficient rehabilitative alimony to obtain meaningful education and training are in a much better financial position a few years after divorce than are women whose economic circumstances force them to take the first job they can find. But short-term alimony is not appropriate for the older, long-term homemaker who lacks skills to make her marketable and who will never be able to make up for the years she invested in unpaid homemaker work for the benefit of her family. Even for younger women who are in the paid work force or who have some expectation of success when they join it, fairness may require a combination of rehabilitative and permanent alimony to avoid the kind of stark postdivorce economic inequities that the *Holston* and *LaRoque* cases illustrate.

Child Support

A subsequent chapter in this book describes the long and ultimately successful battle to secure from Congress the federal Child Support Enforcement Amendments of 1984.[11] The amendments require each state to enact a variety of mechanisms for enforcing child support and to adopt nonbinding quantitative guidelines for support levels or lose federal funding for the Aid to Families with Dependent Children (AFDC) program. Although passage of these amendments was a significant victory for single mothers, it is too soon to know what their impact will be, and the question that must be asked is, What happened in our court system that made it necessary for the federal government to step in to what had always been a state preserve? As with alimony, the regrettable answer is that not only are many judges uninformed about women's earning capacity and the true costs of child raising, but among some judges there is an attitude of protectionism toward men and their money and indifference to the financial struggle of women and their children.

Legally, both parents are responsible for the support of their minor children. If the parents are divorced or have never been married to one another, state laws provide that the noncustodial parent shall make payments to the custodial parent for the support of the child in accordance with the child's needs and the standard of living the child would have enjoyed in a two-parent home. Parents may make a private agreement, enforceable in court, as to the amount and schedule of these payments, or they may be ordered by the court. The history of child support has been that awards do not remotely reflect the true costs of child raising or the parents' incomes. Because children live with their mothers after approximately 90 percent of divorces and in almost all paternity situations, even if the full amount of the award is paid—a rare occurrence—the mother must scramble to make up the difference between payment and need.

In 1979, as the result of a conference on Issues in Federal Statistical Needs Relating to Women, held in 1978, the United States Census Bureau published its first study of alimony and child support awards and compliance. It found that of the 7.1 million women living with children under 21 present from an absent father in 1978, only 59 percent even had an agreement with the children's father or a court award to receive child support. Of the 3.4 million women due to receive child support payments in that year, 49 percent received the full amount due, 23 percent received partial payment, and 28 percent received nothing. The average amount received *per family* (not per child) was $1,800. This represented 20 percent of the mean income, $8,940, of women receiving child support. Never-married women received the lowest amount of child support payments—an average of $980. The mean payment received by white women was $1,860. The mean payment received by black women was $1,290, and by women of Spanish origin, $1,320.

The awards were so low that even if the full amounts had been paid, the mean amount received for all women would have been $2,000, the total amount of money income for women receiving child support would have been $8,900, and the poverty rate of 17 percent for women due to receive child support would not have decreased significantly. Women with voluntary written agreements fared better than those with court orders for child support in terms of receipt of payment, but even among these women, only 68 percent received the full amount due, as compared to 37 percent of women with court-ordered child support.

Repeated Census Bureau studies have yielded similar data. According to the most recent study, published in 1987, of the 8.8 million women living with children under 18 from an absent father in 1985, 61 percent had an agreement or award to receive child support. As with alimony, of the 4.4 million women due child support payments in that year, half received the full amount due, one-quarter received partial payment, and one-quarter received nothing. The average payment received *per family* was $2,220, a drop of 12 percent from the mean dollar amount received in 1983 which, when adjusted for inflation, represented a more than 16 percent decrease in purchasing power as compared to the mean amount received in 1978. Thirty-two percent of women with children from an absent father had incomes below the poverty level. Among these women the mean child support received (by those who received any) was $1,380 per family, about two-thirds the average received by all women. Breaking the data down by the race of women eligible for child support, two-thirds of white women were awarded support and the mean amount received was $2,294; a third of black women were awarded support and the mean amount received was $1,754; and 41 percent of Hispanic women were awarded support and received a mean amount of $2,011. Again, these mean amounts received are all per family, not per child. The Census Bureau reported that $3.7 billion of the child support due in 1985 was not paid.

Amount of Awards. It is hardly news that children are expensive and become more expensive as they grow older. Yet child support awards are rarely commensurate with the true costs of child raising; nor are they indexed for the child's growth or inflation. The Census Bureau reported that the average amount of court-ordered (as opposed to voluntarily agreed upon) child support in 1983 was $2,290 per year, or $191 per month. These awards covered an average of 1.7 children. Based on the federal poverty guideline, the average award provided support at only 80 percent of the poverty level. Moreover, these failings are not being fully remedied in the guidelines that states are establishing in conformance with the federal Child Support Enforcement Amendments.

Some judges and other court personnel charged with handling child support decisions do not even look to the child's needs in making the award but concern themselves with what the father can afford to give without diminishing his own life-style. The father's budget, including expenses for entertainment, is accepted at face value. The mother's budget for herself and the children is scrutinized to the penny, and items such as money to take the children to a fast-food restaurant once a week are rejected with the pronouncement that the woman can cook. A study of support awards in Denver in the late 1970s found fathers paying more for their cars each month than for their children.[12]

The Costs of Child Raising. The estimates of child raising costs that have been used to establish most child support guidelines are based on data developed by the U.S. Department of Agriculture and updated by academicians and others. These estimates are deficient for several reasons. They are based on data that are too old to reflect current spending. Because they are based on expenses in an intact, two-parent, two-child family, they do not take into account the additional costs that arise when there are two households. For example, when two parents are present, one can care for the children while the other does errands or visits the doctor. The single mother may have to pay a babysitter while she attends to these needs. A critical failure of these estimates is that they do not include the costs of child care. The single mother of young children cannot go into the paid work force unless she has full-time or after-school child care. In 1985 the Conference Board, a nonprofit business research organization, reported that child care absorbs 10 to 30 percent of a family's budget, with the majority of parents paying approximately $3,000 per year. A single mother can easily use up her entire child support award paying for child care. These data also omit college costs and needs specific to individual children, such as enhanced education for the gifted child and medical care for the disabled child. They do not include family savings that inure to the children's benefit, such as saving for college, insurance, and pensions, and there is absolutely no reflection of the value of unpaid work the custodial parent does as the primary caretaker.

Child support guidelines which set numerical parameters or establish a formula for support levels will provide greater predictability and uniformity and will increase award amounts for most families. The Bush Institute for Child and Family Policy estimated in 1985 that if all awards were set according to the Wisconsin and Delaware guidelines, the total amount of child support due per year would rise from approximately $10.1 billion to approximately $26.6 billion. But the guidelines will still leave custodial mothers bearing a disproportionate share of child raising costs. According to U.S. Bureau of Labor Services Data on the equalization of family living standards, in a divorced family where the noncustodial father earns $2,000 per month and the mother earns $1,000 per month and cares for two children, the father would have to pay 52 percent of his *gross* income in support in order for the two families to have an equivalent standard of living. No guidelines come even close to this politically unpalatable number.

Enforcement. The New York State Child Support Commission, established in conformance with the federal Child Support Enforcement Amendments' requirement that each state establish such a commission to investigate its own child support collection system, reported in 1985 that judges' unwillingness to demand compliance or impose penalties for noncompliance was the prob-

lem about which it received the greatest number of complaints.
The director of this commission testified to the New York Task
Force on Women in the Courts:

> *It may seem fanatical to allege that the run around these women are*
> *getting in the court is a result of gender bias . . . , but I believe that*
> *what we are seeing is a not-so-subtle form of bias against women as*
> *we continue to see them through this process as litigious, vexatious,*
> *harassing, and a little bit crazy, if they continue to pursue something*
> *to which they are entitled. It is almost like a little game, a game*
> *where a person with power can put his hand on the head of the*
> *person who is angry and let that person flail away, continue to move*
> *until he drops from exhaustion, and many do drop from exhaustion.*
> *In fact, perhaps the most stable of them do drop from exhaustion or*
> *say, "The hell with it, let's let him keep his money."*

New York's secretary of state testified that "Family Court has
made women feel that their attempt to support their children is
vindictive, unimportant or even a joke." The chair of the Coalition
of Women for Child Support, an organization of women from all
walks of life from western New York, testified that on average
members had spent over seven years trying to have court-ordered
child support enforced. Four-fifths of members had to apply for
welfare subsequent to divorce, though none had been on public
assistance before. Echoing the secretary of state, the coalition
chair testified: "Individually we have been told that our unsuccessful attempts to collect uncollected child support build character . .
. . We have also been told that we are vindictive, money-grubbing,
that we made our beds and now we must lie in them."

The administrative judge of New York City's Family Courts
testified that judges so frequently grant adjournments to nonpaying
fathers that mothers abandon their enforcement efforts. These
women cannot afford to pay their lawyers (assuming they could
afford one at all) to keep coming to court, and their own repeated
court appearances jeopardize their jobs. A Rochester attorney
described being at a conference in the judge's chambers on behalf
of a woman who had been attempting to enforce a child support
order for 14 years. The father's attorney said to the judge, "It's
been 14 years, why doesn't she leave him alone?" and the judge
said to the mother's attorney, "Yes, why doesn't she leave him
alone?" Counsel to the New York State Division for women reported:

> *Each year . . . I have spoken to hundreds of women who call and*
> *write the Women's Division and other organizations and attorneys,*
> *seeking help with their child support problem. They have invariably*
> *had a disappointing if not devastating experience in the courts. . . .*

They complain of low court ordered support awards, minimal enforcement of their support orders even after they have secured them, and disrespectful treatment from anyone from guards in the courthouse to judges. A frequent ploy used by fathers to delay or avoid child support enforcement is to allege visitation interference or seek a change of custody. The New York State Child Support Commission noted that although "visitation interference" is often raised as a defense to a petition for child support enforcement, it is rarely raised in an independent action, and failure of fathers to spend time with their children is much more frequent than interference with that time by the mother.

Nothing in this grim litany is unique to New York. Although some judges dedicated to collecting child support hold "Pay or Stay Days" in which delinquent fathers believed by child support officials to have the money are ordered to come to court with a wallet and a toothbrush, prepared to pay or stay in jail, it was the massive failure of court systems in every state to enforce child support that led Congress to enact the 1984 Child Support Enforcement Amendments. Study after study has shown that fathers' willingness to pay has nothing to do with their ability to pay. For example, a 1974 Rand Corporation study of California titled, "Nonsupport of Legitimate Children by Affluent Fathers as a Cause of Poverty and Welfare Dependence" showed how the refusal of fathers with ample incomes to pay child support and the inability of mothers to enforce the awards had driven once economically stable women and children onto welfare. Studies have also shown that in counties where it is known that nonpayers face stiff penalties, there is a high rate of compliance. A study of 28 Michigan counties showed that as the number of jailings for contempt (disobeying the court's order) rose, so did compliance. With seven or more jailings per 10,000 people in the population, there was a 75 percent compliance rate.[13]

The refusal of courts across the country to make and enforce meaningful spousal and child support awards has had profound consequences for single mothers over many decades. A University of Michigan study that followed a large sample of families weighted to be representative of the entire country from 1968 to 1973 found that divorced and remarried men and intact couples had incomes comfortably above need level, but women and children had fallen 7 percent below need, into poverty.[14] A large-scale study of California divorces by University of California, Berkeley researchers in the late 1970s found that in Los Angeles county one year after divorce fathers' standard of living had risen by 42 percent, while that of mothers and their children had declined by 73 percent.[15] In the 1984 Vermont study cited earlier, men experienced a 120 percent increase in standard of living and women a 33 percent decline.

In 1987, pollster Louis Harris published a major survey of the American family, with special emphasis on the state of child rearing. He reported that most people are happy with their spouses, their children, their jobs, their incomes, their homes, and their prospects for the future. But with respect to the group he called "Divorced and Separated," he wrote: "These families . . . are overwhelmingly female (77%) . . . are suffering badly economically (71% with incomes of $25,000 or less), and are more dissatisfied by far with their living facilities. . . . Clearly, by any measure, those divorced or separated, who are mainly women, are hurting badly."[16] Women and children in female-headed households are the fastest growing segment of the poverty population in the country. The courts have played a major role in this statistic.

Custody

Although it is widely believed that it is only fathers for whom gender bias is a factor in custody decisions, mothers, too, may be affected by judges' stereotyped thinking about the true nature and role of women. The cultural stereotype of the good mother is the chaste, selfless woman who is at home and is the caretaker of her children. Women may be deprived of custody because of social relationships and life-styles that are acceptable for men. In a pair of 1984 Illinois cases, a woman lost custody of her three daughters because she lived with a man to whom she was not married, while a man with similar living arrangements was permitted to retain custody of his children. In a 1983 Louisiana case, a woman attorney wanted to move with her daughter to Washington, D.C., where she had been offered a job with the National Labor Relations Board. The judge denounced her as a "careerist" and awarded custody to the father. Similarly, witnesses before the New York Task Force on Women in the Courts spoke of how difficult it is for women to gain permission from the court to move with their children for job opportunities, the courts reasoning that moving would diminish fathers' visitation opportunities, while custodial fathers are allowed to move for work-related reasons, and noncustodial fathers are never required to stay in the area in order to spend time with their children. One attorney testifying on this point stated, "I have often heard women clients referred to as 'corporate gypsies' by male counsel over my objection, yet the same type of pejorative names are not applied to male executives."

A single mother need not even be a careerist to be deprived of custody. Merely working outside the home puts her at risk. Some judges believe that any woman at home is better than a mother at work, so when fathers remarry and tell the court they now have a wife at home full-time and can provide a proper environment for the child, there are judges who go along with this and switch custody. They see no irony in the fact that the father, like the mother, is turning his child over to a caretaker while he goes to work, because that is what men are supposed to do. This woman-in-the-home standard amounts to a paternal preference because rarely is the woman who has been a full-time homemaker awarded sufficient spousal and child support to permit her to remain a homemaker, and men 35 to 44 remarry twice as often as women.

Another growing, unstated, paternal preference is the award of custody to the parent with more money, regardless of who has been the primary caretaker of the child or whether the father has a history of violence. Because fathers almost always are in a stronger financial position than mothers, making money the deter-minative factor amounts to a paternal preference.

In 1986 the California Supreme Court ruled in *Burchard* v. *Garay*[17] that a mother's working outside the home and a father's stronger financial position may never be bases for determining custody. This case began when in 1982 a California trial court, subsequently affirmed by an appellate court, awarded custody of a 3-year-old nonmarital child to a father who had refused to acknowl-edge paternity, pay support, or visit the child until a court-ordered blood test proved him the father when the child was 15 months old. During this entire period the mother was working at two jobs, continuing her training as a registered nurse, and caring for the child with the help of her own father and others.

The trial court awarded exclusive custody to the father on the ground that he was financially better off, that he had married and therefore he "and the stepmother can provide constant care for the minor child and keep him on a regular schedule without resorting to other caretakers," and because he would allow the mother visitation, which the mother had resisted. The supreme court overruled this decision with strong language:

> *The court's reliance upon the relative economic position of the parties is impermissible; the purpose of child support awards is to ensure that the spouse otherwise best fit for custody receives ade-quate funds for the support of the child. Its reliance upon the asserted superiority of [the father's] child care arrangements sug-gests an insensitivity to the role of working parents. And all of the factors cited by the trial court together weigh less to our mind than*

*a matter it did not discuss—the importance of continuity and
stability in custody arrangements.*

Yet so much time—five years—had elapsed since the initial
custody decision that the supreme court did not award the child to
the mother but remanded the case to the trial court to determine
whether it was in the child's best interests to change custody again.
One year later the case was still pending.

The trial court's opinion in *Burchard* v. *Garay* is not an aberra-
tion. Other trial courts have used wealth as their standard, and the
District of Columbia Court of Appeals ruled in 1983 that the fact
that a woman is receiving Aid to Families with Dependent Children can be taken into account.[18] In these cases the inference of
the court is that the woman on welfare is lazy and a poor role
model for her children. The fact that she was driven to welfare
because the father refused to pay child support is ignored. This
creates a terrible catch-22 for the single mother. In order to receive
AFDC, she must reveal the father's name so that the state can
institute a paternity proceeding. But, as in *Burchard* v. *Garay*,
once paternity is established, the father may sue for custody, a
proceeding in which the state provides no assistance, and in which
the mother on welfare is at considerable risk.

The mother who initiates a divorce and seeks custody because
she discovers that the father is sexually abusing the children faces
particular risks. Some judges simply do not want to believe that
sexual abuse and incest are realities, and their attitudes may be
compounded by mental health and social work professionals. Thus,
if the woman reveals her grounds for wanting the divorce, she may
be branded as paranoid or as inventing stories in order to deprive
the father of access to his children. Not merely unsupervised
visitation but custody itself may be awarded to the father. Experts
in the area of child sexual abuse often counsel women not to
acknowledge what they know and to seek divorce on other grounds
in order to avoid this problem.[19]

The welcome facts that fathers are participating more in child
rearing and that there are parents who genuinely want joint
custody and manage it well also have negative consequences for
the single mother. Some judges are so taken with the image of the
new father that they award custody to the father who only became
an active parent at the time of separation. In some cases there may
be good reasons for this, and society as a whole should stop
stigmatizing mothers who have given years of daily care and would
like voluntarily to turn that responsibility over to fathers. However,
in most cases the father's sudden interest should not be decisive,

and some states have adopted a "primary caretaker" rule under which, barring unusual circumstances, custody is awarded to the parent who has taken primary responsibility for daily, ongoing care of the child. This rule minimizes both faddish custody awards and the incidence of "custody blackmail," described above, because the law provides much greater predictability than a generalized "best interests of the child" standard.

For the single mother the problems with imposed joint custody are several. Usually joint custody means that although both parents are responsible for making decisions about the child's welfare, principal physical custody is with one parent, usually the mother. Yet courts are cutting child support awards in joint custody cases as if the mother did not have to continue providing space, food, clothing, etc. for the child on a virtually full-time basis. Imposed joint custody also means that parents who do not get along must agree on decisions about their children. Fathers often use imposed joint custody as a means to continue harassing their former wives, and much repeat litigation is generated, as mothers must seek court approval for everything from braces to special education.

Domestic Violence

Often violence in her home is what precipitates a woman into divorce and single parenthood. But the violence does not always stop with separation and divorce. And never-married women are just as likely to require court protection from violence by someone with whom they are (or were) living or the father of their children.

For most of American history the law condoned or ignored a man's violence against his wife. William Blackstone's *Commentaries on the Laws of England* (1768) approved a husband's right to chastise his wife moderately to enforce obedience. The United States adopted the common law, and in 1824, in the first state supreme court case on wife beating, the Mississippi Supreme Court held that a man was free to "correct" his wife with a stick no wider around than his thumb without being charged with assault and battery. Although an Alabama court held in 1871 that wife beating was "a relic of barbarous and unchristian privilege," men's freedom to assault their wives, former wives, and girlfriends has been essentially unchecked until recently.

The magnitude of the problem is enormous. The U.S. Department of Justice reported in 1986 that approximately 2.1 million women were victims of domestic violence—defined as any rape, robbery, aggravated assault, or simple assault on a married, divorced, or separated woman by a relative or person she knew well—at least once a year from 1979 to 1982, and that 32 percent of these women were assaulted again within six months. The Massachusetts Department of Health reported in 1986 that in that state a woman is murdered by her husband or boyfriend every twenty-two days.[20]

A major focus of women's rights advocates over the last two decades has been the creation and reform of domestic assault statutes. Today, courts in virtually every state are empowered to issue orders of protection directing the batterer to cease harassing, menacing, and assaulting the victim and to leave and stay out of her home. Most states provide domestic violence victims the option of proceeding in either civil or criminal court, and many state laws specifically bar law enforcement personnel, prosecutors, court employees, and other officials from discouraging or preventing anyone who wishes to file a petition or sign a complaint in a domestic violence case from doing so.

Despite these statutory protections, the legal claims of domestic violence victims are often belittled or ignored. Women seeking orders of protection find themselves shunted back and forth between different courts by court personnel and judges who would rather not be bothered with their cases. Criminal courts especially may insist that the assault is simply a domestic matter and doesn't belong in their courts. There is often significant confusion about which court the woman belongs in if she is not married to her batterer. Some women become so demoralized by this process that they abandon seeking court protection.

Judges and court personnel frequently ask women why they have no visible injuries, although menacing and threats leave no marks and the injuries to a victim of domestic violence are more likely to be to her torso than to her extremeties, as is typical of an accident victim. Black women have noted that they are particularly disadvantaged by these inquiries because bruises are not readily visible on their skin.

Victim blaming is commonplace. Women are asked what they did to provoke the violence against them, and batterers are permitted to testify about how they were provoked, often without comment from the judge. In 1983 a Colorado judge sentenced a man who shot his wife five times to two years work release, an illegally low sentence that was subsequently overruled, on the ground that her "highly provoking acts" of leaving without warning, being loving and caring up to the morning she left, and obtaining a protective order and proceeding with a separation without telling him where she was constituted "extraordinary mitigative circumstances."

Even if she is granted an order of protection, the victim may be subjected to comments that trivialize her injuries and concerns. In August 1986, Pamela Dunn's body was found on a garbage heap in Arlington, Massachusetts. She had been shot five times by her husband, who was later imprisoned for her murder. Five months earlier Dunn had left her husband after two months of marriage because of his violence and sought an order of protection. The district court judge granted the order, but when she asked for police protection while she collected her clothing from the marital home because she feared being alone with her husband, the judge reviled her in open court. "If he wants to gnaw on you and you on him, go ahead, but not at taxpayers' expense." There was never any allegation that Dunn had been violent toward her husband. Battered women's advocates throughout the country agree that the judge's denigration of her concerns was a signal to her husband that the courts would take scant notice of any future violence he chose to inflict.

Mutual Orders of Protection

Judicial imputation of violence to women takes tangible form in the issuance of mutual orders of protection, directing the parties not to threaten or assault one another, when no petition is filed against the woman. These orders are seriously detrimental to women in several ways. They are first of all a denial of due process. The woman is "found guilty" without notice of the allegations of violence on her part and no opportunity to prepare to meet those allegations. Mutual orders are often issued when there is *no* allegation of violence against the woman. The batterer or his lawyer simply says he wants a mutual, or the judge issues a mutual on his or her own initiative. A 1986 study of gender bias in the Florida courts found that in Dade County (Miami) it is the policy of the administrative judge and the practice of the other judges to issue mutual restraining orders rather than protecting the moving party, no matter what the circumstances.[21] Mutual orders are held against women in custody disputes. When a woman claims that her husband's violence toward her is a reason why he should not be awarded custody or joint custody, or why there should be supervised visitation, the husband responds that a mutual order was issued, which stands as evidence that she was as violent as he. Mutual orders endanger women. When the police are called in a situation where the woman has a mutual order, the officers are frequently confused, often take no action at all, and sometimes put the children in foster care and both parents in jail.

The director of a Rochester, New York, battered women's shelter played the following tape-recorded testimony from a woman against whom a mutual order was issued for the New York Task Force on Women in the Courts. On several different occasions, Linda S. was strangled and raped and subjected to other types of abuse from her husband. While seeking a divorce and custody, she also sought the protection of the court. She was passed back and forth between family and criminal court. When she tried to file criminal charges for the rape, the county attorney filed the case as sexual misconduct, which carries virtually no penalty. As is almost universally the case, no sanctions were imposed on her husband for his several violations of her temporary order of protection. Several months after the strangling incident, her husband, Keith, said he would agree to an order of protection if it were a mutual order. Linda was not in court when the judge wrote "mutual" into her order and did not know whether her lawyer opposed it or not, but other lawyers for battered women have testified about judges coercing them into accepting mutual orders to keep the docket moving. Some lawyers say they walk out of court without any order rather than accept a mutual because it is so harmful to the woman. One night Linda S. tried to use her mutual order to obtain police protection. This is what happened:

> *About four o'clock in the morning, he was running around my house trying to get into my house, because I had nailed the windows shut so he was having a hard time. He came to my front door and I called the police. When the police got to my house . . . I showed them the order of protection and they laughed saying, "Oh, you know it's a mutual order of protection." And Keith was there outside the house; they said, "Oh, he just wants to talk with you." At four o'clock in the morning, I was scared to death. I was dripping sweat from my head to my toes and I kept on saying, "I don't want to talk to him, I don't want to talk to him." The police just kept saying, "Well, just talk to him and we'll get him away." So I couldn't argue any more with the police so he came into my house and I had to stand there and talk to him, in my bathrobe, with two or three police officers. And I think that was because it was a mutual order of protection. I mean, I wasn't even given respect [by] those police officers. I felt I had no credibility when [the judge] wrote this.*

Special Problems of Rural, Minority, and Divorcing Women

Battered women in rural communities face particular problems. The judge, prosecutor, and police are often fishing buddies of the man from whom she needs protection. It is embarrassing for her to tell the details of her personal life to these men, and they are reluctant to take action against their pal. The practice of shunting women from court to court has even more onerous consequences in rural communities. Whereas the "other court" in a city is downstairs, across the street, or at worst reachable by public transportation, the rural woman must frequently travel a considerable distance to reach the "other court," and the likelihood is that she has no transportation.

Sexism may be compounded by racism for the minority group single mother seeking protection from domestic violence. The attitude of some judges is "that's the way those people are" and there is no point in wasting court time on them.

The woman who seeks an order of protection in the course of a matrimonial action is especially at risk. Many judges assume she wants to bootstrap her divorce case and either refuse to grant the order or issue a mutual. These judges do not understand that divorce is often a time of increased violence. Because the batterer is typically a man seeking to exert control over his wife, if she seeks a divorce or fights him over the financial or custody aspects of dissolution, his violence will flare.

Insensitivity in the Courts

This lack of understanding of the psychology and personal circumstances of battered women and batterers permeates the justice system. A very large percentage of women who bring domestic violence complaints withdraw them, to the understandable annoyance and frustration of the courts. But too little effort is made to understand why this is so and how the courts are themselves implicated in women's decisions not to go forward.

Many judges do not understand that women are socialized to acquiesce in a man's orders, to feel responsible for his dissatisfaction with her and his abuse, and often to believe that violence is part of women's natural lot in life because they have seen their mothers and grandmothers beaten. Most batterers have never been told by anyone that they may not abuse the women in their lives. Some judges are insensitive to the issue of economic duress. Many women lack marketable skills with which to support themselves and their children and are essentially one man away from welfare. Yet support awards are no more generous or effective in domestic violence cases than they are in divorce, and some courts refuse them altogether.

Few judges ask women whether they have been intimidated or

coerced into withdrawing their complaints. Not only is such coercion commonplace, it occurs even in the courts themselves. Court waiting rooms rarely separate victims and assailants. Batterers use this opportunity to cajole, harass, and sometimes even physically attack their victims to force them to withdraw their complaints. The attitude of everyone the victim encounters in the court system is often what drives her to abandon the quest for legal protection. When police, intake personnel, court officers, prosecutors, and judges subject women to ridicule and sarcasm, and when judges tolerate verbally abusive and harassing behavior by the abuser toward the victim in the courtroom, it is no wonder that many women are afraid to initiate or carry through on their charges against the abuser. Courts also sometimes force women into mediation to resolve domestic violence complaints. The imbalance of power between the domestic violence victim and her abuser makes it impossible for the victim to speak freely. Mediation is no substitute for a firm and firmly enforced statement by the court that violence will not be tolerated.

As one New York judge told the New York Task Force on Women in the Courts, many judges believe that "all [these women] have to do is get out of the house. It is as simple as that." This assumption that the violence stops once the parties are living apart is one of the most dangerous myths about domestic violence. Every year cases are reported from all parts of the country, like the Colorado sentencing case described earlier, in which men hunt down and murder their former wives and girlfriends. Courts are insistent on fathers having access to their children, yet when women who have common children with batterers ask the court for supervised visitation, judges often ignore or reject the request. The result is that many batterers use visitation with their children as an opportunity to inflict further violence on the mothers.

Some judges are so indifferent to violence against women that they actually award custody to the batterer. In 1984, for example, a New York appellate court reversed the trial court's award of custody to a man who had undisputedly abused his wife over several years, often in the children's presence.[22] The judge stated in his decision that he had walked past the battered women's shelter to which the woman had fled with her two children and decided that a shelter was unsuitable for children and that the father could provide a better home. In 1986 the Wisconsin Supreme Court overruled a trial court judge who barred evidence of a father's violence against his wife as irrelevant in a custody dispute.[23]

There is extensive evidence showing that children are secondary victims in violent homes. They experience significant physical and psychological symptoms. The boys grow up believing it is acceptable to take out their frustrations on the women in their lives. The girls grow up believing that they must accept violence from the men with whom they live. Domestic violence victims are more likely to abuse their own children. A few states now include family violence in the factors that a judge must take into account in determining custody, and treat violence as evidence of unfitness for custody.

Court Facilities and Attitudes in Family and Housing Courts

Still other problems confront the single mother in the courts. Often she must bring her children to court because she cannot afford babysitters. Yet most courts lack facilities for changing diapers and child care. Many judges will not allow children in the courtroom or become furious and order them out if they cry. Women are afraid to leave children unsupervised in the hallways and sometimes have their cases dismissed because they are ducking in and out of the court to check on a child. Family courts, the courts in which women most frequently find themselves, are often the most dilapidated and dirty in the system, a literal manifestation of the legal system's attitude that family law is second class.

A significant, if not major, proportion of individuals in housing court are women on welfare fighting eviction notices because of late and totally inadequate payments which prevented them from paying their rent. A 1987 study of the New York City Housing Court by the American Civil Liberties Union, "Justice Evicted," found that tenants' ignorance of their rights, lack of legal representation and inequities, and slipshod practices in housing court procedures were major factors in the lack of due process in housing court.

When the New York Task Force on Women in the Courts asked respondents to its attorneys survey to comment on the interrelationship of sex, race, and economic status in gender bias in the courts, several attorneys commented on the family and housing courts. One respondent wrote:

> As a legal services attorney . . . I have found the courts to be
> unresponsive to the special problems of poor people and especially
> poor women. In both family court and landlord/tenant court . . .
> most . . . judges have shown a lack of understanding of (1) the

limited resources poor families and especially single mothers have to
bring up their children, provide necessities and pay their rent and
other bills; (2) the fear and lack of understanding that poor people,
particularly poor women, have about the way that courts function
and their rights.

A second respondent commented:

The court system itself seems to be biased against low-income
minorities. Specifically, the family courts and landlord tenant courts
are dirty, crowded and staffed with personnel who do not respect
the litigants. Here especially sexist comments are prevalent and the
judges condone same.

Reform Efforts and Their Impacts

When the NOW Legal Defense and Education Fund (NOW LDEF) was established in 1970, its founders were acutely aware that the reforms in women's rights legislation then beginning to be realized would be meaningless unless the judges charged with interpreting and enforcing the new laws could be educated about the ways in which gender-based stereotypes, myths, and biases affect judicial decision making and the courtroom environment. NOW LDEF's claim that the judiciary, like the rest of society, was gender-biased met with outright disbelief from many quarters. It took until 1980 for NOW LDEF, in cooperation with the newly formed National Association of Women Judges (NAWJ), to establish the National Judicial Education Program to Promote Equality for Women and Men in the Courts (NJEP), with the goal of putting the issue of gender bias on the national judicial education agenda.

NJEP brought together data from a wide variety of sources to convince the nation's judges and judicial educators that gender bias in the courts was a major problem that could only be amelio-rated if judges had an opportunity to explore and discuss these issues in their continuing education programs. NJEP also stressed the need to develop as much local data as possible in each state in which it made a presentation, in order to counter the resistance and denial that are an unavoidable part of addressing this very sensitive issue. When NJEP began to present programs on gender bias for the judiciary, many knowledgeable people expressed skep-ticism about the willingness of judges to accept this issue as a legitimate topic for judicial education or to engage in the self-examination necessary to eliminate it. Yet in a period of seven years NJEP was able to make gender bias in the courts a national issue and present programming about it at numerous national and state judicial colleges, in continuing legal education programs for attorneys, in law schools, and in programs for judicial screening commissions.

NJEP's emphasis on developing local data for judicial education purposes became the catalyst for a series of task forces appointed by the chief justices of numerous states to document gender bias in their own state court systems and recommend ways to eliminate it. The first three of these task forces, those in New Jersey, New York, and Rhode Island, generated such interest that the NAWJ established the National Gender Bias Task Force to encourage and assist in the formation and operation of new task forces in gender bias in the courts. As of late 1987, the first three task forces had published reports and more than a dozen other state gender bias task forces were beginning data collection. NJEP's efforts to focus attention on gender bias in the courts also led to changes in some states' codes of judicial conduct and codes of professional responsibility for attorneys explicitly barring gender-biased behavior, and to legislation proposing that all reforms in family law statutes must include education for judges about the purpose of the reforms.

Concurrent with the NOW Legal Defense and Education Fund's efforts to launch education for judges about gender bias, women law professors initiated efforts to eliminate gender bias in the teaching of law students. In a panel discussion on the treatment of women by the law held at the annual meeting of the Association of American Law Schools in 1970, it was agreed that, in the words of Professor (now Judge) Ruth Bader Ginsburg:

> *Two jobs merit immediate attention: (1) the elimination from law school texts and classroom presentations of attempts at comic relief via stereotyped characterizations of women; (2) the infusion into standard curricular offerings of material on sex-based discrimination.*

This program, too, took many years to get underway. Although individual law professors, primarily women, sought to raise these issues in their own courses, it was not until the mid-1980s that female law students began to object formally to the denigration of women and women's issues in the classroom, and not until 1987 that female law professors published the first comprehensive study of the treatment of women's issues in a segment of the curriculum: "Sex Bias in the Teaching of Criminal Law" found, for example, that with respect to domestic violence, five of the seven leading casebooks did not mention it at all, one included an author's note stating that spousal battery is no longer permitted, and one discussed battered women's use of the self-defense justification in cases where they assault or kill their abusers. The study explains how this failure to discuss domestic violence both marginalizes an issue of crucial importance to millions of women and deprives law students of the insight into the realities of their clients' lives that is essential to competent representation. It also offers suggestions as to how the many aspects of domestic violence should be taught and the materials available to supplement the casebooks.

The child support crisis spurred the growth of numerous self-help grass-roots advocacy groups made up of women trying to enforce their own child support orders, and extensive reform efforts by a wide range of national women's and children's organizations, culminating initially in the 1984 federal Child Support Enforcement Amendments that are discussed in Chapters 5 and 8. Subsequent to the amendments' passage, many organizations such as the Women's Legal Defense Fund, The Children's Defense Fund, the National Women's Law Center, the NOW Legal Defense and Education Fund, the American Bar Association, and Parents Without Partners have been active in monitoring states' enactments of the enforcement measures required by the amendments and whether these new measures are being implemented at the local level, generating information about optimum child support guidelines, monitoring who in each state is charged with setting guidelines and what is finally adopted, and producing written materials for use by lawyers, custodial parents, and grass-roots activists.

What has all this activity meant for women and children in the courts? With respect to the child support guidelines and new enforcement mechanisms and the efforts to reform law school curricula, it is too soon to know. With respect to the National Judicial Education Program's experiences and the efforts to implement the recommendations of the several task forces on gender bias in the courts, the answers are not quantifiable, but there is evidence that many judges have been deeply surprised by the information brought to their attention and have acted on this information in their own courtrooms. After the National Judicial Education Program's pilot course presented at the California Center for Judicial Education and Research in 1981, the general jurisdiction judges who attended insisted that the segment on spousal and child support be repeated for the family court judges. One judge wrote on his evaluation:

> *I was quite shocked at the information we received indicating the disparity between males and females and the treatment of them in*

the courts, especially the statistics concerning how women fare after divorce as compared to how men fare after divorce after a few years. Many of the myths that are taken as facts by judges were shattered by your presentation. . . .

At subsequent NJEP programs judges have openly stated in response to this material on support awards that they had no understanding of the financial problems facing women after divorce and could think of cases where they had not been fair in their awards. In group discussions judges have been amazed to hear the views of their colleagues about such matters as the division of marital property, and to realize how much case outcome in family law cases depends on the judge in front of whom one appears. In New Jersey, the first state to have a gender-bias task force and where there has been the longest period to implement its recommendations, task force members and lawyers and judges throughout the state report that judges have a new awareness of how they should address and treat women, so that the courtroom environment has improved significantly and there is a dialogue on the many aspects of gender bias in the courts that was unimaginable five years ago. The phenomenal growth of interest in these issues demonstrated by the rapidly increasing number of supreme court task forces on gender bias in the courts and the willingness of the judiciary to include in its own education programs presentations on gender bias in the courts and the economic consequences of divorce is itself a positive sign.

Other signs of change are the inclusion of questions about gender-based attitudes and behavior in New Jersey's judicial performance evaluation criteria, a public forum organized by the Westchester, New York, Coalition on Domestic Violence in which the four candidates for a family court seat submitted themselves to public questioning about their views on issues such as mutual orders of protection and marital rape, and passage of legislation proposed by the California Senate and Assembly Task Force on Family Law Equity that would create funding for family law courses that would include information about gender bias. But for all these positive signs, the problems remain enormous.

Conclusion

Reviewing the myriad ways that courts disserve single mothers, one longs for straightforward means to set things right. Some urge limiting judicial discretion as much as possible, but such inflexibility can also be harmful, and it is illusory to believe that writing something down in a statute book always makes it happen in real life. Moreover, no legislation can reach the many situations that must be the judge's call. Although each state must strive to perfect its statutes and regulations, we cannot escape dependence on the discretion of individual judges, hearing examiners, and court personnel.

Eliminating the gender bias documented in this chapter requires that its recognition and a determination to end it must become priorities at every point in the system. Candidates for the judiciary, whether through election or appointment, must be sounded out on their knowledge and views on matters such as domestic violence and divorce. Everyone in the system—judges, hearing officers, intake officers, support enforcement officers, court clerks, and other personnel must be made aware through repeated education and training of their own gender-based biases and how these are interfering with the performance of their duties, and provided with current, accurate information about matters such as the economic consequences of divorce. We must give up the illusion that law is pure, rational, objective, abstract, and principled, and recognize that although the vast majority of judges are commited to fairness, the vast majority of judges are upper-middle-class white men whose perception of fairness is filtered through the lens of that particular life experience, and who have not been exposed to information that would make them question their perceptions or give them accurate information on such matters as the battered wife syndrome or the costs of child care.

Judicial disciplinary bodies must become responsive to complaints of gender-biased behavior and initiate actions on their own when, for example, a judge makes the front page of his community newspaper for failing to pay his own spousal and child support. Judicial performance evaluation, a growing phenomenon across the country, usually carried out through surveys of lawyers in the community, must include questions about judges' decision-making and behavior toward women litigants, witnesses, lawyers, jurors, and court personnel, as the responses to such questions may reveal gender bias. Family courts must be seen as essential to rather than the stepchildren of the system and accorded the respect, resources, and quality of judiciary that their caseloads and importance in peoples' lives necessitate.

Lawyers must be educated in all the same areas as judges, so that they can properly represent their female clients. Law schools must structure their curricula not only to include the issues that impact women and women as single mothers, but also to present them as part of the mainstream of the law.

It is now two hundred years since the Constitution was adopted. Equality for women is not yet guaranteed by the Constitution; nor has it been achieved in the courts. This is a major failure in our justice system and demands a major commitment to reform.

Endnotes

1. All references to the findings of the New York Task Force on Women in the Courts are drawn from *Report of the New York Task Force on Women in the Courts* (New York: Office of Court Administration, 1986), published in *Fordham Urban Law Journal,* vol. 15 (1987).

2. All references to the New Jersey Supreme Court Task Force on Women in the Courts are drawn from *First Year Report of the New Jersey Supreme Court Task Force on Women in the Courts* (Trenton: Administrative Office of the Courts, 1984), published in *Women's Rights Law Reporter,* vol. 9, no. 2 (Spring 1986): 129–77.

3. For documentation of this data, see, for example, John D. Johnson and Charles L. Knapp, "Sex Discrimination by Law: A Study in Judicial Perspective," *New York University Law Review* 46 (October 1971): 675–747; Norma Wikler, "On the Judicial Agenda for the '80s: Equal Treatment for Women and Men in the Courts," *Judicature* 64 (November 1980): 202–09; Lynn Hecht Schafran, "Eve, Mary, Superwoman: How Stereotypes About Women Influence Judges," *Judges' Journal* (Winter 1985): 12–17, 48–52; Lynn Hecht Schafran, "Documenting Gender Bias in the Courts: The Task Force Approach," *Judicature* 70, no. 5 (February-March 1987): 280–90; Laura Crites and Wendy Hepperle, *Women, the Courts and Equality* (Beverly Hills, Calif.: Sage Publications, 1987).

4. Heather R. Wishik, "Economics of Divorce: An Exploratory Study," *Family Law Quarterly* 20, no. 1 (Spring 1986): 80–107.

5. This and other Census Bureau data are drawn from a series of United States Department of Commerce reports titled and numbered: "Child Support and Alimony: 1978," ser. P-23, no. 112 (1980); "Child Support and Alimony: 1981," ser. P-23, no. 140 (1983); "Child Support and Alimony: 1983," ser. P-23, no. 148 (1985); and "Child Support and Alimony: 1985," ser. P-23, no. 152 (1987).

6. Justice Samuel H. Hofstadter and Shirley R. Levittan, "Alimony: A Reformulation," *Journal of Family Law* 7 (1967): 51–60.

7. *Beard* v. *Beard,* 262 So. 2d 269, 272 (Fla. Dist. Ct. App. 1972).

8. *Otis* v. *Otis,* 299 N.W.2d 114 (Minn. 1980).

9. *Holston* v. *Holston,* 473 A.2d 459, 58 Md. App. 308 (1984).

10. *LaRoque* v. *LaRoque,* 406 N.W.2d 736, 139 Wis. 2d 23 (1987).

11. Pub. L. No. 98–378 § 18, 98 Stat. 1305 (codified at 42 U.S.C. § 667).

12. Lucy Marsh Yee, "What Really Happens in Child Support Cases: An Empiri-

cal Study of Establishment and Enforcement of Child Support Orders in Denver District Court," *Denver Law Journal* 57 (1979): 21–68.

13. David Chambers, *Making Fathers Pay: The Enforcement of Child Support* (Chicago: University of Chicago Press, 1979).

14. Saul P. Hoffman and John Holmes, *Husbands, Wives and Divorce in Five Thousand American Families—Patterns of Economic Progress*, Vol. 4 (Ann Arbor: Institute for Social Research, University of Michigan, 1975).

15. Lenore Weitzman, *The Divorce Revolution: The Unexpected Social and Economic Consequences for Women and Children in America* (New York: The Free Press, 1985).

16. *The Philip Morris Family Survey* (New York: Louis Harris and Associates 1987), p. 11.

17. *Burchard* v. *Garay*, 42 Cal. 3d 531 (1986).

18. *Albergottie* v. *James*, 470 A.2d 266 (App. D. C. 1983).

19. See, e.g., Roland Summit, "Recognition and Treatment of Child Sexual Abuse," in *Coping with Pediatric Illness*, ed. Charles Hollingsworth (New York: Spectrum Publications, 1983); Louise Armstrong, "Daddy Dearest," *Connecticut*, January 1984, pp. 53–55, 127.

20. "Judge Criticized After Woman's Death," *The Boston Globe*, September 21, 1986, p. 1.

21. Charlene Carres, *Gender Bias: Its Effects on Justice in Florida* (Tallahassee: Policy Studies Clinic, College of Law, Florida State University, 1986), p. 11.

22. *Blake* v. *Blake*, 106 A.D.2d 916, 483 N.Y.S. 879 (4th Dept. 1984).

23. *Bertram* v. *Kilian*, 394 N.W.2d, 773, 133 Wis. 2d 202 (1986).

Chapter 4

RESTRUCTURING FAMILY LIFE

Frances Smalls Caple

The day-to-day living experiences of any family depend very much on the availability of internal and external resources. Equally important is the way in which the family utilizes its resources. Resources for a family may exist in the form of people, goods, and services. While there are certain basic minimum needs in these categories, there is no specific formula which defines strength or ensures success for a family. Many myths have been generated concerning the family life of single-parent units. Many of these myths are based on a presumption that there *is* a single formula, particularly as to the number of adult persons present as internal resources to the family. Less attention has been given to basic external resource needs.

This chapter will examine family life in single-parent units in order to detail some realities and dispel some myths about single-parent living. The ultimate goal is to assist in the expansion of basic knowledge and understanding, which is vital to developing plans for addressing unmet needs of single-parent families. In order to accomplish this goal, historical and current statistical facts will be documented, and various family forms will be distinguished. The actual discussion of single-parent family life will include the presentation of pertinent family theory and will examine coping skills and adaptive styles of such families as they face special vulnerabilities associated with socioeconomic status, and special circumstances due to changes in family structure. Finally, availability of and access to potential external resources within a system of social services will be examined with regard to their effects on single-parent family life. Conceptual and research findings, as well as the comments of single-parent family members, will be used to enlighten the discussion throughout this chapter.

The Single-Parent Family: A Broad View

The fact is, there have *always* been single-parent families. This nation was founded, settled, explored, and developed by individuals and family units of all kinds. Some male settlers and explorers never returned to their families because of death or desertion. In war times, soldiers were away for long periods, and some never returned to the young families they were just beginning. The system of black slavery in America was such that stability of the black family was not its primary goal. As a result, black families were often separated when it was expedient for the main economic and political purposes of the slaveholders.

A careful review of history yields evidence of the ever-present issue of single parenthood. For example, although minor children were not involved in all instances, during the 54-year period between 1870 and 1924, the divorce rate was reported as having increased by 400 percent.[1] How could that be, especially when, by comparison, the divorce rate has "merely tripled" in the more modern times of the 49-year period between 1925 and 1974? The historical precedents to the unusually high 400 percent rate have been assessed to the cumulative effects of several events: first, to the Reformation, when marriage was secularized; next, to the Romantic movement, which prompted the end of absolute rule of parents over youths and of husbands over wives; and more recently, to the Industrial Revolution, which not only created urban mobility and instability but also paved the way for potential economic independence for women. Of course, other explanations could also be offered for that dramatic rise in the divorce rate. For example, some association could have been drawn to better reporting procedures, or to the fact that there was greater legal and social permission to air the private affairs of families.

Although, as noted, single-parent family forms have always existed, there is considerable variation in the numbers of these families at different times in history. For example, the number of single-parent families has been steadily increasing since 1970. During the 100 years between 1870 and 1970, the proportion of single-parent families in America held steady at a rate of approximately one in ten families. A major change in this pattern began in 1970, as discussed in Chapter 2.

The trend to increasing numbers of single-parent families is not limited to the United States. The divorce rate has doubled in almost every European country since 1960, tripled in the Netherlands, and increased fivefold in the United Kingdom.[2] Furthermore, single-parent families comprised approximately 40 percent of families in some places in Africa and Latin America, one-third of families in Jamaica, and one-fifth of families in Peru, Honduras, and Cuba. These trends have been attributed to (1) the increasing need for men to migrate, without families, in search of employment; (2) the increasing incidence of divorce; and (3) death of the male spouse.

All told, single-parent families are not new family forms; nor are they confined to a specific geographic area. Why, then, is there such current concern about single-parent families? One response arises from the fact that in recent years families in general have captured the interest of scholars, legislators, and policymakers, much the same as individuals were the focus of attention earlier in the 20th century. Other elements related to the current focus on single-parent families may be found in the distinguishing features of these families and how these features have been viewed by society.

Families: Definitions and Distinctions

The term "single-parent family" conjures up certain negative images: weakness rather than strength, failure rather than success, deficits rather than assets. Single-parent families have been viewed as *being* problems or presenting problems of some kind, although what those problems are is not consistently clear. Comparisons are typically drawn between one-parent and two-parent families. Except for that which is evident in the names of these family forms— the notation of the number of parents present—the distinctions between them are not immediately obvious.

The Idealized Two-Parent Family

The stereotypical, all-American family consists of two people who are living together and legally married to each other and have one or more children of their union. In its most idealized form, the father works and the mother does not, thus enabling her to be available as a full-time homemaker. At one point in America's history, this family pattern represented a statistical mode—a research *fact*. Any deviation from this pattern was viewed as deviance—not just in a statistical sense but, in the case of certain single-parent families, in a social sense as well. Billingsley and Giovannoni suggest that the idealized two-parent family model has been revered because it "has untold social and economic benefits for the society." They state:

> *The breadwinner-father concurrently contributes to the gross na-*
> *tional product and prevents drain on the economy by supporting his*
> *family; the full-time homemaker-mother precludes the need for*
> *economically nonproductive social institutions to socialize and care*
> *for children.*[3]

Such an assessment may well be accurate. If so, it explains, in part, the general expectations that families should be independent systems that pull their own weight and expect nothing beyond general-use public services from society.

The statistical reality of the idealized two-parent family cannot be overlooked. It is a fact that most American children are being reared in married-couple households. But details about household composition tell very little about family life. Family life in two-parent units can only be confirmed by a study of how family roles are assigned and tasks are carried out. One author has noted that during this century, for the first time in history, "the majority of women have had, increasingly, to bring up their children virtually alone."[4] A trend toward the isolation of mothers and children (rather than broader interaction of all family members and with outside systems) is noted to be influenced by such factors as (1) husbands are away at work all day and may only interact with their children on weekends; (2) there may be little or no community or block life; (3) there may be little or no everyday contact with extended family; and (4) children are kept indoors out of concern for their safety outside alone. The fact is that mothers in two-parent families may experience a similar kind of aloneness in the parent/child role interactions that many single parents describe. In addition, mothers in two-parent systems are increasingly partic-ipating in the breadwinner role. Economic realities of life in this society have necessitated shifts in the way *all* families function to meet their needs and personal goals. One point is clear: the number of parents in a family does not guarantee an absence of problems or difficulties.

Characteristics Common to All Families

The tasks for all child rearing families are the same, and from this cursory exploration it appears that many of the concerns may be the same whether there are one or two adults carrying out the role of parent. Our interest in single-parent family life is not one of simple curiosity; rather, we wish to determine the degree to which such family life may lend itself to addressing overall purposes of its individual members, of the family as a whole, and of society. Walsh has concluded from her review of research that all family forms hold "the potential for successful adjustment," and that more important than family forms are family *processes*.[5]

In order to facilitate understanding of processes within single-parent families with minor children, as they are described in this chapter, the following working definition of "family" is offered: A family is a distinctive total unit—a social system—made up of specific component parts comprising two generations and residing together, but not necessarily alone. The system is in constant interaction with external systems such as workplace, schools, extended family, friends, and health care and social service facilities.

The "component parts" of the family include the following:

- Adults, whose roles certainly include "parents" and may include "spouse" (wife/husband).
- Minors, whose roles include "child" (son/daughter) and may include "sibling" (sister/brother).

These roles distinguish this unit *as* a family rather than, say, as a corporation or as a club or any other social system. The interacting roles of parent and child, and the fact that the unit is residing in a single location, further sets the family apart and distinguishes it from other systems or other parts of its environment. There is a relatively stable or predictable pattern of social order among the roles in a family. This pattern of social order describes the family's "organization," not unlike that observed in a corporation: How shall those of us within this system interact with each other and with others outside to achieve our goals?

There is considerable room for variation in how this pattern develops for *a* specific family, taking into account, for example, racial and ethnic cultural preferences, religious imperatives, age, gender, and socioeconomic status. However, in a family, as defined here, major emphasis is placed on the role of parent, which is in a hierarchical position in relation to the role of the child. The parents as originator of family units are vested with extraordinary power and authority and are expected to use this power to ensure that the responsibilities and purposes of the family are met and tasks carried out. While purposes of families will vary, basic purposes include nurturance, support and protection of all members, and guidance and control of minor children in a way that facilitates positive socialization both in the family and in society.

In these essential ways, then, all families are alike. There is no documentation of problems or behaviors that are solely evident in a particular family form or which are the inevitable outgrowth of a particular family form. There are, however, special issues and stresses which single-parent families face to greater degrees than two-parent families and some which two-parent families do not face at all. Some of the uniqueness of single-parent family life can be illuminated by examining origins and development of single-parent families, their structures, special issues and stresses, and their means of coping at critical points.

A Profile of Single-Parent Family Life

Origins and Development

There are numerous variations in how single-parent families are "born" and how they grow and change over time. Single-parent families may *begin* as a single-parent system and remain in that form throughout its life span. Other families will go through several forms between the time child rearing begins and ends.

Some women and men *choose* single parenting as a family form and become single parents through adoption. In addition, an increasing number of adult (rather than teenage) women are reported to be choosing motherhood without marriage. For example, in 1983 more than 200,000 single women over age 25 became mothers by birth, compared to a figure of 80,000 single women in 1975. Given the wide availability of birth control and abortions, an assumption can be made that most of these women are mothers by choice. Some of these women have been interviewed and confirm their choice. Unlike teenagers, these women tend to be educated, confident women who earn good salaries. They may have had prior relationships with men but want very much to have a baby while they are still biologically able to do so. Some adoptive and biological single parents by choice are now married but were living as single adults at the time their families began.

Figures are not available to determine how many single parents by choice were ever married. It is conceivable that single parents by choice could be distributed among all four categories of single-parent families commonly identified by the U.S. Bureau of Census: (1) divorced, (2) separated, (3) widowed, and (4) never married.

Most single-parent families evolved out of two-parent systems and came into existence as a result of divorce, separation, or death. Mortality rates are declining, and therefore the incidence of widowhood. By contrast, even though divorce rates are steadily increasing, the fastest-growing group of single-parent families is the "never-married" category.

Parenthood and marital status appear to be inextricably linked. When the term "single-parent family" is used, most often the discussion is focused on divorced, separated, or never-married parents. There is some basis for this. These family forms are most prevalent. However, some stigma is often associated with the labeling of these particular families as "broken," "partial," "uncompleted," "disorganized," or "unwed-mother" families. Some erroneous assumptions may exist that widowed and adoptive families do not face many of the same problems that divorced, separated, and never-married parents face. But the focus on divorced, separated, and never-married parents may be more a function of an effort to highlight failure in the marriage relationship—either failure to achieve it or to sustain it—than to focus on single parenthood per se. A family's identity and that of its members— especially its young impressionable members—is very much tied to society's descriptive labels and their connotations.

If the term "single-parent family" is used, it must be inclusive of all such families no matter how they developed. If indeed the focus is on actual structure and operation of families at given lengthy periods of times, our analysis of single-parent families would also include some families who are technically not classified as such—for example, families in which a spouse is (1) in military service and living apart from the family; (2) commuting long distances or working long periods of time in distant locations; or (3) incarcerated in a prison or health institution. Also, a group of families not typically counted are those in which single relatives or nonrelated adults assume all but the legal role of parent to minor children. These single adults are just as likely to experience many of the same pleasures and difficulties in their roles as parents that biological and legally adoptive parents describe.

Reported legal marital status tells really very little about actual social status of a spouselike nature within a family structure. The best we can glean from demographic data is information about the population of families at a specific point in time—as the census was taken. In fact, among single-parent families there is considerable progression and change over time regarding single-parent status. There may be varying periods of single parenthood interspersed with periods of marriage or stable cohabitation relationships. So, while approximately one-half of all children by 1990 will live in one-parent households before reaching age 18, this will not necessarily be the only family form they will experience. In fact, most likely they will experience at *least* two family forms. The periods of transition from one family form to another require restructuring and adaptation efforts not typically encountered by families whose forms remain unchanged throughout the life cycle.

Single-Parent Family Structures

As it is used here, "structure" refers both to the composition of the family and to "the invisible set of functional demands that organizes the ways in which family members interact."[6] While the functional demands may not be visible, they are usually conveyed or understood by family members through direct communication or other established patterns of behavior. For example, parental power and control are often conveyed by the ways a parent exercises that power more than by an explicit pronouncement that the parent is in charge.

However, from time to time parents in *all* families may need to remind their children—and, perhaps, themselves—who is in charge within the family. Even though many tasks and responsibilities are shared by all family members, the ultimate responsibility for the maintenance of the system rests with the parents. The parent, as executive of this organizational unit, is charged with the functions of "parenting," defined as

> *a process of providing love and encouragement, the opportunities for experience and growth, the atmosphere of care and concern . . . a process for "making children mind," keeping them from "growing up too fast," and keeping them "on the right track."*[7]

While the parent does not have to do all these things alone, the ideal is that the parent ensures that these processes are carried out on behalf of children.

The essential question regarding single-parent family structure is, How do family members interact with each other and with outsiders to meet the basic needs of the family and its members? It is important to note that in any transition to a one-parent household the pattern of interaction among family members will change. There is at least one less person in the system and this translates into new routines, new schedules, and possibly new living arrangements.

Examination of family structure provides a clear picture of the tremendous diversity among single-parent families. A structural prototype of the single-parent family can be drawn using the basic definition of the term "single-parent family." For example, at minimum, all single-parent families consist of an adult (most likely female)* and one child. In real life, however, structural arrangements of the family may vary a great deal. Mendes has described five variations in single-parent family life-styles—the sole executive, the auxiliary, the unrelated substitute, the related substitute, and the titular parent—and some risks and opportunities associated with each.[8] Her typology is especially applicable to discussion here.

The Sole Executive Parent. The *sole executive parent* is the only adult involved in the basic care of the children in the home. On one end of a scale, the parent may very literally translate her responsibility and view herself as the only actor available to meet family needs and perform household chores. She runs a risk of overloading her personal system on all levels—psychologically, physically, and socially. She may try to do the impossible: be both mother and father to the children in an effort to make up for the loss of the father. This so-called "supermom" is bound to fail if she applies the two-parent role model to the new family form.

At the other end of the scale, the sole executive could view herself as a "contributing coordinator" rather than as a direct supplier of goods, services, and emotions for her children. In this single-parent model, the parent provides what is manageable without undue stress and coordinates the conduct of other family tasks with other competent persons within or outside the family if they exist. In this model, children also act as contributing coordinators according to their abilities to do so. Even very young children help with household chores such as picking up toys and dirty clothes, setting the table, and helping with food preparation. Several examples of this parenting style appear in professional and popular literature; this style is described as a highly effective means of utilizing the internal resources of the family. Overall optimum functioning of the family does require an available extrafamilial support system.

In summary, the sole executive parent may isolate parenting functions in her role and thus risk being seriously overburdened, or she may involve her children and others outside the family to varying degrees in addressing routine family tasks.

The Auxiliary Parent. The *auxiliary parent* is usually the father of one or more of the children, and he does not live with the family but shares one or more parental responsibilities with the single

---

*Since the vast majority of single-parent families are headed by women, the feminine pronoun will be used in subsequent discussion unless a specific example of father-headed families is stated.

mother. This arrangement usually describes a family life-style adopted by the parents rather than one actually ordered by the court, although some such arrangements evolve as a result of court-ordered custody agreements. In order for it to work, there must be parental commitment and agreement to focus on the needs of the children. There are numerous patterns to this type of arrangement, which probably exists with greater frequency than is imagined. Divorced, separated, and never-married parents may actively function in this way, and the auxiliary parent may be "a potent force" in the dynamics of families headed by widows and by adoptive mothers.[9]

In one study of black male children in single-mother homes, the researchers concluded that "physical absence of the father from the home should not be taken as evidence that he has little interest in or contact with his family."[10] In some instances, more than one noncustodial father may have ties to the children in a single-parent family, and each of these fathers may be involved as an auxiliary parent; or one father may assume the role of parent for all the children in the single-parent household. One mother describes such a situation:

> *Both of my children always had a good relationship with their fathers. Just because we didn't get along didn't mean they stopped being fathers. Josh comes by regularly to see Dee Dee. He buys her clothes and gives her spending money and goes to school when she is in plays, and things like that. He always helped make the rules about where she could go. Now, Ross didn't come as often to see Donald, but he was steady. Donald knew what he could depend on from his daddy. And Ross always hated having to think about problems and come up with rules, so he left all that up to me.*
>
> *When Ross moved to Canada two years ago, Donald was real upset. Josh stepped right in to try and console him. Now Josh and Donald have a kind of father-son relationship and it's good. Donald's just not sure he likes having to negotiate with Josh about rules and regulations. He knew so well what he could get by with me.*

The new family structure in cases like these may be confusing, especially for family members. Family theorists have noted that proper family functioning requires that the rules be clear about who participates and how. As a specific point, some theorists consider clarity in this regard of much greater significance than who is actually in the family. Some parents may have difficulty giving up spouse role behaviors as they interact with each other around the needs of their children. Conflict between the parents is very likely to create or sustain conflict between the parents and the child. The potentially positive benefits for the child and for the parents are thus diminished. Along with decisions about how parenting tasks will be handled, restructuring a single-parent family also requires that "spouses disengage from their spousal roles" and that they "develop new rules for their relationship" that will continue regarding the children. [11]

Clarity about rules and manner of participation is especially critical in cases of court-ordered joint custody. In these instances, both parents are required to share equally the responsibility for physical, moral, and emotional development of their children; to share both rights and responsibilities for making decisions that affect their children; and to share joint physical custody by having the child live with each parent for a substantial period of time. In many instances, the child moves back and forth between parents' houses or apartments. In some cases the child remains in one house, and the parents move in and out on a planned basis. In these situations the child may technically be a part of two single-parent families, or of one single-parent family and one step-parent family. Rules and patterns of interaction will obviously be different on some level in the two households.

A major concern that has been expressed about court-ordered joint custody is that it represents an "increasingly frantic legal effort to maintain the illusion of the nuclear family, even when it no longer exists"; that the "term *joint custody* is often applied to a legislated family 'pseudonuclearity.' "[12] This assessment of a societal stance may well be accurate. One safeguard against arbitrary legal decisions may rest in the fact that judges tend not to order joint custody when there is high conflict between parents. At the same time specific help may be essential to facilitate the renegotiation of family structures in these cases. The two households may be strikingly different since the parents are no longer living as husband and wife and therefore would have no need to work on shaping a unified family culture.

The Unrelated and the Related Substitute. The *unrelated substitute* is a person who is not related to the family but shares one or more parental functions. *The related substitute* is a relative who assumes a role of parent to the children. In both of these arrangements either related or unrelated persons assume some responsibility for parental functions, sometimes for long periods of time. These persons might also be categorized as members of the family's support system. Typically, the level of involvement is more intense, however, when the relationship is considered to be that of substitute parent. Both of these arrangements ease the burden of what would otherwise be a "sole executive" in the family.

Clarity about rules and roles may be even more difficult in these situations than in situations involving the auxiliary parent. Unrelated housekeepers or personal friends of the mother may have values and goals in child rearing that are in conflict with those of the parent. These differences may not be immediately evident. For example, the substitute parent may provide excellent physical care but little or no warmth and emotional caring. The mother's need for help with parental tasks may make it difficult for her to challenge the behaviors of this resource person.

The mother's interactions with a related substitute may be guided more by the preexisting relationship between them. A single parent who shares a home with her own parents has additional tasks of participating in the restructuring of her family of origin. The purpose of such restructuring would be to take into account her own parental status. If the restructuring is effective, the single-parent family would be part of a larger household yet maintain its own boundaries of role relationships and authority. This structure is harder to maintain if child care is provided regularly by other adults in the house. Parental authority may be divided and not necessarily negotiated as it might be with a spouse. Confusion about who is in charge may be a constant source of conflict within the expanded family system.

The Titular Parent. The *titular parent* lives with the children but does not function in the parental role. This situation arises out of serious social, emotional, or physical dysfunction of the parent, such as alcohol or other drug abuse, or psychosis. Intervention by public social service agencies may be required if there are no relatives willing or able to provide parental care. In any event, aggressive outreach from formal or informal support systems would be vital to the survival, rehabilitation, or restructuring of whatever portion of the family may be viable.

In summary, the internal resources of single-parent families are shaped and utilized within one or another of these various structures. But structure alone is not sufficient. There is a constant need to respond to change, and the manner in which the family is able to put its structure to work will determine, in part, how it manages.

Stresses of Single-Parent Families

Four sources of stress on a family system have been noted: (1) stressful contact of one member with extrafamilial forces (e.g., school, or workplace); (2) stressful contact of the whole family with extrafamilial forces (e.g., poverty and discrimination); (3) idiosyncratic problems of the family (e.g., a chronic health problem); and

(4) transitional points in the family's evolution.[13] Single-parent families report greatest stress with regard to poverty and discrimination, and to that arising at times of transition. If stresses from each of these sources surface at about the same time, the negative effects are compounded and the family is likely to have great difficulty recovering from these effects.

A review of demographic data about single-parent families suggests that conditions of poverty and potential discrimination due to social status of the family members are likely to be *constant* sources of stress. Discrimination based on gender, racial identification, and age are well known issues of American life.

All socioeconomic levels are reflected among the total number of single-parent families; however, a disproportionate number of them are poor. The facts are that women and children are not only the largest portion of poor people, but also the fastest-growing poverty group in the United States. Most single-parent families are headed by females. In some cases, poverty is a constant condition for the single-parent family, existing for the parents before the birth of children and remaining so throughout most or all of the child rearing life cycle of the family system. In other cases, higher economic levels may have existed before the status of single-parent family was assumed, particularly in families evolving out of two-parent systems; but a state of poverty is likely to exist in any event from several months to four or five years of the initial single-parent status.

Single parents may be any age from mid-teens to 60s or 70s. While the vast majority of single-parent families are headed by women, the *number* of father-headed households is increasing, and this trend is likely to continue. The overall number of single-parent families is increasing at a greater rate, however, so that the *proportion* of father-headed families has shown a steady decrease since 1960. Nevertheless, fathers tend to attract extraordinary media and other attention as single parents. One mother at a parent group meeting in a child care center commented:

> *You won't believe the offers of help John had when he kept the children last year while I finished school. People at the church and in the neighborhood brought cooked food, or invited him and the children to supper two or three times a month. He had offers all the time to babysit or do laundry or help clean house. They all thought it was so wonderful that he was doing this thing—as if the children were not his as much as mine. Don't get me wrong, I thought it was wonderful, too, but not any more than if I did it. I never had any offers like he got. I guess I'm doing what I'm supposed to do.*

This experience is not universal for single fathers, of course. But the experiences of single mothers and single fathers are quite different. The differences may be observed in two major areas: (1) societal attitudes and expectations regarding so-called "typical" male and female roles, and (2) disparity between higher actual income and earning capacity of men over women. Furthermore, women are more likely to remain alone, over time, as a single parent since divorced women are much less likely than men to remarry.

The size of the single-parent family will vary, of course, from one child to any upward number. According to 1984 census data, the highest proportion of female-headed families at that time had only one child under age 18, although approximately 10 percent of the families had more than three children.

All told, economic status and changes in that status, plus the ages and gender of family members, will have critical effects on family structure and adaptation. Since most single-mother families are poor, one common association in discussion of this issue is job and wage discrimination against women. Another factor can be observed in the structure of the single-mother family. With one adult and one or more children, 50 percent or more of the family members are financially dependent and are not employable.

> *Female-headed households must sustain themselves on half the median income of all U.S. households, and on almost two-thirds less than married couples. To augment their slender resources, more than half rely on Medicaid and food stamps, compared to less than 10 percent of married couples. Even in [middle- and upper-] income groups, the descent into poverty immediately after divorce is so sharp that one in seven needs public assistance.*[14]

Recovery from the financial drop after divorce can take several years. The first year can be especially difficult. The pervasive impact of economic condition on all aspects of family life is clearly illustrated in the following summary of an interview by Sheila Kamerman.[15]

> *When Sandy, one of our white single mothers, talked to us about what it was like coping with an active two-year old as a single parent, it sounded overwhelming. . . . She looked more like sixteen than twenty-six. Her husband left her a year ago, and she has received no support from him except twenty dollars at Christmas. Her mother, who lives two blocks away, has tried to help her, but since her own husband became ill she had little time or energy for help, let alone money. Sandy works as the office manager in a law office and makes a good salary, but it's still only one salary and it barely covers necessities. She lives in a one-bedroom apartment, selected because she can walk to work and shopping. She has no car. Her two-year-old, Caroline, is in a day care center, and the fee*

is partially subsidized. Because the day care center is not within walking distance, and Sandy has no car, she has arranged with another mother who lives not too far away to pick up her child and bring her home at the end of the day. Sandy gets up at 6:00 a.m. five days a week, in order to get the baby and herself ready by 8:15, when the child is picked up and Sandy leaves for work. If she's going to work late and therefore going to be late getting home, she phones the woman during the day and asks her to bring Caroline to her home, waiting for a call from Sandy to tell when she has arrived. Sandy pays for this "extra" child care by the hour, in addition to paying for gasoline for the car, for the transportation to and from the center.

Most evenings, when Sandy comes home she bathes the baby first, gets her in pajamas, and then they play for a while. Then Sandy fixes supper and reads to her daughter. Housework and laundry are done occasionally in the evening, but usually Sandy says she's too exhausted to do much. The only real cleaning is once a week on the weekend. She hates the look of "sloppiness" but says it's hard to manage even straightening up during the week. Marketing is a Saturday task for which she takes the baby with her. If the weather is bad or the baby has a cold, it is a problem. Another problem is that the director of the day care center thinks parents should be "participants" and visit the center for parent meetings several times a year, but this requires a sitter to stay with the baby, and that's not part of Sandy's budget. Sometimes her mother sits. The health clinic has Saturday hours, which has made bringing the baby for a checkup possible, but there are always other problems around schedules. It's hard to arrange for repairs if something like the washing machine breaks. Last week the baby was sick and Sandy couldn't get out even to the market. She's just asked a friend to sit for a couple of hours, in return for her doing it with the friend's baby, another time.

The financial picture before separation, death, or divorce can be a complicating factor. If the couple had difficulty managing financially, the economic disruption is greater for the newly formed single-parent family. Case studies documented by Meindl and Getty[16] suggest that low finances of the black two-parent families in their research may in fact have been part of the decision for the father to leave. In his absence the family could be eligible for public assistance. Their income would thus be boosted from the low figure they received from his underemployment in a discriminatory job market.

The economic issues and concerns of single-parent families are most commonly described by them as the central elements of life on a day-to-day basis. However, a more subtle but seriously harmful condition arises when members of society withhold social and emotional supports and promote a stigmatized view of single-parent families as negatively deviant. The status "single-parent" has subjected families summarily to discrimination in housing, the workplace, at school. The following comments speak for themselves:

> *One of my worst days this week was yesterday. I finally found an apartment my son and I could afford, and the landlord said it was mine. I had written a check for first and last month's rent when he asked about Mr. Jenkins. I told him there was no Mr. Jenkins, and he suddenly remembered he had promised to wait to hear from another prospective tenant who just "happened" to call while I was there. Then, when I got back to my friend's place, where I had been staying since we moved here, I had a phone call from my son's teacher who wanted a conference with me and his father about Deke's behavior and his poor adjustment to her classroom. When I said I'd welcome the chance to talk with her but Deke's father was not with us, she replied, "Oh, no wonder he behaves like he does." She never asked about his school adjustment at his last school, or if there were any other concerns I had. I felt so bad I just hung up. I could have told her about Deke's reading problems and this condition they call "dyslexia," but I had to get myself together to see her face-to-face for that.*

Coping in Times of Transition: Identifying and Using Resources

One of the most critical periods of any family's life is that of a transitional point in its evolutionary process. With regard to single-parent families one study discovered that

> *recently divorced, separated, and widowed females are much more likely to experience major life events including income changes, residential relocations, and household-composition changes than are women who have been single for three or more years.*[17]

How the family manages during that time will set patterns for future behaviors. These transitional points in the life of a family may be deceptively complex. Changes in membership and composition of the family are sometimes taken for granted, especially if everyone knew the change was coming. One discussion of stressor events emphasized the increased demands on family members for a reallocation of role assignments when membership changes occur. Family crisis is likely to result from any of the following circumstances:

- *Dismemberment:* a family member dies, moves away, or is hospitalized.

- *Accession:* the family adds a new baby, an adopted child of any age, a new stepparent, a paroled convict, a returning-home military person.
- *Demoralization:* any event interpreted by the family as bringing disgrace.
- A *combination of demoralization plus dismemberment or accession:* desertion, some divorces, imprisonment, suicide, or homocide.[18]

Crisis reactions in families are often complicated by the fact that individual members may be experiencing intense reactions to the event at the same time that the system is undergoing a period of disorganization. A condition of disorganization would not be unusual during the time that resources are being assessed and roles are being reallocated for the new organization which must evolve.

Transitional events are sometimes viewed in one-dimensional terms rather than as the multi-leveled processes that they are. For example:

> *A woman (Jessica) mentioned in casual conversation that she and her husband had gone to court a month before for their divorce hearing. They had been separated more off than on for the preceding 2-½ years and had decided six months before their court date that divorce was the best solution for the difficulties they experienced. Interestingly, her husband moved into the guest bedroom and stayed with the family, without separation, until the day before they went to court. She felt she had accepted the idea of divorce at least a year before she and her husband talked about it. In a way, the divorce spelled relief for her. She had sole custody of their three children and she expected no real differences in their life-style over that of the past 2-½ years. "After all, he was rarely there anyway." She felt she and the children had adjusted well to the divorce, even though she expected there might be some "bad days ahead" based on experience described by her friends. Right now she couldn't be better!*

Adaptation by this family will very likely be marked by a more complicated process than a few "bad days ahead." In order to understand what may occur in this newly formed single-parent family, it is important to recognize divorce as not merely an event but rather as the process which follows the event. A critical task for the family and for its members is to decide and put into effect the way in which it will now be organized, and ways in which family members will interact with each other and with persons outside the household. This process of adaptation could take two to three years or more, as was the case for more than half the families in one five-year study of the effects of divorce.[19] There is increasing evidence of similar periods of transition and adaptation by families after the death of a parent.

A first important step, then, is to recognize the length of time that may be required before a sense of stability is restored to the family. Realistic expectations by the family (and by society) regarding time could help diminish the sense of failure some families describe during this period.

> *The mother of two elementary school-aged children was referred to a school social worker concerning the disruptive behavior of her 12-year old daughter. The mother was obviously depressed. In the course of the interview she described how she and her children had scraped together enough money to move from Wyoming to California after her divorce from the children's father a year ago. Her daughter had vigorously protested the divorce and the move, and only recently had stopped nagging her mother about the divorce. She still hated California. The family had changed residences three times since the move, twice because of her daughter's behavior. Money was a constant problem but the mother had recently got a good paying job in her field.*
>
> *When the social worker commented what a difficult transition she was going through, the mother looked surprised and said, "But I've been out here a year, already! We should be settled down by now."*

Each family is a unique system with unique strengths and stresses. How families adapt to the transitional points associated with evolving from one family form to another will vary greatly. A key to positive adaptation is the openness and willingness to explore alternative patterns of interaction. The "supermom" sole executive who begins to feel overwhelmed and who escalates or holds more rigidly to her assumption of responsibility for all parental tasks rather than seeking help in that role runs the risk of becoming stuck in dysfunctional patterns of interaction.

Restructuring Processes

Every single-parent family moves through a period of transition at the time the family is "born." The transition may be due to the addition of a member as for some never-married and adoptive parents. In most cases the transition is due to departure of a member after death, divorce, desertion, or separation. The family has three overlapping tasks related to the departure of its member. It must (1) attend to and master the disruption, (2) negotiate the transition, and (3) work to create a new, gratifying family. The coping tasks involve managing roles and relationships within the family; helping each family member make a personal adjustment to the change; and locating or reallocating tangible resources, especially those related to economic conditions.[20]

Roles and Relationships. When one parent leaves the family, the relationship between the remaining parent and the children will obviously undergo some change. In some cases, a closer, more intimate social relationship develops between mother and children. One mother noted that when she did not have a romantic relationship with a spouse, she had more time and paid more attention to the children. She was more playful, and time schedules for family routines were not as important. Overall, she spent more time with the children. In the absence of a need to wonder what her husband might say, she was more spontaneously decisive. On the other hand, many single parents are concerned that they do not have enough time to spend with their children once the full burden of economic provider becomes the parent's responsibility.

Weiss described a family life pattern where the children tend to grow up faster than if they were in a two-parent home. Decision-making, which may have gone on just within the spouse system, now might be shared in the parent/child system. Some families develop this pattern without deliberate plans; others may be more direct:

> As soon as I was on my own, I sat down with the children—I always had good rapport with the children—and I told them, "Now things are different. Instead of, more or less, it being a family of mother and four children, we're all one family with all equal responsibility, and we all have a say, and we're all very important. And if it is going to work right, we all have to be able to cooperate with each other."[21]

In this family management style, the children assume a role of partner with the mother with regard to household chores, some of the care of younger children, and the like. Children get themselves off to school and home again.

The positives of such a family life-style are many. Children and parent work together more in a spirit of cooperation than one in which the mother is required to assign tasks and monitor their completion. Household chores are not just the responsibility of the mother.

This management style contains some risks. Because of the structure of the family, it is important that the parent remain in a role of authority at a level necessary to maintain the organization. A child—and a parent—might be confused about the boundary of authority in this family. There may be competition for the leadership role. Role reversals may develop if the parent's needs for adult companionship are not met and if the parent turns to the child for personal comfort. The child in this family may not have as much time for play. Adult supervision during portions of the day may be lifted at an earlier age than might be desirable for the child, the family, or society.

Both the process and the goals for restructuring the parent/child relationship depend very much on the cultural style and values of a family. Other influences in this process are the age and gender of family members and the socioeconomic level at which the restructuring takes place.

Personal Adjustment. There is no common reaction of loss following death, divorce, or separation. The experience may have different meaning to each person in the family. Family members express or experience a loss of companionship, of affectionate expression, of financial or social status, and the mother may experience a loss of sexual intimacy, a "warm body in bed at night," or may simply speak of the loss of "the marriage" or "being married."

There is general consensus that open expression of feelings about the loss in the family facilitates adaptation. Children often have fantasies that dad might come home. In the example cited earlier, Jessica's children had some difficulty accepting the finality of the divorce since their parents' pattern had been one of together/apart for a long time. The fact that dad had been home the entire six months before the divorce left the children thinking he was just away again for a short time.

Not all families have open expressive styles. Members of the support system may be helpful both to the mother who does not want to burden her children with her feelings, and to the child whose mother may be so distracted by her own grief at the loss that she is unable fully to meet her child's emotional needs. These individual responses are a part of what may complicate the process of adaptation for the family.

How children fare over time has been the subject of a great deal of research, and various conclusions have been reached based on what the research sought to discover. In global terms, research has shown that after a period of adjustment, children fare better in the home of a single parent than in the home of two warring parents.

Managing Financial and other Resources. Single-mother families use various strategies to cope with their financial situations. Some of these are evident in Sandy's story. Initial consideration is for a realistic budget which addresses basic needs first. In order to do this, most families must move to more affordable housing. Many families who are unable to maintain a separate household move in with relatives or acquaintances, even though such a move may be less than desirable on a social and emotional basis. Any move means a potential risk of further loss for the family with regard to old neighborhoods, friends, and support systems. A sense of helplessness and vulnerability is often described by single parents as they reflect on a forced move.

Another coping strategy is to seek out other sources of income. Child support is likely to be irregular and to cease altogether within a few years. (An exception to this pattern is in the group of fathers who maintain regular visitation or other contacts with their families.) The lack of dependability about child support payments creates new stresses. Permanent plans for regular purchases cannot realistically be made.

In order to meet financial needs, mothers may go to work for the first time, or they may take a second job. These changes require adjustment in time and may account for a common complaint of single mothers that they do not have enough time for the kind of interaction with their children that they would like.

Teenagers may help by becoming employed, but teen employment increases a risk of school dropout. As the teenager enters adulthood, then, the low-paying jobs of his or her youth may become a lifetime pattern, and a cycle of poverty may thus begin or be perpetuated.

Another source of financial help is government subsidies of cash, food stamps, health services, and housing. There may be new stresses, however, associated with establishing and maintaining eligibility for these subsidies. In some places, it may take three or four years after application for subsidized housing to become available.

Myers noted after his extensive review of research that frequently reported negative effects of single-parent families on Afro-Americans were probably not due as much to the existence of a single-parent as they were due to inadequate socioeconomic, educational, and personal resources, and the unavailability of and support from kin and community.[22]

Altogether, single-parent families tend to be very resourceful in their efforts to supplement their budgets. Certainly single parents are not stubbornly refusing to use financial resources which might facilitate family adaptation. The resources are simply scarce for the identified needs. Stresses in this area are apt to seriously impede the process of adaptation to single-parent living.

The Unmet Needs: A Case for a Functional
System of Social Services

All told, the preceding areas of concern to single-parent families—
the tasks of the restructuring process—speak to the physical,
social, and emotional survival of the system and its members. The
single-parent family, like all families in modern America, does not
have all the resources within the system necessary to sustain it.
External support systems are vital to the adaptive processes of the
family.

Two essential qualities pertain to support systems: they must be
present and they must be *available* for use. Although the internal
resources are limited to those produced by a single adult and
minor children who have little or no capacity to generate tangible
resources, considerable strength is reflected in the coping efforts
of single-parent families. How can these efforts be enhanced? An
obvious resource would be an available network of relatives and
friends. But that resource is simply not available to a large number
of single-parent families.

Kahn has made a case for personal social services which would
"not merely replace or seek to correct the family" but which would
be "new responses to new social situations"—a kind of "social
invention" to address the needs of modern families.[23] A range of
such personal social services which could help improve family life
is evident in the direct reports of unmet needs cited by the
families.

One social invention promulgated by single-parent families
themselves is self-help groups, which typically address one or
more specific areas of need for support. By their existence, these
self-help groups acknowledge the need for external resources "to
strengthen and repair family and individual functioning."[24]

Several institutional responses to otherwise unmet family needs
have been established. For example, several organizations provide
recreational activities for children and families, and these allow
some respite from a constant focus on household tasks and family
problem solving. Big Brother and Big Sister programs provide
another adult relationship for the child, and some relief for the
single parent with regard to maintaining total responsibility in this
area. Greater access to such programs is a specific request of
families in some communities.

Single parents are noted to be "more open to seeking help."[25]
This demographic finding is often translated to suggest that single-
parent families are more disturbed than other families; and certainly during a time of transition a higher than normal degree of

disorganization is to be expected. However, the efforts toward positive adaptation must be recognized as a key element in a family's use of this resource. Despite input from children and extended family and pastors and teachers—much of which may be confusing and unresponsive to the immediate needs of the family— the *parent* has ultimate responsibility to restructure her family in a way that meets all of their needs. A trained professional, who has no emotional investment in the outcome, may be the best resource for problem solving. Outreach programs may be necessary for parents who are experiencing difficulty but have no immediate access to counseling services.

Public and private school systems are fertile grounds for the creation of innovative programs for all families and children and especially for single-parent families in transition. Children are in these living situations most of their waking hours, for most of their childhood years. Furthermore, they are in a position to be observed daily by professionally trained teachers, and occasionally to be observed and attended by other professional staff such as school social workers, nurses, psychologists, and counselors. Full access to schools as service centers will require some new thoughts about what "education" and "learning" really are, and an expansion of those concepts to include the development of knowledge and skill to solve the everyday problems of living. Full access to schools also requires that parents and school staff develop the kinds of partnerships where each person is a vital resource to the other in the process of promoting the positive development of the next generation.

The development of institutional responses to the unmet needs of single-parent families is thus begun. However, social service programs like those described here, and ideas for building new ones, exist in irregular patterns and at various levels of adequacy for the pressing needs of this nation's families. The effectiveness of such programs is limited, then, to those families who have or somehow gain access to them. There are no data to show the total external resources that may be *present* for single-parent families, and of the ones present, which are actually *available* for use. One concern about "availability," for example, has been expressed by many single mothers with regard to public welfare. While this resource is present *and* available to persons able to meet eligibility requirements, many mothers find using this resource a humiliating and frustrating experience. The parents' experiences prompt a question about the purposes of public welfare and the degree to which those purposes have a goal of strengthening family life as is proposed here.

The recommendation which emerges from this study of single-parent family life is that the knowledge about how families function, as structural entities with both constant and intermittent external pressures, be applied to the development of a comprehensive national plan for a system of social services for single-parent families. Such a plan could reduce the fragmentation of services which currently exist. At the same time, it could ensure broader and more consistent access to such services by all single-parent families by proposing, for example, that service centers be located where children and families typically are—at schools, in their own homes, and in other neighborhood bases. The primary purpose of this system of social services would be the enhancement of family life by assisting families to secure necessary resources not otherwise available to them. The already-demonstrated coping abilities of single-parent families could only be strengthened by the known availability of a service of this kind.

Conclusion

America's families comprise the members of American society. Society's neglect of certain of its members is seen, in part, as its having ignored the reality that single parents exist, in favor of its efforts to promote the myth of an all-American family. Efforts have been directed more toward preventing the development of single-parent families than toward strengthening the units that already exist. In general, society has not held its single-parent families in high esteem. Instead, any observation of low self-esteem of family members has frequently been cited as evidence of inherent pathology of the system.

The nature of society's efforts to be or not to be supportive of all its families will have a reverberating impact on society. Already the impact of environmental conditions and society's attitudes has begun to be observed in family life throughout the country. Some common themes emerge, and the large numbers of families involved means they can no longer be denied or ignored. The increasing numbers of these families suggest, perhaps, a survival of the fittest and a positive adaptation rather than an indication of failure. A family life has been forged out for the sake of its members in the midst of what has been observed to be an obstinate "unyielding environment"—an "unresponsive society."[26]

Rather than continuing to focus primarily on the parental *status* of particular families, the nation must focus as well on its families' functioning and potential for stability. The fact that single-parent forms are surviving and continuing to grow suggests potential for effective functioning and stability. Contrary to the value-bound notions of independence, families and society are not that; rather there is an *interdependence* which binds one to the other. The strengths of one will be reflected in the other.

Endnotes

1. These and other general statistics cited throughout this chapter have been compiled from the following sources: Edward H. Thompson, Jr. and Patricia A. Gongla, "Single-Parent Families: In the Mainstream of American Society," in *Contemporary Families and Alternative Lifestyles*, ed. Eleanor D. Macklin and Roger H. Rubin (Beverly Hills, Calif.: Sage Publications, 1983); Sheila B. Kamerman, *Parenting in an Unresponsive Society: Managing Work and Family Life* (New York: The Free Press, 1980); George Masnick and Mary Jo Bane, *The Nation's Families: 1960–1990* (Boston, Mass.: Auburn House, 1980); Esther Wattenberg, "Family: One Parent," in *Encyclopedia of Social Work*, Vol. I, 18th ed. (Silver Spring, Md.: National Association of Social Workers, 1987), pp. 548–55; Alice Lake, "And Baby Makes Two . . . ," *Woman's Day*, January 21, 1986, p. 68; Stephanie Stokes Oliver, "The New Choice: Single Motherhood After 30," *Essence*, October 1983, pp. 131–34; Barbara Kantrowitz et al., "Mothers on Their Own," *Newsweek*, December 23, 1985, pp. 66–67; Ernest R. Mowrer, *Family Disorganization: An Introduction to a Sociological Analysis* (Chicago: University of Chicago Press, 1927), pp. 4, 37; as cited by Catherine Townsend Horner, *The Single-Parent Family in Children's Books* (Metuchen, N.J.: The Scarecrow Press, 1978), p. 51.
2. As cited in *USA Today*, December 1985, p. 1.
3. Andrew Billingsley and Jeanne M. Giovannoni, "Family: One Parent," in *Encyclopedia of Social Work*, Vol. I, 16th ed. (Washington, D.C.: National Association of Social Workers, 1973), p. 363.
4. Ann Dally, *Inventing Motherhood: The Consequences of an Ideal* (New York: Schocken Books, 1983), p. 9.
5. Froma Walsh, "Conceptualization of Normal Family Functioning," in *Normal Family Processes*, ed. Froma Walsh (New York: The Guilford Press, 1982), p. 7.
6. Salvador Minuchin, *Families and Family Therapy* (Cambridge, Mass.: Harvard University Press, 1974), pp. 51–60.
7. Gary Crow, *The Nurturing Family* (Millbrae, Calif.: Celestial Arts, 1980), p. 3.
8. This discussion relies on Helen A. Mendes, "Single-Parent Families: A Typology of Life-Styles," *Social Work* 24 (May 1979): 193–200.
9. Ibid, p. 196.
10. Lovelene Earl and Nancy Lohmann, "Absent Fathers and Black Male Children," *Social Work* 23 (September 1978): 415. These findings are similar to those noted by Thompson and Gongla, "Single-Parent Families," p. 101; and

by Hector F. Myers, "Research on the Afro-American Family: A Critical Review," in *The Afro-American Family: Assessment, Treatment, and Research Issues*, ed. Barbara Ann Bass, Gail Elizabeth Wyatt, and Gloria Johnson Powell (New York: Grune & Stratton, 1982), p. 55.

11. Constance R. Ahrons, "Redefining the Divorced Family: A Conceptual Framework," *Social Work* 25 (November 1980): 437–41.

12. Richard N. Atkins, "Single Mothers and Joint Custody: Common Ground," in *In Support of Families*, ed. Michael W. Yogman and T. Berry Brazelton (Cambridge, Mass.: Harvard University Press, 1986), p. 81.

13. Minuchin, *Families and Family Therapy*.

14. Wattenberg, *Family: One Parent*, pp. 552–53

15. Sheila B. Kamerman, *Parenting in an Unresponsive Society*, pp. 80–81.

16. Nomsa Vanda Meindl and Cathleen Getty, "Life Styles of Black Families Headed by Women," in *Understanding the Family: Stress and Change in American Family Life*, ed. Cathleen Getty and Winnifred Humphreys (New York: Appleton-Century-Crofts, 1981), p. 157.

17. Sara S. McLanahan, "Family Structure and Stress: A Longitudinal Comparison of Two-Parent and Female-headed Families," *Journal of Marriage and the Family* 45 (May 1983): 356

18. Reuben Hill, "Generic Features of Families Under Stress," in *Crisis Intervention: Selected Readings*, ed. Howard J. Parad (New York: Family Service Association of America, 1965), pp. 37–38.

19. Judith S. Wallerstein and Joan Berlin Kelly, *Surviving the Breakup: How Children and Parents Cope with Divorce* (New York: Basic Books, 1980), pp. 304–05.

20. The summary of parental experiences in the discussion which follows is drawn from the following sources: Nancy Eberle, "I Was a Better Mother When I was a Single Mother," *Redbook*, November 1983, pp. 90–91; Robert S. Weiss, "Growing Up a Little Faster: The Experience of Growing Up in a Single Parent Household," *Journal of Social Issues* 35 (Fall 1979): 97–111; Terri Schultz-Brooks, "Single Mothers: The Strongest Women in America," *Redbook*, November 1983; Wattenberg, "Family: One Parent"; and M. Janice Hogan, Cheryl Buehler, and Beatrice Robinson, "Single Parenting: Transitioning Alone," in *Stress and the Family*, Vol. I, *Coping with Normative Transitions*, ed. Hamilton I. McCubbin and Charles R. Figley (New York: Brunner/Mazel, 1983).

21. Weiss, "Growing Up a Little Faster," p. 100.

22. Hector F. Myers, "Research on the Afro-American Family," p. 56.

23. Alfred J. Kahn, *Social Policy and Social Services* (New York: Random House, 1979), p. 16.

24. Ibid.

25. Edward H. Thompson, Jr. and Patricia Gongla, "Single-Parent Families," p. 109.

26. Meindl and Getty, "Life Styles of Black Families Headed by Women"; and Kamerman, *Parenting in an Unresponsive Society*.

Chapter 5

WORKING FOR LESS: SINGLE MOTHERS IN THE WORKPLACE

Teresa Amott

One-quarter of the mothers in the U.S. labor force are single mothers with children under 18. Nearly 40 percent of the single mothers in the workplace fail to earn enough to bring their families above the federal poverty line.[1] Many other single mothers do not participate in the work force and must rely solely on child support payments and programs such as social security, Aid to Families with Dependent Children (AFDC), or Supplemental Security Income (SSI). Over half of the women maintaining households who do not participate in the work force are poor.

In the first half of Chapter 5, we will explore the labor force participation of single mothers, focusing on the types of jobs they do and the wages they earn. We will also examine barriers to labor force participation by single mothers, including high child care costs and lack of access to health insurance. In the second half of the chapter we will evaluate the welfare reform initiatives of the 1980s and their impact on poor single mothers. These new initiatives assume that single mothers should participate in the paid labor force. However, the structure of labor markets makes it difficult to design policies that ensure self-sufficiency at an adequate income for single mothers.

Labor Force Participation

By 1985, the median income for single mothers of children under 18 was only $10,076.[2] Mothers with at least one child under 6

99

averaged an even lower income ($6,472 in 1985), mainly because fewer of these women are able to participate in the labor force and their only sources of income are child support and public assistance. Despite the barriers to working outside the home, over two-thirds of women heading households with children under 18 were in the labor force. Over half of these women worked full-time year-round.

How can we reconcile the high labor force participation of single mothers with their low median income? The answer lies in the nature of the jobs they perform. Single mothers most frequently work in service and blue-collar jobs that offer low pay, unstable employment, and few opportunities for advancement. In this respect, they share the situation of most women in the labor force.

Occupational Segregation in the Work Force

Despite the increasing number of women in high-paying professions such as law and medicine, the overwhelming majority of women continue to do "women's work." This phenomenon is called *occupational segregation*. The majority of U.S. occupations are sex-segregated. As a result, 60 percent of the work force would have to change jobs in order for the proportions of men and women in each occupation to be the same.[3]

Single mothers are distributed across occupations much like female workers in general, with some exceptions. (Table 5–1 compares the occupational distribution of single mothers with all women workers in 1986.) One exception is that single mothers are more likely to be service providers than are all female workers. Nearly 22 percent of single mothers in the work force hold service jobs, compared with 18.3 percent of all female workers.

A second exception is that single mothers are less likely than are all female workers to be found in white-collar jobs. Only 20.5 percent of single mothers were in managerial and professional jobs, compared with 23.7 percent of all female workers. Compared with all female workers, single mothers are underrepresented even in the typically female professions such as nursing and teaching (see Table 5–1). Single mothers are also less likely to work in sales than women workers in general. For instance, retail sales, which employs 8.4 percent of all female workers, employs only 5.7 percent of single mothers in the work force.

A third exception is that single mothers are more likely than all female workers to have blue-collar jobs (see Table 5–1). These blue-collar jobs account for 15.1 percent of single mothers in the

Table 5–1   **Occupational Distribution, Female Heads of Households Compared with All Women Workers, 1986**

Selected Occupations	Female Heads of Households with Children Under 18 (%)	All Women Workers (%)
Managerial and professional	20.5	23.7
Executive, admin. & manag.	8.0	9.6
Public admin. & officials	2.3	4.4
Other exec., admin. & manag.	5.0	5.8
Management related occupations	2.7	3.3
Professional specialty	12.5	14.1
Health assessment	3.3	3.6
Teachers, exc. university	4.7	5.4
Lawyers and judges	1.3	2.4
Technical, sales, & admin. support	42.5	45.6
Technicians and related support	3.2	3.3
Sales occupations	10.0	13.1
Retail and personal sales	5.7	8.4
Administrative support	29.3	29.3
Computer operators	15.1	12.1
Secretaries & typists	9.5	10.0
Service occupations	21.6	18.3
Private household	1.8	1.9
Protective services	0.6	0.5
Food service	7.1	6.6
Health service	4.6	3.4
Cleaning service	4.0	2.4
Personal service	3.4	3.5
Precision production, craft & repair	3.0	2.4
Mechanics and repairers	0.5	0.3
Construction trades	0.3	0.2
Other	2.1	1.9
Operators, fabricators & laborers	12.1	8.9
Machine operators	9.0	6.5
Transportation operators	1.4	0.8
Handlers & equipment cleaners	1.8	1.6
Farming, forestry & fishing	0.3	1.1

Source: Unpublished data, Bureau of Labor Statistics. Author's calculations.

work force, in comparison with 11.3 percent of all female workers. In summary, 36.7 percent of single mothers hold service or blue-collar jobs, compared with 29.6 of all female workers.

If we examine differences in the occupational distributions of single mothers of different races, we see broad diversity. Recent occupational data are not available for Asian and Native American single mothers, so the numbers presented here refer only to whites, blacks, and Hispanics (see Table 5–2). For instance, white women are more than twice as likely as black or Hispanic women to be found in white-collar occupations. In turn, black and Hispanic women are far more likely to be service providers. Their overrepresentation in service occupations extends across the range of high-paying service jobs such as protective service (fire and police) and low-paying jobs such as private household work. For instance, black women are more than four times as likely to hold protective service jobs as are whites. Hispanic women are twice as likely to hold these jobs as are whites. Minority women are also more likely to hold the lowest-paid service positions in the private household sector. Black and Hispanic women are two to three times as likely as white women to be domestic servants.

While white women are overrepresented in white-collar positions, black and Hispanic women are overrepresented in blue-collar jobs. For instance, black and Hispanic women are four to five times as likely to work in construction—even though such jobs employ only a tiny group of single mothers of any race. Black and Hispanic women are also more likely to be machine operators and assemblers than are white women.

The Dual Labor Market

Economists examining occupational segregation view the labor market as divided into a "primary" and a "secondary" sector.[4] The primary labor market offers high salaries, steady employment, and career ladders. Its upper tier consists of professionals and managers, and its lower tier contains unionized manufacturing jobs such as auto and steel production. In contrast, the secondary sector offers low wages, few or no benefits, and unstable employment. Work is often part-time, temporary, or seasonal. Workers receive less reward for education or years on the job. Examples of secondary labor market jobs include domestic service, waiting on tables, migrant farm work, and fast-food counter jobs. The "pink-collar ghetto" of women's service, manufacturing, and clerical work is generally considered part of the secondary sector.

Historically, white men had greater access to primary sector jobs which provided them with "family wages" to support homebound women and children, and even brought some upward mobility over the course of their work lives:

> For organized labor, the continued popularity of the family wage idea afforded male workers an opportunity to further their argu-

Table 5–2 Occupational Distribution, by Race and Spanish Origin, Female Householders with Children under 18, 1985

Selected Occupations	White	Black	Spanish Origin
Executive, admin. & manag.	8.8	3.4	3.7
Managers, officials & admin.	6.0	1.5	2.2
Management related occupations	2.8	1.9	1.5
Accountants	1.4	0.4	0.9
Professional specialty	12.4	7.1	4.1
Health assessment	3.6	1.2	0.4
Teachers, librarians, counselors	5.2	3.7	1.5
Health technologists & technicians	2.1	4.8	2.4
Technologists and technicians, except health	1.2	0.7	1.1
Sales	12.8	6.6	7.1
Supervisors & proprietors	2.1	0.6	0.9
Sales reps, commodities & finance	3.4	0.7	0.7
Other sales	7.3	5.3	5.6
Administrative support	27.4	26.7	24.5
Computer operators	1.4	1.5	3.9
Secretaries & typists	9.1	6.5	6.5
Financial records processing	3.8	2.7	1.5
Other admin. support	13.1	16.0	12.7
Private household	1.8	3.7	5.2
Protective service	0.4	1.8	0.9
Service, exc. private & protective	17.4	25.1	22.2
Food service	7.5	8.1	6.0
Health service	4.4	9.9	3.9
Cleaning	2.4	4.9	9.5
Personal service	3.2	2.2	2.8
Farming, forestry & fishing	0.9	0.3	3.4
Precision production, craft & repair	2.3	2.7	3.7
Mechanics & repairers	0.2	1.0	1.0
Construction trades	0.2	0.9	0.2
Precision production	2.0	0.9	2.6
Machine operators, assemblers & inspectors	8.8	12.2	16.3
Machine operators & tenders	6.2	8.6	13.6
Fabricators & assemblers	1.7	2.8	1.9
Production inspectors	1.0	0.8	0.7
Transportation	1.5	0.8	1.5
Handlers & equipment cleaners	2.1	0.2	4.3

Source: U.S. Bureau of the Census, "Household and Family Characteristics: March 1985," *Current Population Reports,* series P-20, no. 411 (Washington, D.C.: U.S. Government Printing Office, 1986).

*ments for higher wage rates. Male unionists could demand first
rights to jobs and pay increases because married women's employment only supplemented family income, and single women could
expect to marry. . . . The family wage provided a convenient means
for male workers to retain their control of jobs and conditions.*

*The effectiveness of arguments for protection of male positions
had a significant impact upon women workers [in the early twentieth
century. In the 1920s, many] unions simply excluded women entirely
. . . [and] women workers as a category found themselves relegated
to specific sectors of the labor market. . . .*

*During the Depression, use of the family-wage argument to limit
or prohibit women's employment accelerated.*[5]

In this way men came to dominate the more highly paid manufacturing jobs, known today as the lower tier of the primary sector.
Throughout the 19th and 20th centuries, as corporations developed
and employed greater numbers of managers and professionals,
white men also monopolized these jobs.

In contrast, sex and race discrimination, gender roles, and lack
of access to education confined the vast majority of white women
and minority men and women to low-paying, secondary jobs. This
segregation kept minority and white women's earnings far below
those of white men to this day. Confinement to the secondary
sector also creates higher risks of unemployment for white women
and minorities, since by its very nature work in the secondary
sector is less stable (in contrast to the tenure and job security
offered in many primary sector jobs). This lack of job security
explains the fact that single mothers experience unemployment
rates between one-and-one-half to two times higher than those for
all female workers.

As we can see from Tables 5–1 and 5–2, single mothers are even
more likely to be found in the secondary labor market than are all
female workers. Low educational attainment by single mothers
contributes to their overrepresentation in the secondary sector.
Eight out of ten female workers are high school graduates compared with only 65 percent of women maintaining households.
Still, even if single mothers had higher educational attainment, it
is not likely that they would be able to earn "breadwinner's wages"
in today's labor market. Female college graduates who worked full-
time, year-round in 1984 earned only slightly more than male high
school dropouts ($20,257 compared to $19,120).[6]

Child Care Costs

Confined to low-paying secondary labor market jobs, single mothers rarely can earn enough to pay for high-quality child care.

According to a study by the House Ways and Means Committee, annual child care costs can range from $2,000 to more than $6,500.[7] With income averaging under $7,000, a single mother of a child under 6 clearly cannot afford child care unless subsidies are available. The federal government subsidizes child care for low-income working mothers through Title XX. Under the Omnibus Budget Reconciliation Act of 1981, Title XX was folded into the Social Services Block Grant, and funding levels were cut 20 percent. Studies by the General Accounting Office and the Urban Institute show that most states have reduced their spending on subsidized child care as a result.

The other mechanism by which the federal government subsidizes child care for working parents is the child care tax credit. However, as the House Ways and Means Committee found:

In 1982, only 6 percent of those claiming the credit had incomes below $10,000, and for these low-income families, tax savings averaged $256. Because its nonrefundability means that families can benefit only to the extent of their tax liability, the credit provides only limited assistance to the poor.[8]

Ironically, the 1987 tax reforms which lowered the number of working poor families who must pay federal income taxes will limit further the usefulness of the child care tax credit to low-income families.

On the surface, part-time or part-year work would appear to offer some advantages to single mothers. For instance, it can cut down on the mother's need for costly full-time child care and can allow her more time with her children. However, single mothers are less likely to participate in part-time or part-year work than are married mothers. As shown in Table 5–3, approximately 47 percent of single mothers in the work force held part-time or part-

Table 5–3   Work Experience of Single Mothers with Children under 18, by Age of Youngest Child, 1985

Age of Youngest Child	Number of Mothers (thous.)	Working Full-Time		Working Part-Time		Not Working
		Full-yr.	Part-yr.	Full-yr.	Part-yr.	
Under 3	1,873	15%	17%	3%	15%	50%
3–5	1,610	31	17	5	11	36
6–11	2,244	42	16	6	8	28
12–17	2,117	52	13	5	8	21
All	7,845	36%	16%	5%	10%	33%

Source: U.S. Congress, Senate, Committee on Finance, *Data and Materials Related to Welfare Programs for Families with Children*, S. Prt. 100-20, March 1987, p. 174.

year jobs, in contrast to nearly 59 percent of married mothers. Nearly 54 percent of single mothers in the work force worked full-time, full-year, compared with 43 percent of married mothers. The relatively lower representation of single mothers in the part-time, part-year work force is attributable to their need to earn "family wages"—wages high enough to support a family. Part-time workers generally earn less per hour than full-time workers. One study of part-time work by 9 to 5, the National Association of Working Women, found that part-time workers earned, on average, about 58 percent of the hourly wage of full-time workers ($4.50/hour compared to $7.80/hour in 1984.)[9]

Another serious problem with part-time or part-year work for sole-provider mothers is the lack of benefits, particularly the health insurance so necessary for families with children. The National Association of Working Women study found:

> *Since 1981, there have been 1 million fewer workers each year with employer-provided health benefits. . . . The Employee Benefits Research Institute estimates that only 15.6 percent of all part-time workers have direct health coverage under an employer group plan. . . . Only 27.5 percent of part-time workers (working fewer than 1000 hours per year) are covered by employer-provided retirement plans, in contrast to 50.5 percent of employees working 1000–1999 hours a year, who received pension benefits on the job. In 1985, a significant number of women who worked voluntary part-time work schedules averaged just under 1000 hours and thus, by law, never worked enough hours to accrue retirement credits.[10]*

Social Policy Initiatives

Child Support

Since single mothers in the work force generally do not earn a family wage adequate to support their families above the poverty line, legislators have urged an increase in child support enforcement.[11] Child support payments occur, if at all, as a result of a court order or a voluntary agreement between the absent and the custodial parent. This means that a single mother's chances of receiving adequate child support currently depend heavily on the talents of her lawyer, the charity of her judge, and the generosity of the child's father.

In 1984, of the approximately 8.7 million single mothers with children in the United States, 4.0 million were due child support payments. Race, age, and education play a big role in determining whether a mother is awarded child support payments. Two-thirds of white mothers were awarded payments in 1984, compared with only one-third of black and 41 percent of Hispanic mothers. The older the mother, the more likely she was to be covered under a payment plan. And mothers with more education were more likely to be awarded payments. Nearly three-quarters of college graduate women had been awarded payments, compared with 42 percent of high school dropouts.

Of the 4 million mothers who were due child support payments in 1983, only half actually received the full amount they were due, 1 million received less than they were due, and another million received nothing at all. For the 3 million who received any money at all, the mean amount received was only $2,340 per year. In the aggregate, $10.1 billion was due in child support in 1983, but actual payments amounted to only $7.1 billion.

Over the past 20 years, child support legislation has generally been used to enforce the collection of payments from the father only if the mother collected welfare payments in the form of Aid to Families with Dependent Children (AFDC). In fact, child support has been used as a substitute for welfare expenditures, not a supplement. Starting in the 1970s, congressional concern over rising welfare costs led to legislation which required every state to collect child support payments from absent fathers of AFDC recipients.

Today, when a mother applies for AFDC, she signs over her right to collect child support to the state and agrees to cooperate in identifying and locating the father. If she refuses to cooperate, she faces partial or total loss of AFDC benefits. Once the father has been located, the state collects child support payments from him and keeps most of the money as reimbursement for federal and state outlays of AFDC. AFDC mothers are only permitted to keep $50 each month of the child support money collected on their behalf. (But their food stamps are reduced by $0.30 for each dollar of child support received.)

Beginning in 1984, as the poverty of women and children gained national attention, Congress gave the states a variety of new powers to collect child support, including the right to withhold child support payments automatically from the absent parent's paychecks. Congress also made available the federal government's vast computer record-keeping capacity to the Parent Locator Service, an agency which tracks delinquent parents. The 1984 law encouraged states to assist non-AFDC mothers in collecting support, but today the program still serves twice as many AFDC families (over 5 million) as families who do not collect welfare.

Finally, the law required that every state establish a guideline for the amount of child support awards. Several such guidelines are now in use. In some states, such as Wisconsin and Minnesota, child support is set as a flat percentage of the absent parent's income. Other states, such as Colorado and New Jersey, use what is called the "income shares" approach, in which both parents must contribute in proportion to their incomes. Delaware and Hawaii use a complex formula which guarantees a flat dollar amount per child and then supplements the flat amount with an additional "standard of living allowance" which is based on the income of both parents.

Child support awards are generally too low to lift significant numbers of women and children out of poverty, and therefore are not an adequate alternative to AFDC. The Census Bureau has estimated that if every woman who had been awarded child support in the country were to collect the full amount of her award, the number of women and children in poverty would fall by less than 5 percent.[12] The average award—$2,520 per family per year—is simply too low to guarantee an adequate standard of living to these families. The fathers of most poor children are poor themselves, and even when the fathers aren't poor, the courts have been reluctant in the past to make large enough support awards to bring the custodial parent and children out of poverty.

Sometimes the father has very little capacity to pay because he is a teenager, unemployed, or disabled. If the father remarries and is supporting a second family, the courts must choose which family will be without adequate support. The new guidelines may lead to somewhat higher awards, but it is extremely unlikely that awards can be raised enough to equalize income between married-couple and single-mother families.

Welfare

If labor market earnings and child support together are insufficient, women supporting families turn to public assistance. Aid to Families with Dependent Children (AFDC) is the largest income support program for poor families in the United States. Eligibility requirements and benefit levels are set by each state, and the federal government provides half the funds. Almost 90 percent of families receiving AFDC are headed by single women.[13] In theory, 26 states permit a two-parent family to qualify for AFDC benefits if the father is unemployed, but in practice other requirements limit the number of two-parent families who are eligible. There were only 253,000 AFDC unemployed parent cases in the entire United States in fiscal year 1986. The vast majority of AFDC recipients are children. Of the 10.7 million people receiving AFDC in 1986, 7 million were dependent children.

In order to collect AFDC benefits, a recipient whose youngest child is at least 6 years old must also register for work or job training. In many states, such as North Carolina and West Virginia, the recipient must work an average of 20 hours per week in a public sector job in order to collect her benefit check. In these programs, known as "workfare," the recipient does not earn wages and is not eligible for unemployment compensation or other benefits offered to regular employees.

Families must be very poor to qualify for AFDC, since states set limits on recipients' income and assets. The limit on assets means that families must draw down most of their savings before they become eligible. If a family has savings over $1,000, it cannot collect benefits. Under the asset limits, a family with a car valued over $1,500 is also ineligible.

In no state are AFDC benefits high enough to bring a family out of poverty. Thirty states pay less than 50 percent of the poverty level for a three-person family. Like eligibility, benefit levels vary widely across states. In 1987, the lowest payment for a family of three was $118, in Alabama; the highest payment was $833, in Alaska. Even when we add in the value of food stamps, the average state provides benefits equal to $533 per month—only 73 percent of the federal poverty line. Nationwide, 80 percent of AFDC families also receive food stamps.

States are required to provide Medicaid—a program which provides free health care—for all families who qualify for AFDC. For many women who might otherwise take jobs that do not provide health insurance, this is the most important reason for staying on welfare.

The common perception of AFDC is that a large number of recipients stay on AFDC for many years at a stretch. This perception is incorrect: while roughly one-quarter of U.S. households rely on public assistance *at some point* in any ten year period, very few are dependent on assistance for the full ten years. The average stay on AFDC is less than two years. Most welfare recipients apply for assistance because of a major family event such as divorce, separation, or the birth of a child. Once their life circumstances have stabilized, they leave the caseload. Only one in five of all women beginning a stay on AFDC will remain on for more than eight years. [14]

The Dual Welfare System. Sociologist Diana Pearce has observed that welfare systems in the United States correspond to the division between the primary and secondary labor market:

> *The duality in the welfare system complements and supports the inequality in the labor market itself. Over all, the primary sector of welfare seeks to minimize the costs to the individual when the system fails, as when there is high unemployment in a geographically concentrated industry. It seeks to enable workers to move from job to job without impoverishing them or their families.*
>
> *The secondary welfare sector, on the other hand, seeks to provide only the most minimal support necessary to meet basic needs. It also seeks to subsidize low-wage workers (and through them, low-wage industries) by providing some of the support services, such as health care through Medicaid, found in the fringe benefits of the primary sector. . . .*
>
> *These very different goals and patterns of services create two worlds differentiated by poverty rates, gender and race. Men, especially white men, are found disproportionately in the primary sector, while women and minorities are concentrated in the secondary sector. . . . Indeed, AFDC functions as the poor woman's unemployment compensation.*[15]

In the primary sector, benefits (such as unemployment compensation and social security) are considered a right, not a privilege, and the recipients are not subjected to humiliating means tests. In the secondary tier, which includes AFDC, recipients are stigmatized and regulated, and benefits can be withdrawn arbitrarily. To qualify for secondary welfare programs, recipients must divest themselves of assets such as cars and savings accounts with a value over the legislated maximum; this forced pauperization makes it very difficult to escape from the welfare system. For example, cars are necessary to seek paid work in many areas, and a cushion of savings could maintain a family through spells of unemployment or while going to school.

Welfare-to-Work Programs. Periodically, policy-makers in Washington and across the country decide that it is time for a major overhaul of the nation's welfare system. Pressure for the most recent round of welfare reform began building early in the 1980s, when Ronald Reagan was elected President on a conservative platform that included a broad assault on social programs. The prime target of this assault was Aid to Families with Dependent Children. Charging that welfare caused a range of social problems from family breakup to drug abuse, conservatives sparked a nationwide interest in welfare reform.[16] Unfortunately for the conservative case, there is no conclusive evidence that AFDC promotes the formation of single-parent families through divorce, separation, or out-of-wedlock births. High-benefit states, for instance, don't have a greater share of single-parent families than low-benefit states.[17]

The availability of welfare appears to have little impact on the childbearing rates of unmarried women. There has been a rise in the share of births to unmarried women over the past 15 years, but this is mainly due to lower birthrates among married women. As a result, the *share* of out-of-wedlock births has risen. And despite rising media attention to teen pregnancy, teen birthrates (births per 1,000 women aged 15–19) have been declining steadily since the 1970s.[18]

The Impact of OBRA. The Reagan administration took as a policy goal a reduction in the number of families receiving public assistance. One of its first actions toward this goal made it more difficult for families collecting AFDC to participate in the labor force while supplementing their earnings with public assistance. The Omnibus Budget Reconciliation Act of 1981 (OBRA) changed eligibility requirements for AFDC. Prior to OBRA, many low-income families with earnings were able to receive AFDC and Medicaid because a portion of their earnings was "disregarded." This portion was referred to as the "30 and a third" rule, or the "work incentive disregard." The OBRA rules, among other changes, ended the work incentive disregard after the first four months of employment. According to a Department of Health and Human Services estimate, nearly 700,000 families lost eligibility or benefits as a result of these changes, a net savings of $1.1 billion in 1983 to the federal and state governments, but at an average loss in benefits per family of $1,155 per year.[19] Concerned that these changes unfairly penalized low-income families, Congress restored some disregards in 1983, although the new law did not return eligibility standards to the pre-OBRA levels.

Table 5–4 shows how these changes have affected the benefits collected by a single mother, with two children, who works full-time, year-round at minimum wage. In the average state prior to 1981, this mother could have collected $166 in AFDC benefits per month to supplement her earnings—and received Medicaid as a result. Under the OBRA rules, her benefit check was reduced to $66 for the first four months of employment, and then to zero thereafter. Because she received no AFDC benefits, she lost Medicaid eligibility. Under the current law, she can collect $87 in AFDC benefits during the first four months, but still loses her AFDC and Medicaid eligibility thereafter.

Not surprisingly, these changes reduced the number of AFDC

Table 5-4   Calculation of Benefits for a Full-Time Minimum Wage Worker under Pre-OBRA, OBRA, and Current Law, Mother of Two Children

		OBRA (1981–1984)		Current Law		
	Pre-OBRA (Prior to 1981)	First 4 mo.	After 4 mo.	First 4 mo.	After 4 mo.	After 12 mo.
Income:						
Gross earnings	$581	$581	$581	$581	$581	$581
EITC[a]	—	+32	+32	—	—	—
Gross income	581	613	613	581	581	581
Disregards:						
Initial disregards[b]	30	105	75	105	105	75
One-third of rest	184	—	—	—	—	—
Child care[c]	100	100	100	100	100	100
One-third of rest	—	136	0	125	0	0
Other expenses	95[d]	—	—	—	—	—
Total disregards	409	341	175	330	205	175
Net countable income	172	272	438	251	376	406
AFDC benefits:[e]						
$420 payment standard	248	148	0	169	44	14
$338 payment standard	166	66	0	87	0	0

Notes:
[a]The Earned Income Tax Credit is a refundable tax credit for low-income working families.
[b]Pre-OBRA, $30 disregard. OBRA, standard work expense deduction of $75 plus $30 in first 4 months. Current law, standard work expense deduction of $75 plus $30 disregard in first 12 months.
[c]The average amount reported as child care deduction for AFDC families with earnings in 1979.
[d]The average amount reported for AFDC families with earnings in 1982.
[e]The need and payment standard are assumed to be $420 per month, roughly equivalent to the payment level in a high benefit state, or $338 per month, the average payment level for a family of 3 in 1985.
Source: Calculated by the author from data in *Background Material and Data on Programs within the Jurisdiction of the Committee on Ways and Means,* U.S. House of Representatives, Committee on Ways and Means, WMCP: 99-14, March 3, 1986, p. 356, and *Children in Poverty,* U.S. House of Representatives, Committee on Ways and Means, WMCP: 99-8, May 22, 1985, p. 416.

recipients who participated in the labor force. A General Accounting Office study found:

> AFDC recipients who lost eligibility due to the OBRA cuts were more likely to be non-white, younger than those who remained on AFDC. . . . Recipients who lost AFDC eligibility suffered a substantial loss of income which they could not make up by increased earnings or other means. . . . Lack of health coverage was common among these former AFDC recipients. . . . Families terminated from AFDC were more likely to face increased emergency situations.[20]

Once the OBRA changes were in place, and fewer AFDC recipients were participating in the paid labor force, critics began to design welfare-to-employment programs to encourage greater labor force participation among AFDC recipients. Marketed to the public as solutions to a "welfare crisis," the proposals came packaged with slick, Madison Avenue names. Massachusetts offered ET as well as JEDI. REACH and GAIN came from New Jersey and California, respectively, while Illinois sold Project Chance and Missouri marketed Learnfare. The programs all aimed at changing the welfare system from an income support program into a jobs program through a mix of carrots and sticks which are designed to both bribe and compel welfare recipients to find paid employment.

The main element of conservative welfare reform is workfare: forcing welfare recipients to work off their benefits or lose them. In practice, this means that a family receiving $335 in monthly case benefits would have to spend up to 100 hours per month performing unpaid work in a government or nonprofit agency (the number of hours may not exceed the grant divided by the minimum wage).

Liberals add a few carrots like training and child care subsidies to the work requirement stick. But nearly all of the state projects, liberal and conservative alike, make the job programs mandatory, requiring recipients with children over a certain age to participate or lose some or all of their benefits. The experience at the state level in the early 1980s shows that the threat of losing benefits (known as "sanctioning") is very real. In New York City's misnamed "Employment Opportunity" program, over 8,000 families were sanctioned in one six-month period alone.[21]

The Real Welfare Crisis. Most single mothers would agree that there is a welfare crisis, but of a different sort from that envisioned by the designers of welfare-to-employment programs. The real welfare crisis is that tightened eligibility requirements since the early 1970s have squeezed many families off the rolls, while inflation has eaten away at the purchasing power of welfare benefits.

Welfare rights groups organizing among the poor in the early 1970s demonstrated that more people were in need than were receiving benefits. As a result of their organizing, welfare rolls expanded dramatically.[22] Between 1970 and 1973, the average number of recipients rose nearly 50 percent. But since 1973, the number of people on AFDC has stayed constant at roughly 10.7 million.[23]

The stability of the caseload level masks increasing need. Between 1970 and 1985, the number of people living in families below the federal poverty line rose by 41 percent—from 18.3 million to 25.7 million.[24] But caseloads did not grow because increasingly restrictive eligibility requirements such as those in the OBRA law described above held down the number of recipients so that only half of poor families could qualify.

Not surprisingly, combined federal, state, and local spending on AFDC has fallen in real terms since the mid-1970s. In 1975, net outlays on AFDC were nearly $17 billion (in 1985 dollars.) By 1986, outlays had fallen to $14.7 billion.[25] Outlays have fallen because the real value of AFDC benefits has dropped. AFDC benefit levels are set by state legislatures, and no state automatically raises AFDC benefits when prices rise. As a result, the purchasing power of AFDC benefits fell by one-third between 1970 and 1986. (Some states were slightly less stingy. For instance, Wisconsin raised benefits by 10 percent over the rate of inflation in that period. But other states, like Illinois and New Jersey, permitted real benefits to fall by over 50 percent.) Even if we add in the value of food stamps, which are received by most AFDC families, the combined value of AFDC and food stamp benefits still fell an average of 26 percent between 1971 and 1984.[26]

As Diana Pearce pointed out in the dual welfare system analysis above, the welfare system has been used to regulate the supply of workers to employers paying low wages. When there is shortage of workers willing to take low-paying work, government historically tightens eligibility requirements to force more recipients into the work force.

Over the past 15 years, the number of low-paid jobs in the United States has been rising. In a study prepared for the Joint Economic Committee of the U.S. Congress, economists Barry Bluestone and Bennett Harrison examined net employment growth between 1963 and 1985. Between 1963 and 1973, only 20 percent of the new jobs created paid low wages (categorized in their study as less than $7,400 per year in constant 1986 dollars). But between 1979 and 1985, the share of low-wage jobs had risen to 44 percent.[27]

Despite chronically high unemployment rates, the mid-1980s saw a developing shortage of workers willing to take these low-wage jobs.[28] The labor shortage is particularly acute in urban areas where many welfare recipients reside. Employers have responded with minor incentives, but still have difficulty attracting workers. (For instance, McDonald's franchises in Boston now lure workers with scholarship programs and wages near $6 an hour, but help-wanted signs still hang below the golden arches.) The immigration reform bill passed by Congress in 1986 is also expected to contribute to the labor shortage since it will reduce the supply of undocumented workers who do much of the low-wage work in the United States.

Welfare mothers represent a labor pool to be tapped by these low-wage employers. Some welfare reform proposals, such as New Jersey's REACH, require employment or training for mothers of children as young as 2. New Jersey's plan even provides the jobs: new casinos in the Atlantic City area have agreed to employ 1,500 graduates of the state's AFDC work and training program. In fact, the REACH plan is administered by Private Industry Councils dominated by local employers.

One of the reasons economic compulsion is no longer sufficient to generate enough low-wage workers is that the real value of the minimum wage has fallen even faster than the value of welfare benefits. (The minimum wage lost approximately 30 percent of its purchasing power to inflation between 1981 and 1987.) In 1981—the last time the minimum wage was raised—monthly earnings from a full-time minimum wage job were frozen at $581.[29] At that time, average AFDC benefits per family were $277, 50 percent of earnings from minimum wage work. Since then, benefits have fallen in real terms but risen in relation to the minimum wage. By 1985, AFDC benefits were worth 61 percent of minimum wage earnings. It is estimated that approximately one million women heading households worked at minimum wage jobs in that year.[30]

So despite the falling value of AFDC benefits, the financial advantage of employment has declined for welfare recipients. This is particularly true when the value of other benefits is taken into account. For instance, increased cash income reduces the amount of food stamps a family can collect, so what they gain through wages, they lose in food stamps. When families leave the welfare rolls to take paid employment, they also lose Medicaid benefits, but few low-wage jobs provide company-paid health care. Many low-wage jobs are in the service sector, which provides health insurance to roughly one-third of its employees. In contrast, 80 percent of manufacturing sector employees have employer-provided health plans.[31] Welfare recipients are thus faced with a choice between providing health insurance for their families and taking paid jobs. Another problem for welfare recipients, as for all working mothers, is the high price of child care described earlier in this chapter.

Squeezed between low wages and high work expenses, there is often little economic gain—if any—for a welfare mother who takes a paid job. Table 5–5 illustrates the problem, using data for Massachusetts, whose welfare reform program (the Employment and Training Choices Program, popularly known as ET) is widely

Table 5–5 Comparision of Welfare Package with Low-Wage Employment, Hypothetical Mother of Two in Massachusetts

Welfare Package		*Employment Package*	
AFDC grant	$491	Gross monthly pay	$1,015[b]
Food stamps	141	Net taxes	– 136[c]
Fuel assistance	50	Net monthly pay	$ 879
Clothing allowance	25[a]	Food stamps	62
Total income	$707	Fuel assistance	50
		Total income	$ 991
No taxes		Work expenses:	
No work expenses		Childcare	72[d]
		Health insurance	217[e]
		Transportation	22
			$ 311
Welfare Package	$707	Employment Package	$ 680

Notes:

[a]Massachusetts pays a clothing allowance to AFDC recipients which is an addition to the basic cash grant and is intended to provide winter clothing.

[b]Monthly gross pay is based on an hourly wage of $5.90, the average hourly salary for 1986 graduates of the Massachusetts Employment and Training Program for welfare recipients, and an average workweek of 40 hours.

[c]Taxes include state, Social Security, and federal taxes, including the end-of-year child care credit. This family earns too much to qualify for the Earned Income Tax Credit.

[d]The family would qualify for subsidized child care provided by the state of Massachusetts. Expenses are based on the weekly fees paid by a mother of one pre-school and one school-age child with monthly gross pay of $1,015.

[e]Average family health insurance premiums are assumed to be $217 per month, based on a survey by the Massachusetts Group Insurance Commission. The calculation here assumes that the worker's employer does not contribute to the premiums. Forty-five percent of the graduates of the Massachusetts Employment and Training Program are uninsured and must pay an average of this amount for health insurance.

Source: This table draws on data collected for Jean Kluver, "A Feminist Analysis of Welfare Reform," unpublished paper for the Department of Urban Studies and Planning, Massachusetts Institute of Technology. The table is an updated version of an earlier calculation by the author and Jean Kluver in *ET: A Model for the Nation?* (Philadelphia, American Friends Service Committee, 1986).

considered one of the most successful in the nation. Despite annual earnings averaging over $13,000, and equal to the median annual income of single mothers in the work force, a mother of two graduating from the ET program would actually be worse off financially than she would have been on public assistance, assuming that her job did not offer employer-paid health insurance. In fact, that is likely, since a Massachusetts Welfare Department survey of recipients placed in jobs showed that only 55 percent had any health coverage where they worked and only 14 percent received benefits paid in full by the employer.[32] The calculation in Table 5–5 also assumes that subsidized child care is available. However, as described earlier, many states have insufficient subsidized slots since Title XX has not kept pace with the demand for child care by low-income working mothers.

Welfare reform proposals fail to address these realities of labor force participation for single mothers adequately. Most states offer only short-term training programs, and usually prepare recipients for sex-stereotyped jobs in the secondary labor market, such as nurses' aide or file clerk. The child care benefits allowed to recipients while they attend training programs are far below the cost of enrolling a child in a day care center. Finally, the most any state programs offer for health coverage is a grace period during which the recipient can continue to receive Medicaid.

Conclusions and Prospects for the Future

Recent studies suggest that there will continue to be large numbers of single mothers. A researcher at the National Institute of Child Health and Human Development projected that 70 percent of white children born in 1980 (and 94 percent of black children) will have spent at least some time with only one parent before they reach age 19.[33] The vast majority of those children will remain with their mothers.

A look at the economic status of single mothers over the recent past makes clear the need for dramatic changes in our social policy. Table 5–6 illustrates how single-mother families have lost ground

Table 5–6   Mean Real Income of Families with Children (1984 Dollars)

	Percentage Change		
	1967–73	*1973–84*	*1967–84*
All two-parent families with children	+ 17.8	− 3.1	+ 14.1
White	+ 17.2	− 3.6	+ 12.9
Black	+ 28.0	+ 3.9	+ 33.0
Hispanic	n.a.	− 2.5	n.a.
All female-headed families with children	+ 1.3	− 7.8	− 6.5
White	+ 0.1	− 7.8	− 7.7
Black	+ 7.4	− 9.4	− 2.9
Hispanic	n.a.	− 13.1	n.a.

Source: Sheldon Danziger and Peter Gottschalk, "Families with Children Have Fared Worst," *Challenge*, March–April 1986, p. 41.

compared with married-couple families over the past two decades. Between 1967 and 1984, the income of single-mother families declined by an average of 7 percent. In contrast, married-couple families increased their income by 14 percent. If we divide the period into two halves, we see that both married-couple and single-mother families lost ground between 1973 and 1984, and that minority single-mother families fared worst of all. A new national family policy which simultaneously assists single mothers in earning higher wages and supplements their wages with public assistance income is urgently needed if those children and their mothers are to achieve an adequate standard of living.

Such a family policy would recognize that a secondary labor market job is not an automatic ticket out of poverty for single-parent families. A meaningful system of income supplements for low-income families, such as the European family allowance system, comes closer to what is required. In this system, the government pays a uniform subsidy to all families with children. In Western Europe as a whole, between 1 and 2 percent of gross national product is devoted to family allowances.[34] Devoting the same share of GNP to alleviating family poverty in the United States would require between $40 and $80 billion, roughly twice what we are currently spending on AFDC and food stamps.

Some valuable lessons in how to design such a policy can be learned from Sweden, which combines children's allowances with housing subsidies and a form of child support known as "advance maintenance." Starting in 1964, the Swedish government set child support at 40 percent of the Swedish reference wage (an indexed amount used as the basis for all social benefits) per child. The state guarantees this amount to single-parent families for each child under 18, regardless of whether paternity has been established or a court order is in effect. The amount is independent of the income of the custodial parent, and the program has no stigma attached to it. Payments are administered by the Swedish counterpart of the U.S. Social Security offices. Costs are partially offset (approximately 50 percent) by contributions from the absent parent, but the family receives the payment regardless of whether the absent parent pays his or her share or not.

Roughly half of all children in single-parent households receive payments under the plan, while the other half receive voluntary contributions from the absent parent in an amount equal to or greater than the state guarantee. Every Swedish child under 18 also receives a children's allowance of close to 400 dollars per year, regardless of family income. In addition, low-income families qualify for housing allowances which are based on the amount of rent paid. As of 1983, approximately one in three households with children received housing assistance.

The Swedish system is universal, covering all children as a matter of right, while ours is "means-tested," serving only those with low incomes. (In fact, eligibility for AFDC benefits is so stringent that only half of the poor children in the United States can qualify.) The Swedish system operates to diminish inequality by establishing a fairly high and uniform level of assistance. Benefits under the U.S. system vary dramatically by state, by race, by age, and by education of the parent. As a result, our system reproduces inequality from one generation to the next. Rather than building an income maintenance plan for children around child support enforcement, and reinforcing the most regressive aspects of U.S. policy toward children, we should be seeking to establish a universal plan that guarantees an adequate standard of living to all children.

In the short run, AFDC benefits should be made more uniform across states, and raised, at a minimum, up to the federal poverty level. Eligibility should be expanded to include two-parent families and families with low earnings.

If the policy goal is to expand the labor market options available to welfare recipients, the most important consideration should not be welfare reform, but rather raising the effective wages of the work that is available. Such a change, which would affect all single mothers, not merely those collecting public assistance, would begin with the important first step of raising the minimum wage.

Second, labor law reform is needed if we are to expand union representation in the workplaces where single mothers are most often found. In the United States, in contrast to other Western industrialized countries, unions must organize workplace by workplace. For instance, each individual nursing home in a national chain of nursing homes must vote separately on whether or not to become a union worksite. The process of setting up an election in which workers vote for or against union representation is extremely lengthy and offers many opportunities for employers to delay the vote. Still, union representation pays off for female workers. In 1985, for instance, union women earned on average more than $4,000 per year than nonunion women.[35]

Third, publicly provided health care and child care programs are needed if women are to support themselves and their families through participation in the labor market. Among Western industrialized countries, only the United States and South Africa fail to provide national health care coverage to all their citizens. Child care must also be available for low-income working women. First steps toward the establishment of a national child care system include the extension of Head Start, a federally funded program for economically disadvantaged preschool children. At present, Head Start only reaches one in five eligible children. More federal funding for Head Start and for Title XX would allow states and localities to provide affordable, high-quality child care to children of low-income working mothers. In addition, the Childcare Tax Credit should be converted into a refundable credit so that low-income workers can receive benefits from the credit.

Finally, payment of equal wages to men and women doing work of comparable worth (also known as "pay equity") would help the 80 percent of women trapped in traditional women's jobs.[36] Studies have shown that pay equity would raise wages in female-dominated jobs by about 20 to 30 percent. One route to pay equity is the use of "job evaluation" techniques. Most large employers determine appropriate pay scales for different jobs by assessing the amount of effort, skill, and responsibility called for in each job. Points are assigned to each of these factors, and pay is determined by the number of points each job receives in the evaluation process. Many cities, counties, and states, and some private employers have extended the use of job evaluations to ensure that men and women receive equitable pay for jobs of equal effort, skill, and responsibility. For instance, women employees of the state of Washington will receive nearly $500 million over a seven-year period to close the gap between their pay and pay in male-dominated occupations.

For too long social policy has assumed that single mothers should derive income from either the labor market or the state. For example, changes in AFDC eligibility under OBRA forced women to choose between public assistance and employment. Today's welfare-to-work programs presume that paid employment will end women's need for government support. However, the reality for most single mothers is that neither labor market income nor public assistance at current levels can adequately support their families. A meaningful family policy would expand the opportunities and the income available to women with children—both from the labor market and from the state.

Endnotes

1. The federal poverty line is a threshold figure, below which families are deemed to be too poor to satisfy basic needs. The figure is determined by calculating the cost of a basic food basket which is sufficient to meet minimum nutritional needs. The cost of the food basket is then multiplied by 3, on the

assumption that low-income families will spend roughly one-third of their total income on food. In 1986, the poverty line for a two-person family (e.g., a woman with one child) was $7,133; for a family of three, $8,738; and for a family of four, $11,168.

2. This income figure takes into account all single mothers, whether they are employed or not. Unemployed mothers and those not in the labor force have lower incomes than those who are employed. Employed female householders average higher incomes, primarily because of their higher wage and salary earnings. White women heading households had median earnings of $17,160 in 1985, compared to black women's earnings of $12,094 and Hispanic women's earnings of $13,179. See U.S. Bureau of the Census, *Current Population Reports,* ser. P-60, no. 154, 1986, Table 1.

3. Francine Blau and Marianne Ferber, *The Economics of Men, Women and Work* (Englewood Cliffs, N.J.: Prentice-Hall, 1986), pp. 166–68.

4. An excellent history of U.S. labor force segmentation into different occupations is David M. Gordon, Richard Edwards, and Michael Reich, *Segmented Work, Divided Workers* (New York: Cambridge University Press, 1982).

5. Martha May, "Bread Before Roses: American Workingmen, Labor Unions and the Family Wage," in *Women, Work and Protest: A Century of Women's Labor History,* ed. Ruth Milkman (Boston: Routledge & Kegan Paul, 1985), pp. 12–13.

6. U.S. Bureau of the Census, "Money Income and Poverty Status of Families and Persons in the United States: 1984," *Current Population Reports,* ser. P-60, no. 149 (Washington, D.C.: U.S. Government Printing Office, 1985), Table 7.

7. U.S. Congress, House, Committee on Ways and Means, *Children in Poverty,* 99th Cong., 1st sess., 1985. Committee Print 8, p. 372.

8. Ibid., p. 374.

9. "Working at the Margins: Part-Time and Temporary Workers in the United States," The National Association of Working Women, Cleveland, Ohio, September 1986, p. 18.

10. Ibid., p. 21.

11. This material appeared in longer form in Teresa Amott, "Put Responsibility Where It Belongs," *Dollars and Sense,* October 1987.

12. U.S. Congress, House, Committee on Ways and Means, *Background Material on Poverty,* 98th Cong., 1st sess., 1984, Committee Print 15, p. 138.

13. Data in this section are found in *Data and Materials Related to Welfare Programs for Families with Children,* S. Prt. 100-20 (Washington, D.C.: U.S. Government Printing Office, 1987).

14. Greg Duncan and Saul D. Hoffman, "Welfare Dynamics and the Nature of Need," Institute for Social Research, University of Michigan, Ann Arbor, mimeo, 1986.

15. Diana Pearce and Harriette McAdoo, "Women and Children: Alone and in Poverty," National Advisory Council on Economic Opportunity, Washington, D.C., September 1981.

16. Frances Fox Piven and Richard A. Cloward, "The Contemporary Relief Debate," in *The Mean Season* (New York: Pantheon Books, 1987), p. 45.

17. William Julius Wilson and Kathryn M. Neckerman, "Poverty and Family

Structure: The Widening Gap between Evidence and Public Policy Issues," in *Fighting Poverty: What Works and What Doesn't*, ed. Sheldon H. Danziger and Daniel H. Weinberg (Cambridge, Mass.: Harvard University Press, 1986), p. 249.

18. Ibid.
19. U.S. Congress, House, Committee on Ways and Means, *Background Material and Data on Programs within the Jurisdiction of the Committee on Ways and Means, 1986 edition*, 99th Cong., 2nd sess., 1986. Committee Print 14, p. 403.
20. Ibid., p. 404.
21. For a description of the consequences of the New York program see "Hope or Hassle?" Statewide Youth Advocacy, Albany, New York, 1987.
22. Frances Fox Piven and Richard A. Cloward, *Regulating the Poor* (New York: Pantheon Books, 1971).
23. U.S. Congress, Senate, Committee on Finance, *Data and Material Related to Welfare Programs for Families with Children*, 100th Cong., 1st sess., 1987, Committee Print 20, p. 18.
24. U.S. Bureau of the Census, "Money Income and Poverty Status of Families and Persons in the United States: 1985," *Current Population Reports*, ser. p-60, no. 154 (Washington, D.C.: U.S. Government Printing Office, 1986), p. 3.
25. Finance Committee, *Welfare Programs for Families*, p. 25.
26. U.S. Committee on Ways and Means, *Background Material*, pp. 378–79.
27. Barry Bluestone and Bennett Harrison, "The Great American Job Machines," study prepared for the Joint Economic Committee, U.S. Congress, 1986.
28. See, for example, "Help Wanted: America Faces an Era of Worker Scarcity that May Last to the Year 2000," *Business Week*, August 10, 1987.
29. Congressional Budget Office, *The Growth in Poverty: 1979–1985, Economic and Demographic Factors*, Washington, D.C., 1986.
30. Diana Pearce, "On the Edge: Marginal Women Workers and Employment Policy," in *Ingredients for Women's Employment*, ed. Christine Bose and Glenna Spitz (Albany, New York: State University of New York Press, 1987), pp. 197–210.
31. U.S. Bureau of the Census, *Statistical Abstract of the United States: 1986* (Washington, D.C.: U.S. Government Printing Office, 1986), p. 421.
32. Commonwealth of Massachusetts, Department of Public Welfare, "An Analysis of the First 25,000 ET Placements," Boston, 1986.
33. U.S. Committee on Finance, *Background Material on Welfare Programs*, p. 65.
34. Robert Kuttner, *The Economic Illusion: False Choices Between Prosperity and Social Justice* (Boston: Houghton Mifflin, 1982), p. 244.
35. Fact Sheets on Women in the Workplace and Childcare, prepared by the National Commission on Working Women, Washington, D.C., 1987.
36. For detailed information about pay equity, see Teresa Amott and Julie Matthaei, "Comparable Work, Incomparable Pay," *Radical America*, September–October 1984.

Chapter 6

THE SEARCH FOR AFFORDABLE HOUSING

Elizabeth A. Mulroy

Historically, the "American family" has been valued as a national resource. Public policies were enacted to stimulate homeownership, considered the ideal way to shelter a family. However, significant transformations in family life—specifically, marital disruption—have altered traditional family form, creating a burgeoning subpopulation of poor families headed by women who have immediate unmet housing needs.

The demand for affordable housing has been increasing during a time when the supply has been reduced by decisions in the private housing market and by cutbacks in federal housing programs. Yet federal housing policy has not been formulated to take the housing problems of this growing population into account. In large measure this is because little is known about the housing needs of single mothers. Therefore, the policy debate regarding allocation of limited resources in a period of concern about the national budget deficit has proceeded largely uninformed in regard to housing problems of the nation's largest subgroup in poverty.

Some single mothers and their children reside in single-family homes in the suburbs. Following separation and divorce, these formerly upper-middle-class households are now among the "nouveau poor" struggling to keep up mortgage payments, taxes, and maintenance on severely reduced incomes. Low-income single mothers live primarily in the private rental market in urban neighborhoods. They are heads of households paying a disproportionately high percentage of their low incomes for rent and utilities. Many other single mothers, often in transition, are without conventional housing and thus slip through the cracks of those traditionally "counted" as heads of households; they form subfamilies who are doubling up in the households of parents, relatives, or friends. They move frequently. They may double up in already crowded public housing units, live temporarily in shelters, and are increasingly found among the homeless. To relieve their housing problems, low-income single mothers across the nation apply for conventional public housing and for the Section 8 Rental Assistance Program, which subsidizes rental units in the private rental market. Both large and small housing agencies in many metropolitan areas report waiting lists for these housing programs of anywhere from 2 to 20 years.[1]

In the face of demonstrated need, there is a troublesome disparity between the large volume of income-eligible single mothers who try to use the Section 8 rent subsidy and the paucity of those who are ultimately successful in using the program. In 1985, nearly half of all households who searched in the greater Boston area with a Section 8 certificate failed to access the program.[2] The underlying reasons why some searchers succeed and others fail to access the only remaining federal affordable housing program is of concern to housing policy experts, housing program administrators, public welfare practitioners, and social service providers whose caseloads are bulging with families who are homeless or at risk of homelessness.

Critics contend that these low participation rates in the Section 8 program demonstrate that there is no need for additional public investment in low-income housing programs because the poor, even when given the opportunity to receive a substantial rent subsidy, *choose* not to participate. Other controversies exist over the effort expended by the poor: if they fail to use the rent subsidy, it is because they did not try hard enough. There is also the argument that everyone has freedom of choice in making residential location decisions, limited only by the constraints of cost. Therefore, given the dollar value of the Section 8 rent subsidy, low-income households have had the cost barrier removed and can compete like other renters in the marketplace. Still others contend that the single problem with participation is diminished supply of low-income housing. Increase the supply and single mothers will be able to fully utilize the rent subsidy.

Chapter 6 will examine how, in a tight housing market, low-income single mothers access the Section 8 Rental Assistance Program. The chapter will begin by describing the intended goals that the Section 8 Rental Assistance Program set out to achieve. Then it will report findings of a study of single mothers searching for affordable housing through the Section 8 Rental Assistance Program.[3] Conducted in eastern Massachusetts in 1985–86, the study sought to better understand housing decisions of low-income single mothers, to determine their preferences and motivations for seeking Section 8 rental assistance, and to learn more about rental practices as they occur from the viewpoint of the intended program user. The chapter is organized around four themes: (1) how single mothers organize and carry out a search; (2) the motivations and expectations of single mothers for rental assistance; (3) what single mothers perceive to be the barriers to participation; and (4) implications for improving program utilization.

Affordable Housing as Social Policy

The objective of the housing reformers of the 1890s was to improve physical housing conditions. Regulations were tightened on profit-making developers so that the condition of housing in urban slums would create a "decent environment" that would resolve other difficulties such as overcrowding and poor access to sanitary facilities. The Housing Act of 1937 and the New Deal provided the first federal subsidy for housing.

Since the early days of public housing in the 1930s, low-income households have sought relief from high housing costs through publicly assisted programs. The National Housing Act of 1949 set a national goal of "a decent home and suitable living environment for every American family." Policies to implement the goal conform to societal guidelines, with reliance on the private market and government taking a subsidiary role.

Section 8/Existing Rental Assistance Program

When initiated in 1974, the federal Section 8/Existing Rental Assistance Program was a significant policy and programmatic departure from the conventional public housing model. It was intended to counteract the problems associated with conventional public housing such as expensive new construction, costly maintenance, and concentrations of minority populations in urban high-rise enclaves. Its intent was to reduce public expenditure for low-income housing by using individual leases and contracts for units already in existence in the private rental market. Theoretically, the stock of affordable housing would be effectively expanded as each low-income household located a moderately priced unit that met minimum standards for its physical condition, called housing quality standards.

Deconcentration and Housing Choice

A significant feature of the Section 8 program is its intent to maximize a household's mobility and freedom of choice in each community. A major criticism of conventional public housing is the concentration of projects in the worst sections of cities, or the isolation of projects in remote areas of cities far removed from adequate public services. In the Section 8/Existing Rental Assistance Program, households can move or stay put; families are supposed to obtain affordable housing that is in decent, safe, and sanitary condition in neighborhoods of their choice.

Housing policy-makers and administrators anticipated that the one-by-one deconcentration of low-income and minority families from deteriorating inner-city neighborhoods to better city neighborhoods and to the suburbs would facilitate racial and economic integration. The resounding political resistance by suburban communities to new construction projects specifically targeted for low- and moderate-income households would thus be avoided.

Program Characteristics

Rent could not exceed what the federal Department of Housing and Urban Development (HUD) determined to be the "fair market rent" for moderately priced market-rate rentals in the community.[4] The rental unit then became affordable because the household paid no more than 25 percent (later amended to 30 percent) of income for rent and utilities. Using federal funds, the local housing authority then subsidized the balance of the rent by making a direct payment to a landlord for the difference between the fair market rent and the renter's 30 percent contribution.

Each household searches with a Section 8 "certificate"—a document verifying low-income eligibility.[5] The program is time-limited, giving 60 days to locate an acceptable unit. If a household is unsuccessful in finding a unit in 60 days, extensions not to exceed 120 days can be granted. Households that find a unit within the fair market rent guidelines, then submit a "Request for Inspection" form to the housing authority. This initiates the administrative process of inspecting the physical condition of the unit to certify that it meets housing quality standards. When repairs are neces-

sary, the landlord is responsible for making them. Those households unsuccessful in locating a unit which meets all Section 8
requirements within the 120 days have their certificates terminated and their search ends.

A Program for Women

Women who head households have always been a significant proportion of Section 8 Rental Assistance Program beneficiaries, a fact
not usually recognized in discussions of policies affecting women.
The preponderance of households who apply to the Section 8
Rental Assistance Program are single mothers. In 1976, two years
after program inception, 70 percent of those participating nationwide were female heads of households.[6] A decade later, of those
new households participating in a Section 8 Rental Assistance
Program administered on a statewide basis by the Massachusetts'
Executive Office of Communities and Development, more than
three-quarters were female heads of households. Therefore, both
those who succeed in accessing program benefits and those who
fail to participate are primarily single mothers and their children.

The Massachusetts Experience: A "Worst Case" Scenario

A study of the housing search of 56 single mothers and their
children, conducted in eastern Massachusetts in 1985–1986, presents a "worst case" scenario, in that low vacancy rates and skyrock-
eting rents created housing search problems for many of the area's
market renters as well. The plight of low-income, Section 8 certificate holders was accentuated in this market, giving way to a more
optimistic scenario for certificate holders in other, less active real
estate markets. Nonetheless, 57 percent of searchers succeeded in
accessing Section 8 program benefits, while 43 percent returned
their certificates unused.

Reduced Supply of Housing

The Commonwealth of Massachusetts recently experienced a statewide economic recovery that has affected the affordable housing
market in several ways. The city of Boston has witnessed a real
estate boom and is considered one of the "hottest" real estate
markets in the country. However, "hot" real estate markets tend
to create investment opportunity in impressive downtown revitalization projects, often made possible by demolition or conversion

of low-income housing to office space or condominiums for the luxury housing market. Rental housing comprises 70 percent of Boston's housing stock, but this inventory is diminishing. Between 1980 and 1983 almost 14,000 condominiums were created, and virtually all were conversions as opposed to new construction.[7] Loss of units has also occurred by redevelopment in the public sector and by expiring regulatory controls in the federal HUD-assisted inventory. Additional units have been lost because of "gentrification," which occurs when units in transitional urban neighborhoods are rehabilitated and then either purchased or rented to upper-income households, resulting in more displacement of low-income households. The federal response to diminished supply has been to slash allocations for housing programs, yielding no replacement of lost units, let alone expansion of stock.

Characteristics of Searchers

The most striking characteristic of the 56 single-parent families embarking on their Section 8 search in this tight housing market was their heterogeneity. The population as a whole had only one thing in common: their poverty. Beyond very low income eligibility requirements—which is 50 percent of area median income—there is great diversity relative to personal and background characteristics.

Age. Heads of households ranged in age from 20 to 60 years old with a median age of 32. Not all heads of households turned out to be mothers. There were some grandmothers who ranged in age from 41 to 60 who had either custody or were primary caretakers of grandchildren.

Family Size. Over half of all families were small households consisting of a mother and her one or two children. These mothers formed and were currently maintaining independent households. A third of all families contained four or five members. However, 33 percent of these were mothers with one or two children who were doubling up as subfamilies in the households of others. Only 13 percent of the sample were larger families, and they were composed solely of mothers and their 5, 6, or 7 children.

Location of Residence and Racial Distribution. Within the sample as a whole, 59 percent were nonwhite, and 41 percent were white. Of the nonwhite households, three-quarters were black. Locations of residence at the time the search began show patterns of racial segregation in housing. Nearly three-quarters of all minority households lived in predominantly black neighborhoods of Roxbury, Dorchester, and Mattapan in the city of Boston.

The rest of the minority families were residentially scattered in a variety of smaller cities in the metropolitan area. A few lived in rural areas, and one black family lived in suburbia. Conversely, 75 percent of all whites lived in smaller cities, in rural communities, and in suburbia. About one-quarter of white families resided within Boston city limits in predominantly white neighborhoods of Hyde Park, East Boston, and Dorchester.

Marital Status. About one-third of the women had never been married, and close to two-thirds were either separated or divorced. Widowhood was an insignificant cause of female headship in this sample. All but one respondent remained single during the two-and-one-half-year wait on the waiting list, suggesting, in the short term at least, that single parenthood is not a transient status.

Income Levels and Sources. Annual household income ranged from $4,128 to $19,200, depending on household size, with a median income of $6,048. More than three-quarters of families relied on Aid to Families with Dependent Children (AFDC) as their source of income. Wages were earned by one-quarter of the heads of households. Most who were employed worked part-time. Of those in the labor market either full- or part-time or both, only one-third received employee benefits of any kind. That is, most were not accruing fringe benefits which help to economically stabilize a family.

Only 13 percent of single mothers received child support. Of those who were formerly married, an astonishing 88 percent report that their former husbands were unemployed at the time the marriage ended. Not only does this high incidence of unemployment among "breadwinners" disable fathers from making child support payments, but it further distances the family from work-tied benefits that help to protect children after marital dissolution, such as health care plans, workplace savings plans, or social security benefits.[8]

Education. About half of mothers were high school graduates, with a median level of education of 12 years. Sixteen percent had a ninth grade education or less, and 16 percent had some college education. About a quarter of respondents were enrolled in an educational program of some kind while they were conducting their housing search. Educational pursuits ranged from studying for a high school equivalency diploma (GED), English as a second language, community college courses, professional training certificate programs, to bachelor's and master's degrees.

This chapter will now examine how respondents organized and carried out their search and what the impacts were on search outcome.

Organizing and Carrying Out the Search

Having eagerly waited for at least two and a half years for the
opportunity to get subsidized housing, mothers embarked on the
search with high expectations. Driven by unmet housing needs
and preferences which placed a priority on residential mobility,
women organized their search around four considerations:

1. Where do I want to live?
2. What personal constraints do I have to look there?
3. Where will landlords let me live?
4. Where will Fair Market Rents let me live?

These decision rules resulted in a search which evolved in three
distinct phases. Phase 1 consisted of the first 60 days in which
women's expectations for choice in the determination of where
they would live collided with discriminatory rental practices. Phase
2 consisted of the 60-day extension period which most searchers
requested. In this phase searchers reassessed their housing preferences and expectations for the rent subsidy and some shifted
search strategies. Phase 3 was entered only by those who had
found a willing landlord and a unit at the Fair Market Rent: it
involved accessing the Section 8 administrative system—the housing agency apparatus. Most who entered phase 3 became program
participants. It was possible, however, to sustain the three phases
of the search and still fail to participate in program benefits, to be
discussed further on.

Each phase was like a maze: complex, stressful, difficult to
navigate, and lengthier to complete than anticipated. Each maze
contained obstacles where major decisions had to be made. These
decision "pinchpoints" determined the next direction taken, affected future opportunities in succeeding phases, and impacted
program outcome. This chapter will now examine each phase of
the search from the viewpoint of the women involved in it. It will
look at the decision pinchpoints they confronted and will analyze
impacts of decisions made.

Phase 1: The First 60 Days

The head-of-household role carried primary responsibilities for
caretaker, nurturer, provider, and shelterer of children. Executing
these multiple roles on very low incomes appeared to heavily
influence motivations for seeking the rent subsidy and for viewing
Section 8 as a broad-based housing resource (see Table 6–1).

Table 6–1 Frequency Each Preference Is Cited by Location of Residence in June 1985 When Search Began

		Preferences					
Location	*Low Rent*	*Better Apartment*	*Better Neighborhood*	*Better Housing Environment*	*Less Crowding*	*Stabilize Housing*	*Relocate Near Work*
Inner City Boston (N=30)	18 60% (53)	16 53% (70)	16 53% (70)	10 33% (77)	8 27% (53)	7 23% (58)	2 7% (100)
Other areas (N=26)	16 62% (47)	7 27% (30)	7 27% (30)	3 12 (23)	7 27% (47)	5 19% (42)	0

Note: Multiple responses were allowed.

Motivation for Seeking Section 8 Assistance.   Social factors, in addition to economic factors, motivated low-income single mothers to seek the Section 8 rent subsidy. Mothers regarded traditional criteria of housing cost and physical condition of their units to be important reasons to obtain subsidized housing, but additionally, inadequate neighborhood conditions, no locational choice to escape those conditions, and frequent residential mobility and instability associated with lower economic and social status after separation and divorce were serious problems for which they also sought relief.

Irrespective of where they lived, about 60 percent of respondents cite lower rent as a reason for wanting rental assistance. Even though all respondents were very low income according to federal guidelines (and had median incomes of only about $6,000 a year), 40 percent did not mention lower rent as a reason for seeking Section 8 at all. This suggests two things: (1) some respondents do not believe they are burdened by high rents; and (2) there are compelling housing problems other than cost for which single mothers seek a remedy. The number and the type of these unmet housing needs are more clearly evident in a breakdown by race and residential location.

Motivation for seeking Section 8, beyond cost, is tied to race and location of residence. In this sample, 80 percent of inner-city Boston residents were minority. As Table 6–1 indicates, residents of neighborhoods within Boston city limits, and particularly those living in minority-dominated neighborhoods of Roxbury, Mattapan, and Dorchester, cite more reasons for wanting the subsidy than those living in cities, towns, and rural areas outside Boston city limits. These multiple preferences appear to result from living arrangements which give rise to different unmet needs and preferences. First, nearly three-quarters of respondents in inner-city Boston live in the private rental housing market. Most are heads of households. Others are doubling up as subfamilies in the households of others. These respondents express preferences for lower rents, better quality apartments, reduction in overcrowded conditions, and relocation out of deteriorating housing in neighborhoods they do not consider safe. Second, the remainder live in public housing owned by the Boston Housing Authority, in HUD-subsidized housing, or in low-rent boarding houses. These respondents already have a low rent. Their expressed reasons for wanting Section 8 are to escape what they consider to be a bad housing environment. As one 34-year-old black mother of one 14-year-old daughter put it:

This building is owned by HUD. It is in terrible condition. It is drug-infested and has bad tenants. I want a better environment for my daughter, a better life. Also, the neighborhood is rough. I have to keep a tight rein on her. I work part-time, so I have my daughter come right home from school to take care of her grandmother and I have the grandmother take care of my daughter. Then I have my sister take care of both of them. We look out for each other.

Those who preferred to move to a better neighborhood or better housing environment expressed similar expectations to relocate out of deteriorating neighborhoods with substandard housing stock. However, those who expressed the desire to relocate to a better housing environment, like the woman above, viewed housing itself as a "package" of services and resources. These respondents had big dreams for improving many aspects of their lives, and locational freedom was perceived as the chance to "trade up" their entire housing package by relocating to an area of their choice. The new environment would then provide multiple benefits, including good schools for the children, neighborhood amenities, including safer streets, better recreational opportunities, good public facilities, and less density—in sum, a better life.

Those living outside Boston city limits, who were predominantly white, report an equally frequent preference for low rent, but they do not display as much interest in either relocating to a better apartment, better neighborhood, or better housing environment. These residents appear to already have greater access to newer housing in smaller communities. Minority respondents who lived outside the city of Boston, however, continued to express preferences for better neighborhoods and better housing environments. They also lived primarily in cities.

The notion of stabilizing after separation and divorce as an expressed reason for wanting the rent subsidy reflects an emotional component of housing as both a real and symbolic representation of social well-being, following a period of residential mobility, instability, and family disruption brought about by separation and divorce.

One-fifth of all respondents, and over half of respondents who lived in inner-city Boston neighborhoods, sought rental assistance as a resource to combat these negative impacts experienced by changes in household composition and frequent mobility. Two-thirds of the total sample moved at least once during the two-year period they were on the waiting list; a third moved at least twice or more; and a fifth moved three or more times. This level of residential mobility is consistent with that found in previous studies of female-headed households.[9] However, locating affordable housing in which a mother can *plan* to reside for at least one year with the expectation of an indefinite stay is, in her view, a necessity in order to stabilize her family in transition. For this subgroup of certificate holders, the expressed need to stabilize the family causes her to perceive and then seek the rent subsidy as an important resource to obtain a more permanent housing solution, and in this sense, it becomes a preference.

The expectation that employed women in this sample would show an attachment to the labor force which motivated them to either move closer to or remain near their place of employment was not confirmed.

Those who had multiple preferences were more prone to encounter multiple barriers as they began to contact landlords in the private rental market, particularly when one preference was locational freedom. The decision "pinchpoint" in phase 1 was the amount of emphasis a respondent decided to place on seeking locational freedom and housing choice. The extent to which she shaped her search to achieve this goal determined the ease with which she negotiated phase 1. Those who did not have this preference proceeded on to phases 2 and 3 faster and with less hassle than those who did.

Multiple Barriers and a Search Hassle. Ninety percent of all respondents experienced at least one of the following barriers in their search: landlords who refused to rent to them because of low fair market rent levels; landlords who, as a standard rental practice, refused to participate in the Section 8 program; and landlords who had perceived biases against them because of their single-parent status, their race, their public welfare income, or the presence of children. Most respondents reported experiencing multiple barriers. For example, in the sample as a whole, 79 percent were thwarted by landlords who refused to participate in Section 8, and 77 percent by low fair market rent levels (see Table 6–2).

Only a third of minority respondents reported encountering racial discrimination as a barrier. However, at the end of the study, the spatial distribution of searchers was drawn clearly along racial lines. This suggests that racial discrimination was subtly masked and incorporated into other, more easily recognized barriers, such as rejection based on fair market rent levels, or the catchall category of not participating in Section 8 as a rental practice. Searchers expressed the fear that this wholesale barrier encompassed a multitude of biases without admitting to prejudice against AFDC recipients, presence of children, racial minorities, or single mothers. Furthermore, it was pervasive and experienced by

Table 6–2 Frequency Distribution of Barriers by Program Outcome

Participant Outcome	FMR's Too Low		Landlords Say No Section 8		Won't Take Children		Bias Against AFDC Status		Bias Against Single-Parent Families		Racial Discrim-ination	
Succeed N = 32	21	65.6%	23	71.9%	15	46.9%	14	43.8%	9	28.1%	3	9.4%
Fail N = 24	22	91.7%	21	87.5%	17	70.8%	13	54.2%	9	37.5%	9	37.5%
Total	43	76.7%	44	78.5%	32	57.1%	27	48.2%	18	32.1%	12	21.4%

Note: Multiple responses were allowed.

searchers in all geographic areas—inner-city Boston, smaller cities, suburbs, and rural areas.

Section 8 as the "Scarlet Woman."   Possession of the Section 8 certificate itself hindered search efforts in the first 60 days as it negatively labeled searchers as a class of poverty-stricken women to whom undesirable tenant characteristics were ascribed. Searching with the certificate was like wearing the Scarlet Letter—that is, searching with a moral stigma. An encounter between a woman with a certificate and a landlord not only resulted in immediately eliminating the woman's chances for tenant selection, but also put her through a humiliating and demeaning experience. One mother who sought locational freedom explains:

> *Landlords blatantly discriminate against Section 8. They told me plain and simple they don't take Section 8; that's their policy. I told them it is illegal to discriminate. I even threatened to file a complaint against them. But they held firm.*

There are several possible reasons why landlords do not want to participate in Section 8 as a rental practice. Apart from considering fair market rents too low, government intervention in the housing market is resented by many landlords. Searchers report that landlords do not want to be bothered with government red tape, do not want their units inspected, and "won't play games for the government." One white respondent expressed it this way:

> *When I first talked with landlords, they would tell me the apartments were beautiful. When I told them I would be using Section 8 they got rude and told me the apartments had lead paint. Using Section 8 labelled me poor and to landlords that meant I was a bad tenant. When they found out that I have kids and am a single parent they were ugly to me. They treated me very badly. They implied I would be irresponsible, wouldn't take care of my children, and would throw wild parties. I had to look at more than 25 apartments before I could find one landlord who would go below his asking rent and would take kids and me. It was very demoralizing.*

Another respondent seeking housing in the suburbs felt that landlords were interrogating her in inappropriate ways that they wouldn't ask of non-Section 8 applicants. For example, she reports:

> *The application was too personal. They said, "Why aren't you with your husband? Give your medical history and doctors' references. Are your kids noisy?" I don't think they would ask that of everybody.*

This woman also found that landlords were holding to very high rents for places that were "dumps" and sticking to security deposits and first and last month's rents "upfront" to protect themselves from having to take Section 8 tenants.[10] This respondent concludes:

I finally found a place that was at the fair market rent and I felt it would pass inspection. Then the landlord asked me for a security deposit, and first and last month's rent upfront—this came to $1,300. I told him I could only leave about $100, according to Section 8 regulations. He said that wasn't enough. He gave the apartment to two stewardesses who came in right after me who gave him $1,300 cash on the spot.

Most searchers encountered multiple barriers similar to those described above. Two black respondents searching in Roxbury and Dorchester areas of inner-city Boston describe how they experienced being screened out of particular housing:

Newspaper ads for apartments have phone numbers to call. When I called, there was this recorded message asking you to leave your name, address, and phone number, the number of children you have, how you are going to pay for the apartment, and your place of employment. So you say, I'm Jane Doe, of Shawmut Ave, Roxbury, I have four children, I'm using Section 8, and I'm not employed. Landlords don't call you back.

The second black respondent looking in the inner-city of Boston reports:

Landlords discriminate against Section 8 because they think Section 8 "people" will destroy property. My friend went over to look at an apartment and the landlord checked over her kids and said they were too dirty. So I called the landlord and asked to see the apartment. She asked right away if I had Section 8. I said yes. So she said come over for coffee and let's talk about it. So I dressed myself and my kids up in our best and lectured them to be quiet. She looked us over, up and down—examining us. She found us OK, and told me I could have the apartment. Then the rent was over the fair market rent and she wouldn't come down.

Other searchers report being "put off" by landlords, which causes serious problems in a time-limited program. For example, respondents report finally finding an apartment that they like, with an agreed-upon rent that is acceptable for Section 8 fair market rents. The all-important Request for Inspection form that must be signed by both prospective landlord and prospective tenant is left with the landlord to send in to the local housing agency, demonstrating that an inspection of the unit is requested. Several days, then weeks pass. The agency receives no form. One respondent recalls, "Then you call and you call. Finally the landlord says, 'Sorry, I rented the apartment to Aunt Mary,' and you've lost precious time waiting. You're at their mercy."

Another respondent reports:

*The landlord told me that I didn't need to bother coming down to
see the apartment because it needed repairs. He said he didn't want
to make any repairs. He said, "I can get high rents without making
repairs, so why bother with Section 8?"*

According to one black respondent from the Roxbury section of
Boston who restricted her search to Roxbury because she had no
transportation anywhere else, the problem of using a Section 8
certificate is compounded by the way realty offices in her neighborhood do business:

*The real problem is that realty companies want "upfront" money
plus commissions. They won't consider anything else. I could have
had three or four nice apartments if I could have paid the $900 they
were asking. This is the way realty companies function out there.
We're at a disadvantage anyway of being looked down on as a
Section 8 "person," meaning poor. Two strikes against you for being
black. Three strikes and you're out without "upfront" security, first,
and last.*

The question is raised as to whether realty offices who follow
these practices are doing it intentionally to steer Section 8 certificate holders away or due to lack of understanding about the
security deposit provisions in the Section 8 regulations which offer
protection to landlords against damages and receipt of first and last
month's rent.[11]

The search was a particularly dejecting experience for large
minority families in the inner city of Boston. One recently divorced, black 31-year-old mother of five, whose children ranged in
ages from 1 to 13, wanted to find another apartment anywhere in
the Boston city limits. She reports:

*I searched for four months and couldn't find a place to rent because
I have five kids and landlords didn't want them. I didn't want to lose
my certificate so I tried to use it here where I have been living for
the past 10 years, but the place couldn't pass inspection.*

Biases against children left single-parent mothers in a precarious
position, and found several mothers being asked to make trade-offs
with landlords. One reported that a landlord asked her for $25
extra for each child. "The rent was $500. But with each child an
extra $25, the rent would have been $600 for me."

Discriminatory barriers were also strongly evident for smaller-
sized minority households in other cities and in the suburbs. One
29-year-old black mother of two, an AFDC recipient, actively
sought to move out into the suburbs:

*I looked in the better neighboring cities and suburbs in order to get
my children into a good school district and a safer neighborhood. I*

looked in Belmont, Cambridge, Arlington, Lexington, and Acton and no one would take a Section 8 at $650 for a three-bedroom apartment.

Her search was over before she realized that there was no way she could break into a better suburban community using Section 8. She still wouldn't compromise her housing goal of relocating to a better environment, and she is bitter about her experience trying to use Section 8 under the myth that it is possible to find affordable housing of standard quality in an area of one's choice.

Discriminatory barriers were in place in the suburbs also for one black 28-year-old mother of two who already resided in a desirable suburb. After her divorce three years ago, she moved back into her mother's home until her Section 8 certificate came through. The respondent worked full-time in Boston, and her mother provided child care. Therefore, for consistency in child care, she wanted to use her subsidy in a town close by. She found several barriers working to exclude her, as she explains:

The worst problem was discrimination against blacks on the South Shore, combined with using a Section 8 certificate. The fair market rents on the South Shore are far below real rents. Landlords just laughed at Section 8 rents. The only alternative would be to go back into Dorchester or Cambridge where blacks can find a place to rent.

But she was unwilling to do that. She decided that the costs of using Section 8 outweigh the benefits if you are black and want to live in the suburbs. She returned the certificate unused, and remained doubled up in the suburbs, where she was at least able to keep her job by keeping her support system for child care intact.

Even a new state-subsidized mixed-income development built in the suburbs to house a mix of low income and market rate households rejected this respondent's application for tenancy. It also rejected another respondent, an employed 27-year-old white from another South Shore suburb. In addition to all of the barriers they experienced in the private market, they were thwarted again by rigid tenant selection screening criteria in a suburban, subsidized mixed-income housing development targeted to serve them.

Phase 2: The Second 60 Days

The exigencies of the search in the first 60 days left most respondents in need of a time extension in order to keep looking. The "pinchpoint" in phase 2 was deciding what to do in the face of discriminatory practices: (1) to passively accept rejections by landlords for reasons not selected and continue searching in the areas of choice; (2) to shift search strategies and look in areas where fair market rents appeared to be more in line with market rents; or (3) to confront landlords about repeated rejections and try to convince them of tenant worthiness.

A Shift in Search Strategy.   Most who passively accepted rejection and continued to look only in better areas, hoping to eventually find a willing landlord, ultimately failed. Those who shifted search strategies and decided to compromise their expectation of locational freedom experienced one of three outcomes: some found a unit at fair market rent, but the landlord refused to make necessary repairs; others still couldn't locate a unit at fair market rent; and finally a few did locate a unit at fair market rent and the landlord did make necessary repairs. Those that shifted strategies at mid-point to look at areas not of their preference were more likely to succeed than those who did not shift geographic boundaries of the search.

Social Negotiation: Success for Gatekeepers.   Most who challenged landlord barriers and tried to negotiate a tenancy in spite of rejections failed to break through those barriers. Landlords effectively served as gatekeepers of the private rental market and were rarely persuaded to negotiate tenant selection with searchers at all.

Those respondents who attempted to negotiate tenant selection on their own with landlords tried to convince landlords of their tenant-worthiness. They offered goodwill, or promise of help in the form of physical labor to make necessary repairs. Two respondents tried to solicit the goodwill of landlords in the following way:

> *Landlords are afraid of Section 8 people. They think we're uneducated, dirty, and throw wild parties. I tried to sell myself—that I'm in college, recently separated from my husband and have lived locally for a long time. I had to tell them that I'm a good person and a good tenant.*

One black mother of five was repeatedly rejected by landlords, first for having so many children, and then for her single-parent status. When she finally found a single family house that she wanted to rent, she felt the need to dispel some stereotypes in order to convince the landlord that she is a worthy person:

> *I pulled out the kitchen chair, sat down with the landlord and tried to sell myself. I'm a college graduate. I explained what my goals are and what I'm trying to accomplish; that I wanted to get out of the city to make a better life for my kids. I've always been employed, and never been on public welfare. I started back to college for a*

*master's degree in Education—even with a 6-month-old baby—so
that I can teach eventually.*

This woman broke through barriers of biases against children,
against being poor, single and black, but not without a caveat. The
landlord agreed to her tenancy, but didn't totally trust the substance of the exchange, and asked her to sign an agreement that
she would move out in a year. She signed the agreement.

In Brockton, a city southwest of Boston, a white mother of two
children, who completed nine years of schooling, had been rejected throughout the search because she couldn't get landlords to
reduce their asking rents. All were above the fair market rents.
She tried to negotiate with each landlord, but none would come
down, even $8. She had moved eight times since applying for
rental assistance, and each move was an eviction because of rent
increases beyond her ability to pay. She offered promises of help—
of physical labor—around which her negotiation proceeded:

*Finally I saw an ad in the newspaper for an apartment that was in
the fair market rent. I immediately stopped and called from a pay
phone. When I got there, there were roaches crawling everywhere,
falling from the ceiling. It was in terrible shape. But the landlord
said he'd consider Section 8. So, I tried to present myself with
confidence. I suggested that my family and I would help with
repairs; so much had to be done before it could pass inspection.
Everybody worked together alongside the landlord. We all pitched
in. It was compromise; you do this, I'll do that. Finally, it all worked
out.*

The infrequency of attempts to break through landlord barriers,
and the paucity of success rates for those who try, suggest first,
that the matter of renting to poor single mothers with Section 8
certificates is not yet considered a negotiable subject, and second,
that single mothers are unequal communicators with landlords in
the process of social negotiation. Program participation was facilitated not by breaking barriers, but by finding alternate paths to
more cooperative landlords. Some searchers continued to call
landlords indiscriminately. Others, demoralized by continuous
rejections, gave up on the private market. They decided to avoid
pitfalls of random searching by seeking assistance from the housing
agency, or from landlords known to them through networks of
contacts. At this point in the search, those who did not contact the
agency for assistance, or who knew of no landlord contacts to
pursue, failed to ever access the private rental market.

Phase 3: Accessing the Section 8 System

Bureaucracy as Maze. Irrespective of whether they succeeded
or failed, mothers who conducted the search experience in phase

2 exacted a high personal cost, but the search was still not over. As the end of the 120-day time limit approached and no desirable housing had been found, searchers scrambled to submit a Request for Inspection form for any available unit. This form represented entry into an administrative maze filled with negotiating requirements, technical inspection regulations, time limits for housing repairs, inspection failures, loss of units, delayed occupancy, and the threat of having to start all over again.

The complexity and uncertainty of getting a match among fair market rents, housing quality standards, a willing landlord, and a vacant unit created a new "pinchpoint" that asked: Will fair market rent and inspection decisions be made in time or will the unit be rented to someone else? Having competed and finally been selected for tenancy, searchers were vigilant because pressure from market renters continued to be strongly felt as the certificate holder's file slowly grinded through the bureaucratic maze.

In desperation, some mothers submitted a Request for Inspection form for their own substandard units. Those whose own landlords were willing and able to make necessary repairs to bring the substandard properties up to housing quality standards were able to succeed as program participants. Those who had landlords unwilling to make repairs or whose housing still couldn't be brought up to code after repairs failed to participate.

Trying to bring these properties up to housing code was often a difficult and lengthy process. Also, important decisions had to be made with respect to trade-offs, as one Hispanic mother of three reports:

> I wanted to get a better and larger apartment so my three teenagers would have more room. Even though this neighborhood is going downhill, I don't mind staying here because I am near the stores, public transportation, and the police station is across the street. I couldn't find another apartment, so when I asked the landlord to make all the repairs for this place to pass inspection, he raised the rent by $150 and told me I had to sign an agreement to stay five years if he made the repairs. I signed the agreement, he made the repairs and it's still not a good apartment.

A few respondents entered phase 3 of the search, attempted to meet all program requirements, and still failed to participate in program benefits. One example is that of an employed 20-year-old black woman with a new baby who was doubling up with relatives in an overcrowded apartment. She searched for a small apartment in inner-city Boston and found one below the fair market rent, but the landlord refused to make needed repairs. Even though she worked full-time and had a baby to care for, she found a second apartment, also within rent guidelines. This time the landlord did agree to make repairs. On inspection, the unit failed because several code violations still were not corrected. The landlord said he had done all he was going to do. The mother could not take the apartment because it still didn't meet Section 8 housing quality standards.

She continued to search and several weeks later found a third apartment, also within the fair market rent guidelines, but also in need of substantial repairs. The landlord agreed to make the repairs. On first inspection by the agency, the unit failed to meet minimum standards. The landlord was provided with a list of code violations and advised to contact the agency when the repairs were done. Two months passed and the landlord still had not done the repairs. Three months later, the landlord reported that violations were corrected. The housing agency inspector went out to check again. On second inspection the unit failed to pass. More work needed to be done. Five months later the landlord reported all repairs were finally done. On third inspection the unit failed again because all violations were still not corrected. The unit never passed inspection. The tenant finally moved into the apartment anyway, without benefit of the rent subsidy. She did manage to reduce her formerly overcrowded conditions by establishing herself as head of household, but she is now living in a substandard unit and paying a very high rent relative to her level of income.

The final resolution to this respondent's Section 8 search took seven months from the day she began her search. She is statistically recorded as a "failed" respondent. Like many others who searched and failed, she was unsuccessful as a result of not being able to find a perfect match between *all* Section 8 program characteristics—not just fair market rents—and the marketplace, which is required in order to make the Section 8 program work.

Bureaucracy as Resource. A significant difference in search behavior between those who failed and those who succeeded in entering Phase 3 was observed by their use of the local housing agency as an information and referral service for listings of vacancies and as a mediator to "broker" rent negotiations and inspection schedules with landlords.

During phase 2, a third of all those who ultimately succeeded still had not found an acceptable unit on their own. These searchers asked the housing agency to talk to landlords to explain program benefits and try to negotiate rents on their behalf. Housing agency representatives were successful in bringing landlords' asking rents down to acceptable fair market rent levels in 85 percent of the cases. Of those respondents who failed, very few sought agency help with this component of the search.

Agency assistance continued with "brokering" inspection schedules. Units that failed inspection precluded occupancy and thus required careful mediation between a tenant anxious to move in and a landlord reluctant to make repairs but eager to receive rents. Had searchers not sought agency intervention, the success rate in this sample would have dropped from 57 to 36 percent.

One successful searcher only used listings from the housing agency bulletin board to guide her search. A 27-year-old black mother with one child felt that it would be useless to bat her head against a wall trying to rent apartments from landlords who didn't want her, so she made a list of posted vacancies, assuming that if these landlords were advertising units in the Section 8 office they were familiar with program requirements and would accept a subsidized tenant. She structured her search to look only one to five miles from where she was then living in inner-city Boston, constrained by the fact that she had to do all of her searching either by walking or public transportation. Her motivation to use Section 8 was to get out of overcrowded conditions. She was doubling up with family members and wanted to be on her own. Employed for several years, she applied for both Section 8 and AFDC after she was laid off. She was not deterred by neighborhood conditions. Using her search method, she found a willing landlord, an acceptable unit, and was receiving Section 8 rent subsidy benefits in 81 days. The median number of days to search and succeed was 103. The 60-day time limit turned out to be an unrealistic time limit in this tight housing market.

Highly focused, well-organized search behavior enabled the above mother to receive the rent subsidy relatively quickly. However, it was her use of the local housing agency for *access* services to the private rental market that facilitated her successful search. Leasing requires more intervention and support services from the local housing agency than anticipated. The extent to which local housing agencies provide access services and the extent to which searchers utilize them will be a key factor to increasing program participation rates.

The Search Ends

Three-quarters of those who failed to access the Section 8 program had multiple housing preferences, but also three-quarters of those who failed had personal constraints that inhibited their ability to search. Conversely, among all those who succeeded, half also had personal constraints in their search, but most had only one housing preference. Therefore, they were not burdened by as many expectations and needs as those who failed.

Role Burden Syndrome

Overall, these constraints derive from a generalized burden of roles and responsibilities created by being the sole family provider, protector, nurturer, and shelterer on median incomes of less than one-quarter that of families as a whole in the Boston Standard Metropolitan Statistical Area.[12] For example, 60 percent of *all* searchers had no access to child care while they searched. Transportation problems provided another serious constraint for one-third of all searchers. Nearly half of all respondents relied on public transportation to conduct their search, and a third relied on being driven by friends or relatives. This dependence on transportation provided by others, be it public or private, presented a serious obstacle to scheduling appointments. It created barriers to conducting a search of any geographic distance because of length of time it takes to travel by public transportation to and from various points in the metropolitan area or to rely on someone else's schedule to drive.

Additional geographic restrictions were imposed by mothers who wanted to remain in the same school district boundaries in order to retain educational continuity and stability for children; by those who found the cost of searching beyond their local neighborhoods too expensive; and by those who needed to stay near shopping or transportation services. More than one-fourth of respondents, restricted by having neither driver's licenses nor their own cars, wanted to live in neighborhoods where they could obtain food, clothing, and other necessities and conduct the business of their daily lives without having to drive. Because of their very low incomes, it is not surprising that only one-fourth of all respondents own cars, but only 43 percent of respondents had a valid driver's license. Those who succeeded did not show a greater percentage of either car ownership or licenses than those who failed. The distribution was equal in the two samples.

Fragile Social Support Systems: Caretaking and Caregiving. More than a third of all respondents displayed "hovering phenomenon" behavior.[13] That is, they restricted the geographic boundaries of the search in order to stay near social networks of family and friends from whom they derive emotional or physical support.

An additional constraint was experienced by one-quarter of respondents in this study—a "care-giving" role that required mothers to render help to extended family in need. Care-giving activities were usually rendered to ill or disabled parents, grand-parents, or to young children of brothers, sisters, aunts and uncles who were unable to take care of their own children. Care-giving responsibilities were time-consuming and distracting during the limited 60- to 120-day search, putting competing pressures on certificate holders, by requiring them to be support systems for others. In some cases, care was given on a daily basis for the duration of the search, suggesting an intensive daily regimen for these mothers.

A case example of how the multiplicity of personal constraints are interrelated, and how fragile support networks impact search behavior can be seen from the experience of the following respon-dent, a white 49-year-old woman who lives in a deteriorating neighborhood of inner-city Worcester (a city west of Boston), and who had been given custody by the courts of her two preschool-aged grandchildren. Her apartment was too small for her enlarged family. In order to qualify for the Section 8 subsidy, she needed to move to a larger apartment of standard quality in a better area of Worcester. She had multiple roles and responsibilities. She at-tended college and worked part-time, in addition to parenting. She needed her new apartment to be near the child care facility for the stability of the children already uprooted by changes in household composition. She also needed to stay near family be-cause she helped her daughter (who was disabled) with another grandchild who was also disabled, and she provided this care on a daily basis. This grandmother also needed to stay close to medical and social support systems for herself. She relied solely on public transportation to get her from home, to the day care center, to work, to school, to her daughter's house, and to her own appoint-ments.

She could not find an apartment at the fair market rent in the areas in which she was restricted to look. She explains:

> *These aren't even good areas at all. The real estate market in Worcester has skyrocketed because investors are buying up the three-deckers, raising the rents, then turning over the properties. Three-deckers are selling like hot cakes and the rents keep on rising, but the condition of the apartments isn't changing and the neighbor-hoods are still run down.*

She felt that if she moved to a worse area she could find an apartment within the fair market rent, but that new location and the transportation problems that would ensue would break a link in the fragile support network that had to be in place in order for her to meet all her responsibilities and commitments. Ultimately, she had to return the certificate unused.

Differentiation by race suggests that whites usually are more isolated from their extended families and from networks of support systems, and are involved less in care giving than are minorities. More bound into a mutual self-help relationship, minorities who had the preference to move to better neighborhoods and better environments found this preference in conflict with the care-giving role.

Limited Resources. Some 16 percent of the total sample expressed concern that they really did not know how to go about conducting a search such as locating vacancies, contacting landlords, or getting selected for tenancy. This lack of familiarity with the rental market was compounded in several cases by no access to telephones. For many searchers, all contacts with landlords were made on pay phones or on telephones belonging to family or friends, as the next respondent reports:

> *I have no car and no phone, so I had to go to friends' homes to make and receive phone calls to landlords. Then I had to ask relatives and friends to drive me around. The search was extremely complicated from beginning to end. It was frustrating and hostile.*

The totality of constraints depicts a formidable search process for certificate holders and creates conflict between housing preferences and obstacles to achieving them for the "role burdened." A tension emerges which pits the certificate holder's desire to improve her standard of living against personal responsibilities and expectations that others in her extended family have of her. When combined with constraints imposed by transportation problems, or by a misconception of the program requirements, the "role-burdened" certificate holder is at a severe disadvantage in the search process. She has more decision points to confront, more obstacles to overcome, and more tension in the search than those who have very few or no constraints. The role-burdened certificate holder is a disabled searcher as she tries to compete with market renters.

Search Intensity

Differences in search behavior between those who succeeded and those who failed can be measured by the intensity of their search. That is, observed differences can be seen between (1) the number and kinds of resources they used to locate vacancies, (2) the number of landlord contacts made, (3) the amount of time they allocated for searching, and (4) the number of miles away from their original residence they extended the geographic search.

Those who succeeded had a more focused search than those who failed. They spent fewer days searching and more hours per day working on the search, called fewer landlords, and saw fewer units than those who failed. They devoted between three to five hours per day working on their search, a more concentrated and efficient use of time than those who failed who spent only one to two hours per day for more days. Newspapers were the most frequently cited method used to locate vacancies, both for those who succeeded and those who failed. However, about half of those who succeeded leased the apartment from someone they knew, thereby relying less heavily on blind leads obtained through conventional methods. About half of those who failed called more than 20 landlords but got to see only between one and five apartments. This suggests that respondents get screened out at the point the *initial* phone call is made.

Geographic Boundaries. Those who succeeded extended the geographic boundaries of their search to a slightly wider area than those who failed (see Figure 6–1). The fact that about one-fifth of those who succeeded did not search at all is indicative of their prior relationship with a prospective landlord; either they intended to lease where they already lived or they knew the landlord and the unit in advance and had the commitment previously arranged. Sixty percent of those who searched and succeeded and 70 percent of those who failed—all of whom engaged in a search—restricted the geographic boundaries to within 10 miles of their residence. For those living in inner-city Boston, this means that searchers were looking primarily in neighborhoods within the Boston city limits and in neighboring cities bordering Boston, such as Cambridge, Watertown, or Somerville.

Search by Public Transit. The fact that 70 percent of those who failed restricted their search to a 10-mile radius of where they live is consistent with the constraint that nearly one-half relied on public transportation to search, and that 50 percent of all of those who failed restricted their search because of transportation problems. Since the neighborhoods in Boston and close-by cities are accessible by public transit, they may represent the only neighborhoods this group could get to. Those who succeeded, having more modes of transportation available to them, were able to extend the search farther. For those living in the Boston neighborhoods of

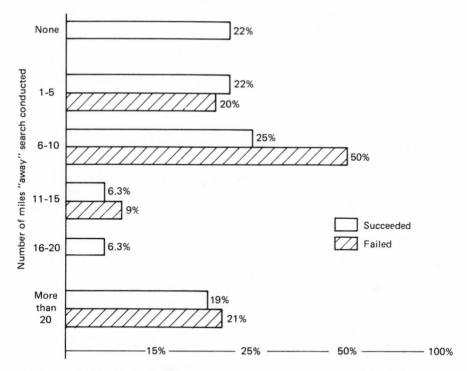

Figure 6-1 Number of Miles the Search Is Extended by Percentage of Certificate Holder, by Program Outcome.

Dorchester, Roxbury, Mattapan, or East Boston, looking 20 miles away or more brought them through to the suburbs and finally to cities like Brockton and Lynn, where many looked. But, if they were minority and poor, the farther they looked away from central cities, the more apt they were to be perceived by landlords to be "out-of-place—a suspect category," and hence more apt to encounter failure.

It is surprising to find that those who failed extended their geographic boundaries as far as they did, in view of the multiplicity of constraints, specifically that of transportation. It appears that they were very highly motivated to relocate to other neighborhoods and suburban communities, particularly within a 10-mile radius of where they lived, and they made serious efforts to look there. The fact that they looked for only a few hours each day, rather than the three to five hours spent by the successful searchers, appears to have fragmented the intensity of their search, requiring an investment of more days and an overall less organized search.

Four-Way Outcome

Looking at the outcome in only two categories of "succeed" and "fail" is to miss some important and subtle distinctions found as a result of this study, as well as to misunderstand the heterogeneous nature of the subpopulation of single mothers. Moreover, these distinctions point to the basic strengths and weaknesses of the Section 8 program. For single mothers in this sample, the confluence of housing preferences, of limitations of economic and personal resources, of barriers in the private rental market, and limited supply of affordable housing stock give rise to four categories of program outcome, not just the expected two. The categories are the "successful," the "successful-but-stuck," the "failed-but-succeeding," and the "failed-and-trapped."

The Successful. The criteria used to evaluate program outcome are based on respondents accessing *all* intended Section 8 program benefits—that is, affordable, safe, and sanitary housing in a location of choice—and having all of their own expectations met. Seventeen single mothers met these criteria—representing about half of all those officially regarded as successful and 30 percent of the total sample. Race, location of residence, level of income, household size, mobility, and motivation for seeking the rent subsidy program were found to be predictors of program outcome.

Forty-one percent of the searchers were white, living in communities outside the city of Boston, but they comprised 77 percent of the "Successful" subcategory. The Successful were the poorest and smallest households. Those a little bit better off were less likely to be Successful. More than three-quarters of those who were Successful had annual incomes of between $4,000 and $6,999. The remaining one-quarter had incomes of between $7,000 and $10,999. This illuminates the need for the main housing preference among Successfuls as lower rent. It also suggests that the more important lower rent is to a respondent, the greater are her chances of success, yet the more important other considerations become, the more her chances of success are likely to diminish. Furthermore, when a searcher has only one housing preference, and that preference is for lower rent, it can be predicted that she is more likely to succeed than to fail.

Eighty-five percent of the Successfuls had moved at least once while on the two-and-a-half-year Section 8 waiting list, and more than a third had moved twice or more. Sixty-three percent of those who failed did not move at all while on the waiting list. High mobility rates were often generated by rent increases beyond the tenant's ability to pay, culminating in the doubling-up phenomenon. Smaller household size—meaning a mother and one, two, or three children—made moving and searching easier. It is likely that a household with fewer children would be more acceptable to landlords who fear the destructive tendencies of children. Four black households who had the same very low income level, same limited preferences, high mobility pattern, and small household size as white households were Successful program participants. The goal of moving out of inner-city Boston to improve the quality of their housing environment was not an issue for any of the minorities who were Successfuls. Whites demonstrated more mobile behavior in using the program, relocating to different cities and out of central city to rural areas, whereas blacks relocated within inner-city neighborhoods only.

Successful-but-Stuck: Leasing Out of Desperation, Not Choice.

The "Successful-but-Stuck" are also program participants; what distinguishes them from the Successfuls is that they did not achieve all of their own expectations nor all the Section 8 policy objectives. Sixty percent of respondents in this subcategory were very low income minority families with larger households than the Successfuls and who had multiple, competing preferences. They lived primarily in inner-city Boston and expressed a great need for lower rent, for better housing, and for a better location. Unable to relocate to better quality housing or better locations, many of these searchers opted to lease their own units, so as to take advantage of at least much-needed lower rent. For example, an Hispanic mother of four reports:

> *I looked for three months to find better housing and I couldn't find anything in Everett [a neighboring city bordering Boston]. I was about to lose the Section 8 certificate, so I sent in the Request for Inspection form for my own apartment, even though I wanted to get out. I had to restrict the areas I looked in so the kids could stay in the same schools.*

A white, 33-year-old mother of three was recently separated from her husband and had no child support. She was paying 80 percent of her income toward rent. She wanted to move to a better apartment in a better neighborhood in the city of Lynn. She found two places, but neither one could pass the Section 8 housing quality standards. She used Section 8 where she was living because she needed the rent subsidy to reduce her rent burden. She got the lower rent, but neither the apartment nor the area of her choice.

And finally, a black mother of four who lives in the inner city of Boston explains:

*My apartment was in bad condition. I paid $250 a month for rent.
The landlord agreed to fix up the apartment for Section 8 if he could
increase the rent to $450. He brought in a construction crew and
they fixed the place up. Now I live in a better apartment in a bad
neighborhood. I still want to move and will look again when the
lease is up.*

Most minorities who became Section 8 program participants in
this study are Successful-but-Stuck. This suggests that the only
way most central-city minority single mothers with larger households can utilize Section 8 is to already live in units that can be
brought up to housing quality standards by willing landlords. The
dilemma is that so few live under these conditions.

Failed-but-Succeeding. A subgroup of searchers (representing
14 percent of the total sample)—the preponderance of whom were
minorities who lived in cities other than Boston or who lived in
the suburbs—when unable to access the private market in these
same areas, chose to drop out of the search in phase 2. They traded
off all Section 8 program benefits rather than move back into an
area of Boston where they perceived minorities could utilize the
subsidy. These respondents had slightly higher incomes than those
who succeeded, and smaller household sizes than most of those
who had failed. While motivated by multiple expectations for using
Section 8, the main housing preference for more than half of those
in this group was to move to a better neighborhood or housing
environment. Some were doubling up so their living arrangements
precluded using the subsidy at their present apartment. Those
who were heads of household knew that either their landlord
would not "take" Section 8, or the unit could not pass housing
quality standards.

One head of household, a 35-year-old separated black mother
with a 15-year-old son from the Mattapan section of inner-city
Boston, takes public transportation to a college in the suburbs
where she is studying for her nursing degree. Her son takes public
transportation to the prestigious Boston Latin School, which is a
selective public high school. Her preferences were for low rent, a
better apartment, and a better neighborhood.

Her search was restricted by the fact that the apartment and
better neighborhood had to be on a transportation line so that both
she and her son could continue their education uninterrupted.
Furthermore, while her college is located outside Boston in a
desirable suburb, to relocate there would take her son outside the
Boston city limits and make him ineligible to stay at Latin. She
explains, "I want him to stay at Boston Latin. To move out of the
city would not be good for his education at this time." Not being

able to find an affordable apartment in the areas in which she looked, she traded off program benefits for the stability of staying put until she can move to a location of her choice on her own.

One 33-year-old black mother of two reported that she was on AFDC after her divorce, and is now working full-time while the Department of Social Services is subsidizing her child care expenses to help with the transition. Her living arrangements include doubling up in a small apartment with her parents who receive social security. The total family income is over $16,000. While her main housing preference was to get out of these overcrowded conditions and be on her own, she also placed a strong value on moving to a place that would be a good environment with good schools for her children. She is already living in what she perceives to be a nice, though small, apartment in an attractive building in the city of Watertown, and she couldn't find anything better at the fair market rents in the neighborhoods and communities she wanted. In the final analysis, she decided that moving to a "bad" area where she could get an affordable apartment was not worth the social costs, and there were social benefits to be obtained by enduring the overcrowding and staying put. She concluded, "Even though we're overcrowded now, the landlord is nice, the building is nice, and the place is near my child's day care center and my work. Also, I can take care of my father, who is ill."

The Failed-but-Succeeding represent one-third of all those who failed to participate in Section 8. They have multiple housing preferences that place a higher priority on housing choice than on low rent. They focused their search to obtain a good housing environment, and traded off program benefits of affordability when their hopes were dashed for relocating in an area of their choice. Neither the whites nor blacks would lower their expectations for an improved quality of life nor lower the standard of living that they already achieved. Social factors were important in their housing decision: need for a safe area for the children, proximity to family support systems, stability in day care, and quality education.

Failed-and-Trapped. The remaining two-thirds of those who failed were nearly all minority households (94 percent) clustered in inner-city Boston. "Failed and Trapped" respondents are burdened with multiple areas of housing deprivation. They perceive the most significant to be poor housing conditions; deteriorating, unsafe neighborhoods; and overall poor quality of the housing environment, which they feel is detrimental to their well-being. The Failed-but-Succeeding also have a compelling interest in improving their housing environment, but they are in a position to consciously choose not to take the subsidy. The Failed-and-Trapped do not aspire to relocate to the suburbs, but they do want to relocate to affordable housing of standard quality that is located in decent city neighborhoods of Boston that are safe. Their households were both small and large in size, and overall they had a higher level of income than those who succeeded, in large measure, because of combined sources of incomes in larger households. A few respondents entered phase 3 of the search and came close to leasing a unit, as told in the story of the 20-year-old mother of the new baby presented earlier. Multiple personal constraints, plus a diminished supply of physically adequate affordable housing in the central city prevented relocation to units of standard quality for minorities, making their use of the Section 8 program impossible.

In sum, single mothers who expect Section 8 to remedy multiple housing problems are unlikely to succeed in the Section 8 program. Furthermore, minority respondents who sought Section 8 rental assistance to relocate to communities of their choice did not achieve their expectations. No minority respondent whose main housing preference was either to relocate to a better neighborhood or better housing environment succeeded in achieving these preferences in the Section 8 search.

The Successfuls, unburdened by as many unmet housing needs, looking primarily for lower rent and standard apartments, were able to search with fewer expectations of the Section 8 program and with fewer competing constraints that limited the geographic boundaries of their search.

This chapter will now examine the policy implications of the above findings, and then make recommendations for program changes.

Policy Implications

Rental Assistance: A Viable Program

Housing conditions of more than one-half of all single-parent families studied improved as a result of program participation, and thirty-two units were added to the supply of affordable housing stock. Since rental assistance has been found to be more cost-effective than new construction,[14] it should be viewed as a viable model of affordable housing which needs to be improved and expanded so benefits can be more equitably spread over a wider population of single-parent families in need. The goal to increase program participation, then, can be justified on grounds of equity and efficiency.

Guaranteeing that fair market rents keep pace with private market rents and increasing the supply of affordable housing stock by multiple means are crucial and clear-cut points of intervention, but they will not be enough. Results of this study demonstrate that understanding the social aspects of housing decisions among the largest population of searchers will also be needed so that remedies can be formulated that take social factors into account.

Importance of Social Factors

We now know that four dimensions of single mothers' housing search go unattended by the Section 8 program. First is the importance placed on relocating out of a deteriorating neighborhood environment, with its attendant lack of locational freedom to escape that environment. Second, racial discrimination continues to create an intransigent barrier through which minority single mothers are unable to penetrate. Third, single mothers perceive housing as part of a larger "bundle" of services and resources which include proximity to public facilities such as transportation, stores, child care centers, and schools so they can execute their daily head-of-household responsibilities in a geographically limited area on very low incomes. Fourth, the need for single mothers to maintain personal connectedness with others further defines where they can live. They may need to stay close to family/friend social and economic support networks both for receiving help and for giving help to others. The extent to which these factors are used to shape policy changes, to reformulate programs, and to change implementation practices will have a certain impact on increasing participation rates among single-parent families.

Remedies to alleviate or eliminate the forces of social exclusion should be targeted to local neighborhood and community rental practices. The dilemma is that national housing goals conflict with local rental practices.[15] Federal goals of Section 8 set forth fundamental rights to equal housing opportunity, to economic considerations of cost, and to physical considerations of objective housing quality standards. Local implementation issues involve (1) deteriorating neighborhood environments stemming from "filtering" down of housing stock; and (2) exclusionary rental practices that serve to maintain social distance between populations that are perceived to represent a transitional, or a "mixed" economic or social category. Local housing agencies are enmeshed in the social provision of housing. Implementing the Section 8 program inherently entangles the agency in economic *and* social housing mix. Yet local housing agencies perceive their mission to be the physical provision of housing, serving a pass-through function to redistribute income and monitor the physical condition of the stock.

Federal cuts in administrative fees allocated to local housing agencies by HUD have made it more difficult to perform efficiently administrative tasks related to the above functions, let alone take on a social services function as well. Between 1985 and 1987 local housing agencies sustained up to a 15 percent cut in administrative fees during a period of increased demand for services from anxious Section 8 searchers and a proliferation of new state-mandated programs for the homeless. But, findings from this study point to the pivotal role local housing agencies played in facilitating program participation. Therefore, empowering local housing agencies with greater resources to administer the Section 8 program is the first strategy on which others can be built.

Searchers in this sample were motivated to succeed with their Section 8 certificates; they conducted long and intensive searches to compete with market renters. However, they were caught up in the conflict between national goals and local practices. Households behaved as if the Section 8 certificate gave them the freedom to choose where they would be housed. To the contrary, minority searchers who sought locational freedom ended up neither achieving national goals of deconcentration, nor improving shelter for the half of searchers who failed.

These results suggest two important considerations for policy: first, failure rates among certificate holders should be understood to mean that searchers *wanted, needed, and tried diligently to get rental assistance benefits, but were unable to participate by a combination of program characteristics and social forces in the private market.* When certificates are returned unused, this should not be construed to mean that there is no *need;* rather, it means there is no *access* to the private rental stock. When policy-makers or critics of social programs note that AFDC recipients may be a statistically small sample of program participants nationally, this should not become an argument that AFDC recipients do not bother to avail themselves of existing rent subsidy programs, but understood to mean that they were unable to *access* rent subsidies.[16] Second, the market functions imperfectly, and the scope of expectations for rental assistance will have to be scaled down. Local housing agencies are in a most perplexing spot: if they encourage searchers to reach for maximum freedom of choice, they risk setting searchers up to fail; if they encourage them to set their sights low, they will find more searchers succeeding, but they will have discouraged success for the few who might have broken through discriminatory barriers. Changes in larger institutions will have to take place to support the equity objectives of the National Housing Act, which, in turn, would support Section 8 policy intent.

Recommendations

The crisis in affordable housing and the lack of adequate supply clearly demand an increase in new production, in rehabilitation, and in retention of existing units in central cities, suburbia, and in rural communities. The purpose of the following recommendations is to suggest some organizational and regulatory changes affecting implementation strategies at the local level that could increase program participation in the short and long term.

The U.S. Congress and the Department of Housing and Urban Development need to articulate, as an explicit goal, their intention to increase program participation in the Section 8 Rental Assistance Program. The following set of recommendations could then be used to help HUD achieve its intended mission.

Increase Administrative Fees

The trend to diminish administrative fees must be reversed and administrative fees increased. Reduced fees diminish resources needed to successfully implement the Rental Assistance Program and implicitly doom it to failure. Increased fees could be used to provide access services and collaborative management.

Access Services. Access services include active outreach to the private landlord and property management community to increase the number of *landlords* participating in the Section 8 program and to increase the geographic range of their units. Landlords with standard quality rental units need to be brought into the program from *all* city neighborhoods, from the suburbs, and from rural areas. This is a task for the local housing authority, which can market the advantages of the program to prospective landlords. If the housing authority collected enough landlord "clients" with standard units in a wide geographic area and shared this knowledge and information with searchers before the search began, it is predicted that searchers would find fewer substandard units and fewer rejecting landlords, thus making the search process more organized, less aggravating, and more successful for searcher, landlord, and agency. This landlord-as-client approach requires ongoing, careful monitoring so that searchers' information is *always* current relative to vacancy status, rent levels, and geographic location of available units. Housing agency staff are spreading knowledge and creating linkages[17] which serve to access the searcher to an expanded supply of affordable housing. The 60- to 120-day time limit of the program requires attention to accuracy and timeliness of information provided to searchers.

Collaborative Management. Access to the Section 8 Program could be facilitated with change on the management level as well as on the direct services level above. Social services and housing agencies serving the same low-income clients need to collaborate on finding the housing solution. Just as local housing agencies have not seen their mission in social terms, social service agencies have not traditionally seen housing as part of their mission. Yet the increasing population of the homeless and near-homeless served by public welfare agencies, by public and private social service organizations, legal assistance corporations, women's resource centers, shelters, and housing agencies should force all organizations serving the poor to recognize that housing is a commonality. Frequently, these human service providers are working independently of each other, yet with the same goals. Modern bureaucratic complexity and a multiplicity of new state programs have created gaps in interagency working relationships.

Since Section 8 can be administered as a statewide, regional, or local community-based program, it is recommended that a consortium of service providers be convened at each of these levels of service delivery. The purpose is twofold. First, managers from interdisciplinary fields of interest (such as public interest law, public welfare, housing, child care, social services, mental health) have the opportunity to learn about housing-related resources and programs often provided by each other's agencies. Second, the networking effect could produce collaborative intervention strategies formulated to bring a wider array of needed services to families engaged in the search. The point is that valuable resources exist, but they are underutilized by housing agencies. For example, if agencies working with the same family were aware of each other's interest, Section 8 program managers could link searchers with needed resources provided by child care agencies or transportation services which exist, but may not be known to searchers. In addition, the housing agency could encourage immediate reporting of discriminatory rental practices and referral to legal assistance corporations and fair housing commissions to investigate and prosecute suspected landlord violators. This would be followed up by counseling and case management. The fragmentation of the far-flung public and private human service network would be better harnessed to address the fundamental goal—to increase Section 8 program participation. The more knowledgeable all housing and human service managers become relative to the full range of delivery systems available to low-income households, the more resources can be mobilized to facilitate program access.

Expand HUD Evaluation Criteria

Local housing authorities are highly motivated to comply with HUD audits because of the sanctions imposed for not meeting standards of administration, particularly in matters of finance and enforcement of housing quality standards. Therefore, if HUD were to enforce fair housing initiatives, local housing authorities could also be evaluated on measurable tasks they accomplish to expand housing choice for searchers seeking to relocate out of deteriorating central city neighborhoods to areas of their choice. A three-pronged approach is recommended:

Fair Housing Compliance. A local housing authority could be rewarded for efforts it undertakes to break local discriminatory rental barriers. For example, records could be kept of the local housing agency's role in referring discrimination complaints to commissions against discrimination, of the investigations in process, the number of cases being prosecuted, and the number successfully resolved.

Agency Outreach to Landlords in All Neighborhoods. HUD could measure the output of programs local agencies put in place (with increased administrative fees) to capture more landlords with standard quality units in *all* city neighborhoods, in the suburbs, and in rural areas.

Expand Criteria for Agency "Success" Rates. If local implementation efforts are to be measured in terms of success in reaching the goal of expanding housing choice for all searchers, then a reconceptualization is needed in how HUD defines local agency success. That is, HUD currently determines a local agency's success by a ratio which measures the number of units the agency has under lease against the number of units HUD allocates to be leased. A 95 percent lease rate is considered successful. However, since roughly only one out of two searchers in the metropolitan Boston area studied succeed in program participation, agencies must continuously send out hundreds of searchers in a revolving-door approach in hopes that it will send off enough to reach its 95 percent lease requirement. (One agency found it had to take 10 families off the waiting list to get one leased.)

A more equitable approach would be to intervene in the search on behalf of *all* who are looking, particularly the role-burdened, those least able to negotiate the marketplace on their own, rather than sit back and rely on the Social Darwinian "survival of the fittest" doctrine which is currently in place. A 95 percent lease rate might still be reached through implementation of all the foregoing recommendations. But the outcome in terms of the equity goal of expanding housing choice would be substantively different. The extent to which the sample of searchers were able to relocate out of deteriorating neighborhoods to areas of their choice should be considered a "success" factor.

Indeed, enforcement of federal civil rights laws and state laws that prohibit discrimination in housing have the power to alter the existing spatial distribution in the marketplace.[18] Local housing agencies are integral to this process, and with adequate administrative fees and commitment from HUD, can be instrumental in bringing about changes in the social environment and, thereby, greater program utilization.

Strive Toward Making Program Characteristics Reflect the Market

In a tight housing market a landlord's interest in a Section 8 tenant appears to diminish as the number of procedures required of the landlord differ from the norm for those involved in renting to market tenants. Lower fair market rent levels, inspection and repair requirements to meet housing quality standards, and low security deposit provisions create bureaucratic hurdles and complaints which are disincentives that work to weaken a landlord's interest in selecting a Section 8 tenant, even if the landlord feels she will be a good tenant. Therefore, if rental assistance is to be viable, these program characteristics need to more closely reflect market rents and practices.

HUD needs to monitor fair market rents more frequently and approve increases in certain areas as needed. Security deposits reflecting one month's rent could be arranged with vouchers to conform to rental practices. Continued close scrutiny of housing quality standards will be needed to ensure physical adequacy of units. However, with increased fair market rents and security deposit vouchers, landlords may be more amenable to speedy compliance with housing quality standards.

Conclusion

Low-income single-parent families are an "unsheltered" subgroup of the poor to whom special policy attention should be drawn.

Section 8 rental assistance originated in the early 1970s as a less expensive alternative to reduce federal spending within the many publicly supported new construction programs. It was not designed specifically to target single-parent mothers.

In the sample studied, rental assistance had trouble meeting the housing needs of many minority low-income single-parent families because their housing problems are set in larger systems of discrimination and poverty, which the Section 8 program does not address. Their unmet housing needs are a function of cost, but also of their gender, life-cycle position, race, and location of residence. New policy responses to their housing plight must be fashioned to reflect these race- and gender-related concerns.

The overriding policy issue is that millions of families headed by mothers with children remain inadequately housed at a point in national history when a federal theme is reverence for the American family, and where federal policies are sought which purport to strengthen family life. Attention should be directed to the housing plight of poor families headed by women so that unmet housing needs of these households—also American families—will become a priority on the national housing agenda.

Endnotes

1. In a six-month period from September 1984 to March 1985, 80,000 families filed applications for housing assistance with the New York City Housing Authority. The waiting list for Section 8 certificates is approaching 200,000 applicants. On a first-come first-serve basis, it will take 20 years from date of filing to the point of getting an apartment, according to John Simon, general manager of the New York City Housing Authority, in testimony before the congressional Subcommittee on Housing and Community Development in March 1985.
2. Francine Price, *The Adequacy of the Section 8 Fair Market Rents for the City of Boston,* Report prepared for the Boston Housing Authority, 1986, p. 1.
3. Sixty-seven respondents were randomly selected through the statewide Section 8 program administered regionally by the Massachusetts Executive Office of Communities and Development. Their housing search was monitored for a 10-month period from May 1985 to March 1986 when the last respondent's status was determined to be a program participant or nonparticipant. The survey instrument was administered to 56 searchers, representing an 83.6 percent rate of response.
4. From May 1985 to January 1986 in the Boston Standard Metropolitan Statistical Area (SMSA), HUD-determined fair market rents were $533 per month for a two-bedroom unit and $652 for a three-bedroom unit, including utilities.
5. Very Low Income Guidelines in the Boston SMSA in May 1985 could not exceed:

1-person household	$11,300	5-person household	$17,450
2-person household	$12,900	6-person household	$18,750
3-person household	$14,550	7-person household	$20,050
4-person household	$16,150		

6. U.S. Office of the Comptroller General, "Major Changes Are Needed in the New Leased Housing Program," Report to Congress by the Comptroller General of the United States, 1976.

7. Emily Achtenberg, *Preserving Affordable Housing in Boston,* Report prepared for the Boston Rent Equity Board and the Mayor's Housing Advisor, 1984, p. 1.

8. See also Susan Anderson-Khlief, "Income Packaging and Life Style in Welfare Families," Family Policy Note No. 7: Joint Center for Urban Studies, Cambridge, Mass., 1978, p. 14.

9. See Martin Rein et al., "The Impact of Family Change on Housing Careers," Unpublished report, prepared for the Department of Housing and Urban Development by the Joint Center for Urban Studies, Cambridge, Mass., 1980, pp. 2–8; Susan Bartlett, "Residential Mobility and Housing Choices of Single-Parent Mothers," Unpublished paper, Joint Center for Urban Studies, Cambridge, Mass., 1980, pp. 21–30; and Mary Jo Bane and Robert Weiss, "Alone Together: The World of Single Parent Families," *American Demographics* (May 1980): 11.

10. Section 8 regulations allow a tenant to leave a security deposit equal to her 30 percent share of the rent or $50, whichever is greater. The first month's rent is paid as soon as the unit passes housing quality standards inspection and the lease and contract are signed. The last month's rent is guaranteed to the landlord per terms in the lease and will be paid up to the date the tenant vacates the premises.

11. When a tenant damages a unit, the agency guarantees the landlord up to two month's rent worth of damages, minus the tenant's security deposit. The agency then draws up a repayment agreement with the tenant for repayment of damages directly to the agency.

12. Median income of families in Boston SMSA was $22,848 (Summary of General Population Characteristics: 1980, Massachusetts Data Center Bureau of the Census [PHC 80-3-23]).

13. Susan Anderson-Khlief, *Divorced But Not Disastrous* (Englewood Cliffs, N.J.: Prentice-Hall, 1982).

14. John Yinger, "State Housing Policy and the Poor," in *The State and the Poor in the 1980s,* ed. Manuel Carballo and Mary Jo Bane (Boston: Auburn House, 1984), p. 35.

15. William Grigsby et al., *Rethinking Housing and Community Development Policy* (Philadelphia: University of Pennsylvania, 1977).

16. Charles Murray argues that social programs of the past 30 years have stifled productivity and motivation among "deserving" minorities. In reference to a case study on AFDC benefits and income packaging derived from public transfers, he notes, "She is eligible for substantial rent subsidies under the many rent subsidy programs, but only a minority of AFDC recipients use them." (*Losing Ground* [New York: Basic Books, 1984], p. 159).

17. For a thorough discussion of access services, see Alfred J. Kahn, *Social Policy and Social Services* (New York: Random House, 1979), p. 29.

18. For example, Massachusetts Law Chapter 151B bans discrimination in housing on the basis of race, color, religious creed, national origin, sex, age, presence of children, ancestry, marital status, veterans status, public assistance recipiency, blindness, or deafness.

Part III

A CALL FOR FEDERAL
AND STATE ACTION

Chapter 7

THE ROLE OF THE COURTS IN WELFARE REFORM

Barbara Sard

The potential for social change through the courts is often greatly exaggerated. Nonlawyers, especially, often look with envy, or resentment, at the apparent power that courts have to declare rights and order remedies which seem impossible to accomplish through legislative or administrative avenues. On the other hand, legal commentators are often as pessimistic as nonlawyers are optimistic, arguing that the last 20 years of welfare litigation show precisely how limited court rulings are, even for accomplishing paper gains, and that even these are often destroyed in the administrative process.[1]

This chapter will argue that the truth lies in between. In the social welfare area, courts will not, and cannot, accomplish social change in a vacuum. But litigation has been in the past, and can be in the future, a valuable tool for expanding welfare benefits, particularly in combination with the efforts of concurrent social movements or political coalitions.

The primary period of expanding welfare benefits through court action was in the late 1960s to mid-1970s. "Welfare" in this chapter refers to the federal-state Aid to Families with Dependent Children, or AFDC, program, which is the primary source of financial support for poor single-parent families. Two-parent families in which one parent is incapacitated, or, at state option since 1961, unemployed, are also eligible for assistance. In fact, welfare programs include any financial assistance provided on the basis of need, rather than on the basis of prior contributions, such as social security and unemployment compensation. On the federal level, other welfare programs include food stamps, which has essentially universal eligibility based on need alone, and supplemental security income, or SSI, which provides financial assistance to the aged, blind, and disabled. Some states also have a general assistance program, which may provide universal assistance based on need, or may be limited to narrow groups or short periods of time. Other federal and state need-based programs provide specific kinds of direct or in-kind assistance, such as housing subsidies, medical assistance, child care, etc.

As a direct result of judicial decision, as well as from the indirect effects of the publicity and increased legitimacy stemming from such litigation and the concurrent welfare rights organizing, literally millions of needy families received welfare benefits, and the benefits received by many increased. The first part of Chapter 7 will examine these initial court challenges to the administration of the welfare system and arrive at some generalizations about the nature of the claims likely to meet with judicial success.

After a hiatus in successful affirmative litigation efforts in the late 1970s and early 1980s, when most court action was defensive, a new period of judicial decision-making expanding welfare benefits appears to be unfolding. Unlike the primary thrust of the initial period, the current phase of affirmative welfare litigation is based on state rather than federal law, and is taking place in the state as opposed to the federal courts. Moreover, it is directly targeted at increasing welfare benefit levels as well as at creating additional "entitlements." The second part of this chapter will look at this new phase in the use of the courts, focusing on the recent landmark decision of the Massachusetts Supreme Judicial Court declaring the right under state law of needy families to a level of welfare benefits or other assistance sufficient to enable families to live in permanent housing. Based on the historical analysis in the first part, the second part of Chapter 7 will attempt to outline some directions for areas of possible future successful state court affirmative welfare litigation.

The First Phase of Welfare Expansion: 1960s to 1970s

Litigation and the Welfare Rights Movement

Prior to 1968, the United States Supreme Court never considered a case involving the Aid to Families with Dependent Children

(AFDC) program, even though the program had been in existence since 1935. Indeed, prior to the mid-1960s, there were barely any legal actions involving the AFDC program in any courts. The reason is simple: the poor had no lawyers. It was not until the early 1960s when the federal government started to provide funding for lawyers to work in poor neighborhoods that lawyers became available to represent poor families seeking welfare benefits.

The lack of court action was not because of any lack of legal issues. Once workers in storefront offices began in the early 1960s to try to assist the poor to obtain the means of basic survival, the problems of arbitrary denials of benefits and harassment by welfare departments became obvious. Lawyers were one tool to help people navigate the welfare system and to challenge intimidating practices. For example, after the first year of having social workers assist neighborhood families with welfare problems, in 1962, the Mobilization for Youth program on the lower East Side of Manhattan hired two lawyers, and then more, to back up the social workers. The lawyers challenged welfare department practices such as shipping welfare applicants out of state and midnight raids in which welfare workers would enter the homes of AFDC mothers in the middle of the night, with no prior notice, in order to see if they could catch a man on the premises.[2]

By 1966, a number of legal issues had been identified that, if successfully litigated, would dramatically change the welfare system's arbitrariness, harassment of applicants and recipients, and moralistic exclusion of masses of needy children based on their mothers' presumed sexual behavior or other conditions unrelated to need.[3] While the proposed legal actions would all have created very significant changes in the program, largely by enabling far more families to receive benefits, it is noteworthy that the overall level of benefits eligible families were entitled to receive would barely have been touched by the proposed legal actions.

Perhaps more important than the identification of possible legal issues for the purpose of bringing test case litigation was the significance of the fundamental underlying premise—that welfare applicants and recipients had some "rights" under statutory or constitutional law—and its effect on the groups of welfare recipients beginning to organize at the very same time. From a few local groups in the early and mid-1960s, welfare rights organizing mushroomed, so that by 1967 local groups had coalesced into the National Welfare Rights Organization (NWRO), with tens of thousands of dues-paying members.[4]

The idea that the Social Security Act or the Constitution or even the state's own welfare regulations gave poor families some rights against the arbitrary and harassing actions of state and local welfare agencies was tremendously empowering. Instead of begging charity in shame, people could demand benefits and dignified treatment as their *right*. It was no coincidence that the welfare rights movement came on the heels of, and in many ways grew out of, the civil rights movement, which had also empowered people to act by convincing them that they had a legal as well as a moral right to better and equal treatment.

The idea that literally millions of poor families were being denied the AFDC benefits to which they were legally entitled under the Social Security Act was in many ways the motivating force behind the welfare rights movement. The movement began based in large part on the hypothesis put forth by sociologist Richard Cloward, who had worked with Mobilization for Youth, and political scientist Frances Fox Piven, that the welfare rolls could be doubled if even currently eligible families were enabled to receive benefits. As movement strategists saw it, such a doubling of the welfare rolls had both a short- and a long-term goal: some of the hardship of poverty would be alleviated for millions of families. At the same time the enormous expansion of benefits would create a fiscal crisis in the major urban areas, which would create a powerful constituency for "real" welfare reform: a guaranteed minimum income for all.

The lawyers' identification of legal issues in the welfare system and the recipients' adoption of a strategy to expand drastically the rolls and increase the amount of benefits paid were intertwined. George Wiley, the head of the welfare rights movement, and Ed Sparer, the leading welfare lawyer, worked closely together, and Sparer presented his ideas for lawsuits challenging the welfare system to the first meeting of the National Coordinating Committee of the National Welfare Rights Organization in February 1967. Some of the initial proposed lawsuits were essential to stop the midnight raid-type harassment and the thoroughly arbitrary denials, which had to be overcome to implement the Cloward and Piven "break the bank" strategy. Others, while aimed at actually expanding entitlements by invalidating existing restrictive provisions in state law or welfare regulations, shared the same goal as NWRO organizing: the more families found eligible for AFDC, the greater the fiscal pressure, they thought, to develop a more fair and equitable system of income maintenance. Thus, "[a]lthough the ultimate objectives of those who sought to legalize welfare were unquestionably radical—assuring a minimally adequate grant to everyone in need—the relief poor people's advocates sought from courts was limited, incremental, and process-oriented."[5]

Why limited relief was sought, and obtained, will be discussed in the sections below. However, despite the fact that this first phase of welfare litigation did not mount a direct attack on the adequacy of welfare benefits, its achievements were substantial. In the five-year period 1967–1972, the AFDC caseload nationally more than doubled, increasing from 5 million to 10.9 million families. This dramatic increase was due both to a higher percentage of applicants being found eligible, and a substantial increase of applications from potentially eligible families—that is, the complete vindication of at least the basis of the Cloward and Piven strategy that the welfare rolls could be doubled simply by getting the eligibles on aid. While welfare rights organizing, community action advocacy, publicity, and changing views of rights all played some role in bringing about this enormous increase, Piven and Cloward themselves give significant credit for this change to legal challenges—both directly by changing rules and indirectly by limiting administrative arbitrariness and harassment. They cite estimates "that at least 100,000 persons annually had been denied aid because of residence laws," and that "tens of thousands of families were denied aid under employable mother rules." Regarding the 16 to 23 percent increase in the rate of approvals of AFDC applicants in various areas of the South in this period, Piven and Cloward state:

> *The Southern increase, we suspect, resulted mainly from legal services, the predominant form of welfare rights activity in the South. Much of the important litigation originated there, since the legal structure of the Southern welfare system was the most restrictive. When substitute-parent policies, employable-mother rules, and other restrictive practices were challenged, approval levels jumped, and the Southern rolls rose even though the volume of applications did not greatly increase.*[6]

Finally, in considering the court decisions discussed in the sections which follow, it must be kept in mind that no litigation occurs in a vacuum. Just as the civil rights movement's litigation strategy to end segregation and discrimination paralleled the direct action efforts, drawing strength and a changing public and judicial consciousness from them, so has welfare rights organizing of recipients and coalitions of groups been interwoven with successful affirmative welfare litigation to expand benefits. While the analysis which follows will focus primarily on legal questions and the possibilities and limits of judicial action, there should be no misimpression: these are not pure, immutable questions. What relief courts may be persuaded to grant has something to do with legal doctrine and much to do with the current political situation, ideology, and the economic interests at stake.

The Concept of Entitlement

Perhaps the major accomplishment of the early welfare litigation was the legitimation, by judicial acceptance, of the very premise which underlay the legal actions: that receipt of welfare benefits was a "right" of those in need of aid and not merely a privilege or gratuity. The thoroughness with which this premise has been incorporated in our consciousness within such a short period of time is, in fact, astonishing. This is particularly true when the short life of the "rights" notion is juxtaposed to the more than 350-year history of public assistance efforts from the Elizabethan Poor Laws in the early 1600s until the late 1960s. During this entire period, including the first 35 years of administration of the Social Security Act, it was widely believed that dispensers of aid acted with virtually unfettered discretion. Although it was the government dispensing benefits, the aid received was nonetheless viewed as charity—and no one, by definition, could claim a "right" to charity.

For example, the prevailing judicial view that welfare benefits were discretionary is well illustrated by this excerpt from the federal court argument in one of the earlier welfare cases in 1966:

> *[Lawyer for the recipients]: Your Honor . . . our contention is that if a person is eligible under the conditions laid down, then that person has a right to welfare.*
> *The Court [Holtzoff, J.]: No—welfare is discretionary of course. . . . The rules as to eligibility are there to exclude anyone who is not eligible. . . . It doesn't mean that everybody who is eligible has a right to sue for relief if it is refused, for example.*[7]

It was not only the courts that took this view. The federal Department of Health, Education and Welfare (HEW, now the Department of Health and Human Services, or HHS), the agency charged with the oversight of the state AFDC programs, also took the position that the provisions of the Social Security Act were merely the outer limits of what the federal government would reimburse—that is, it was a federal ceiling, and not a federal floor or guarantee, of who was eligible for benefits or what they should receive.

The intellectual backdrop to the movement to make welfare

benefits an entitlement was provided by Yale Law Professor Charles Reich. In an extremely influential article in 1964, entitled "The New Property," Reich argued why it was essential to the preservation of the zone of individual liberty in a society of greatly increasing government power for the "largess" distributed in nearly infinite forms by government to be considered as the property of the recipient, with the attendant rights attached to property in our society. Although Reich wrote about such varied forms of government "largess" as government jobs, licenses, franchises, contracts, agricultural and airline subsidies, postal services, and savings bank insurance, his special concern was reserved for recipients of welfare and related benefits:

> *The concept of right is most urgently needed with respect to benefits like unemployment compensation, public assistance, and old age insurance. . . . Only by making such benefits into rights can the welfare state achieve its goal of providing a secure minimum basis for individual well-being and dignity in a society where each man cannot be wholly the master of his own destiny.*

In 1965, Reich went a step further, and, while again analogizing the rights of welfare recipients to the automobile dealer's franchise, the doctor's and lawyer's professional license, the farmer's subsidy, etc., he declared:

> *Such sources of security, whether private or public, are no longer regarded as luxuries or gratuities; to the recipients they are essentials, fully deserved, and in no sense a form of charity. It is only the poor whose entitlements, although recognized by public policy, have not been effectively enforced.*[8]

Reich's concept of entitlement implicitly incorporated three potentially different meanings. First, and most broad, is the essentially normative concept, in the nature of a "natural right," that "[t]he idea of entitlement is simply that when individuals have insufficient resources to live under conditions of health and decency, society has obligations to provide support, and the individual is entitled to that support as of right."[9] If carried out, such a concept would obviously go far beyond the eligibility restrictions of existing welfare statutes and programs. It would amount essentially to the "right to live," which Sparer identified as the long-range legal and political goal of the early welfare rights lawyers as well as of the recipient movement. Second, the concept of entitlement implied a basis for establishing as yet undeclared constitutional rights of welfare recipients against the arbitrary or harassing actions of welfare agencies. This meant the right not to be deprived of their benefits without due process of law, and the right to privacy and dignity in their receipt of benefits. Third, and at the very least, the concept of entitlement implied the right to receive benefits within the bounds of statutory authorization, rather than benefits being a matter of official discretion.

As it turned out, by the early 1970s, the Supreme Court had adopted, with some important provisos, the second and third elements of the entitlement concept. However, it squarely rejected any notion of entitlement that would significantly expand the statutory limits of eligibility or affect benefit levels. In the Court's 1970 constitutional declaration of the due process rights of welfare recipients in *Goldberg* v. *Kelly,* the Court finally laid to rest the right/privilege distinction in the area of welfare benefits. It stated that welfare benefits "are a matter of statutory entitlement for persons qualified to receive them." The Court in a footnote explicitly and favorably acknowledged Reich's writings, and stated: "It may be realistic today to regard welfare entitlements as more like 'property' than a 'gratuity.' "[10]

Thus, within a few short years, the centuries' old principle that welfare benefits are discretionary had been overturned. While the acceptance of the premise that eligible needy families have a "right" to welfare benefits does not in itself transform the restrictive eligibility conditions of the program or increase inadequate grants, it is nonetheless a fundamental change. Poor people, just like everyone else in this society, were now "entitled" to their "property." They could enforce this entitlement in the courts. How far the courts would go, and to what extent they would continue to be limited by prevailing notions of just how "deserving" of public assistance poor people are, are the issues to which we now turn.

The Limits of Constitutional Adjudication

For what has turned out in retrospect to be a historically brief period, the United States Supreme Court in the 1950s and 1960s found in various provisions of the United States Constitution protections for the rights of the historically powerless.[11] Some welfare rights advocates hoped for a few years in the late 1960s that the Court could also be persuaded to establish a right to basic minimum subsistence, or a "right to live." Such a legal right, if adopted by the Supreme Court, would have been the effective tool for accomplishing, at least in part, the fundamental goal of a minimum adequate income for all, which otherwise eluded the welfare rights movement and welfare rights lawyers.

But the Supreme Court, while establishing the procedural, or due process, rights of welfare recipients, drew the line at constitutionally expanding substantive entitlements. With minor exceptions, the Court refused to use the Constitution to expand welfare eligibility or increase grant amounts. These basic issues remained the sole province of the "democratic" branches of government— the legislature and the executive. To understand how the Court drew this line, it is necessary to take a brief detour through some basic principles of constitutional law.

Equal Protection Analysis. The Fourteenth Amendment to the United States Constitution states in part that no State shall "deprive any person of life, liberty or property, without due process of law; nor deny to any person within its jurisdiction the equal protection of the laws." The manner in which the Court has construed the due process and equal protection clauses of the Constitution is the critical factor in determining the potential success of constitutional claims for relief by the poor. Because it is the equal protection clause which has the greatest impact on substantive, as opposed to procedural, claims, it is the standard of court review of claims of denial of equal protection that is the most significant here.

Our legal system operates on the basis of what is called a "hierarchy of laws." Under Article VI of the United States Constitution, applicable federal law is supreme over all state law. The federal Constitution supersedes all other law. Therefore, only a theory based on the federal Constitution could overcome the eligibility restrictions of the federal Social Security Act. (At times, state courts have held that the provisions of state law impose independent duties on state welfare agencies, even if federal reimbursement is not available because the requirement is not authorized by the Social Security Act. Such state-based challenges are, however, relatively rare, and at any rate cannot work wholesale changes in the AFDC program.) Due process arguments on their own do not generally expand who is eligible for benefits or increase benefit levels.

A claim of denial of equal protection is essentially an argument that first, a governmental rule or practice creates two classes of persons, those with a particular benefit or burden, and those without it, and second, that this classification is "invidious." The key is whether the claimant can establish that the obvious or proven discrimination between the two groups is somehow "invidious." To assist it in making this determination, the Court has established certain principles that determine the level of scrutiny which the Court will apply. As it has turned out, it is actually the level of scrutiny applied which for the most part determines the result in the case.

If a claimant belongs to what is considered a "suspect" or "quasi-suspect" class, or if the right asserted is considered to be a "fundamental" right, then the Court applies what is called "heightened scrutiny," which is "strict" for suspect cases and "intermediate" for quasi-suspect cases. When a classification adversely affects a "suspect" class, unless the governmental interest in maintaining the discriminatory classification at issue is found to be "compelling," the claimant will win and the discriminatory rule or practice will be invalidated. As a practical matter, virtually no alleged governmental interest is ever found to rise to the level of "compelling." However, in *Roe* v. *Wade*, the Court did find that the state had a compelling interest in the health of the mother after the first trimester of pregnancy, making reasonable health-related regulation permissible, and in the third trimester of pregnancy, a compelling interest in the preservation of life which permitted the state to prohibit abortions unless necessary to save the mother's life or health.[12] The application of the strict scrutiny test, then, almost always results in victory for the claimant. When a quasi-suspect class is involved, the governmental interest must be "important," and the classification must be "substantially related" to its achievement or the plaintiffs will win.

A suspect class is one which has historically been subject to discrimination, or which has obvious, immutable, or distinguishing characteristics that define them as a discrete group, or is a politically powerless minority. So far, only race and alienage have been found to be suspect classes. Sex and illegitimacy have been found to be "quasi-suspect" classes, deserving of intermediate scrutiny. Alternatively, if the claimant is not found to be a member of a suspect class or to be asserting a fundamental right, the Court will apply what is called the "rational basis" test or "minimal scrutiny." Under this test, "[a] statutory discrimination will not be set aside if any state of facts reasonably may be conceived to justify it."[13] As a Court can virtually always imagine some rational basis for any governmental rule, the adoption of this test generally signals defeat for the claimant.

Thus, the key question for welfare lawyers raising an equal protection challenge is how to get their case put in the strict scrutiny, or at least the intermediate scrutiny, box. In *King* v. *Smith*, the first AFDC case to reach the Supreme Court, the plaintiffs had argued, and had persuaded the lower court, that Alabama's policy of denying AFDC eligibility to families in which there was a so-called "substitute father" was a denial of equal protection.[14] The Supreme Court ruled for the plaintiffs solely on the grounds that the state policy violated the Social Security Act. As a result, there was no opportunity to establish the principle that the equal protection clause applied to the categories of families eligible for AFDC, which Sparer and others had hoped could be the basis of an equal protection challenge to the very nature of a categorical, as opposed to a universal, program.

In the challenge to state residency laws for AFDC, *Shapiro* v. *Thompson,* which was the first AFDC case decided by the Supreme Court on constitutional grounds, the welfare lawyers succeeded in having the Court apply strict scrutiny to their claim. The Court ruled that needy families moving across interstate lines had a fundamental right to travel based on the United States Constitution. It ruled that the asserted state interests in a time-specific residency requirement prior to eligibility for aid, which was permitted by the Social Security Act, either were not constitutionally permissible or did not rise to the level of compelling. In a dash of the pen, so to speak, the Court eliminated one of the major, centuries' old restrictions on public assistance eligibility. While the financial implications for state budgets were obviously significant, the Court dismissed this issue, stating simply, "The saving of welfare costs cannot justify an otherwise invidious classification."[15]

The Demise of Equal Protection Challenges. But the blush of success quickly faded. One year later the Court dashed any hopes that the equal protection clause would be a powerful tool on behalf of poor people. In *Dandridge* v. *Williams,* the Court squarely rejected a constitutional challenge to the maximum grant limitation imposed by Maryland (and similarly by 20 other states), which effectively discriminated against children in large families, as families of more than a certain size did not get any grant increase to account for the needs of the additional children. Although some lower federal courts, including the court in that case, had been applying a stricter standard of review in equal protection cases when the claim involved a deprivation of minimum subsistence, the Court put a quick end to such theories, as well as to the grander hope that the Court would declare a constitutionally based fundamental "right to life."

In *Dandridge,* the Supreme Court adopted the minimum rationality test, which had for decades applied to economic regulation cases. The Court acknowledged that "[t]he administration of public welfare assistance, by contrast [to state regulation of business or industry], involves the most basic economic needs of impoverished human beings." But the majority concluded: "We recognize the dramatically real factual difference between the cited cases and this one, but we can find no basis for applying a different constitutional standard. . . . [I]t is a standard that is true to the principle that the Fourteenth Amendment gives the federal courts no power to impose upon the States their views of what constitutes wise economic *or social* policy."[16] The Court went on to find sufficient justification for the maximum grant policy in the state interest in avoiding paying any family welfare benefits at a level higher than the minimum wage, although the Court acknowledged that there were no employable persons in any of the plaintiff families.

The next year, the Court also laid to rest any hope of getting around minimal scrutiny in welfare cases by showing that, at least in some states, welfare rules had an adverse racial impact. In *Jefferson* v. *Hackney,* the Court rejected an equal protection challenge to a Texas decision to pay AFDC recipients, who in Texas were predominantly non-white-Anglo, only 75 percent of need, while paying the aged and the blind and disabled, who were primarily white-Anglo, 100 percent and 95 percent of need, respectively. The Court held that a racially disparate impact, if not proven to have been intended by the state, did not justify strict scrutiny analysis.[17]

A small wedge in this otherwise solid wall of constitutional hopelessness in terms of equal protection challenges exists only when a statutory provision adversely impacts the quasi-suspect classes of women or illegitimates. In *Westcott* v. *Califano,* the Court invalidated the congressional restriction of the optional AFDC-Unemployed Parent program to families where the father is the unemployed individual. It ruled under heightened scrutiny analysis that "Congress may not legislate 'one step at a time' when that step is drawn along the line of gender, and the consequence is to exclude one group of families altogether from badly needed subsistence benefits."[18]

In 1981, Congress restricted the financial implications of this decision by requiring that the unemployed person must have been the "principal earner," that is, the parent who earned the greater amount of income, in the two years prior to the application for AFDC. Thus, a family that relied on the income of both parents, in which the mother loses her job, but where the father had had the greater income over the prior two years taken as a whole, would not be eligible for AFDC. Moreover, simply having an unemployed parent in the home has never been sufficient to enable needy children to be eligible for aid: the "unemployed" parent has to have had a fairly recent and extensive work history for the three years prior to applying for aid. Nor are low wage-earning intact families eligible for supplementary aid under the AFDC-U program, as any family in which the "principal earner" works more than 100 hours per month, regardless of income, is automatically disqualified.

Thus, the equal protection clause has proved to be of very limited use in expanding welfare eligibility, and of no help whatsoever in challenging the amount of welfare grants. Despite the current claims of conservatives decrying law-making by the courts, the Supreme Court has always been very reluctant to move far away from the views of the majority. This is particularly true when the implications for requiring increased expenditures are clear. Furthermore, the political consensus as to whether welfare recipients are "deserving" of aid is shaky at best. While there is a strong belief in the importance of the social safety net, there is also a strong suspicion of whether welfare families are really "needy," which is highlighted by any case that raises the relation between welfare and encouraging employment, as did *Dandridge*.

The "Federalization" of Eligibility

An examination of court decisions involving challenges to state rules or practices which are inconsistent with the federal Social Security Act reveals an avenue of legal action that not only has had enormous effect in the past, but also holds significant potential for the future. The recent conservative turn in federal welfare legislation, in which Congress has added numerous specific restrictions on AFDC eligibility, rather than the prior type of broad statutory language, may make successful statutory challenges based on federal law unlikely, at least in the short run. However, the basic mode of analysis which proved so effective in the first phase of welfare litigation may hold enormous potential for challenging state welfare rules and practices based on inconsistencies with *state* law. This section will explore the reasons for the success of an expansive statutory mode of analysis in the initial federal law-based challenges. The second part of this chapter will explore the potential for utilizing state law in a similar fashion to expand welfare rights and benefits.

To understand why arguments challenging state welfare rules and practices as inconsistent with the Social Security Act had such great effect, it is first necessary to understand the legal structure of the AFDC program. The Aid to Families with Dependent Children program is what is known as a federal grant-in-aid program. It was established by Congress in 1935, as Title IV-A of the Social Security Act. Conceived as a program to aid children in families lacking a wage-earner, AFDC eligibility was initially restricted to children whose parent (understood to mean father, but written sex-neutrally) was continually absent, by death or otherwise, or incapacitated. In 1950, Congress made the caretaker relative of the children (generally the mother, although not necessarily a parent) eligible for benefits as well, and in 1961 families in which a parent was "unemployed" were made optionally eligible for assistance. Thus, AFDC is a "categorical" aid program: families must have certain characteristics, independent of financial need, to qualify for assistance.

States are free to choose whether or not to participate in the AFDC program. (All states do.) If a state wishes to participate, it must submit its plan for its state AFDC program to the governing federal agency, now the Department of Health and Human Services (HHS), for approval. HHS must grant its approval if the state plan conforms with the terms of the Social Security Act and the implementing regulations promulgated by HHS. For AFDC expenditures made under an approved plan, the state will receive 50 percent or greater federal reimbursement. This legal structure is what courts have called "a scheme of cooperative federalism."[19]

Despite this legal structure of governing federal law, states have a great deal of latitude in defining their AFDC programs. Sometimes the language of the Social Security Act explicitly grants states a choice whether to adopt a particular aspect of the program. Implicitly in the statute, and explicitly under the federal regulations, states have the power to determine their own "standard of need" and level of benefits. The "standard of need" has been defined by the courts as the amount deemed necessary by the state to maintain a hypothetical family at a subsistence level. However, neither federal law nor judicial interpretation currently require a state to set its standard of need based on the real cost of minimum subsistence. Currently, only two states even set their standard of need at or above the federal poverty level; all states pay AFDC benefits that are below the poverty line.

Unlike many statutes, the AFDC provisions of the Social Security Act were written in broad, prescriptive terms: for example, that aid "shall be furnished with reasonable promptness to all eligible individuals." This normative, goal-oriented style was continued by HEW in the interpretive rules it issued to the states in the first several decades of the program. Despite this hortatory approach, HEW played a basically hands-off supervisory role over state AFDC programs during the first 30 years of the Social Security Act. It rarely disapproved any provisions of state AFDC plans. In general it took the legal position that the eligibility conditions set forth in the Social Security Act operated as a ceiling on what payments were eligible for federal reimbursement, not as a mandate regarding who must be considered eligible for benefits or how a family's amount of benefits was to be determined.

Thus, when lawyers first confronted the Social Security Act in a systematic way in the mid-1960s, they faced a statute and body of written interpretations which together appeared to create broad rights on behalf of AFDC applicants and recipients. Yet the lawyers had to deal with the history of virtually nonexistent federal enforcement, or even federal approval of all manner of restrictive state rules. The primary legal question, then, was whether the language of the Social Security Act was to operate as a mandate upon the states, or merely as a weakly enforced outer limit on their discretion.

In *King* v. *Smith*, a unanimous Supreme Court articulated for the first time what was to become a tremendously potent tool for welfare recipients: that states are required to grant AFDC benefits to families eligible for aid under the federal definitions contained in the Social Security Act. The case involved a challenge to the Alabama provision denying aid to needy children found to have a "substitute father," on the grounds that such children did not meet the parental absence requirement of the program. Despite the lack of any definition of "parent" in the Social Security Act, and the lack of any indication that the "eligible individuals" clause was intended by Congress to imply a federal rather than a state definition of eligibility, the Supreme Court ruled that Alabama had no discretion to define "parent" more narrowly than the federal statute. Since the federal statute required that aid be granted "to all eligible individuals," children in families meeting the federal standards could not be denied aid. Thus, without any explicit justification of its federalization of the "all eligible individuals" clause, the Court overturned more than 30 years of administrative practice in which HEW had permitted states to define eligibility far more narrowly than the federal statute would appear to authorize.

Alabama defined a "substitute father" as a man with whom the child's mother had sexual relations, regardless of whether their "cohabitation" occurred in the home where the children lived. It was irrelevant to the Alabama provision whether or not the so-called "substitute father" actually contributed to the children's support, and it was stipulated in the case that the man was not the father of any of the children, did not live in the home, did not contribute any money to their support, but in fact used his meager income to support his own nine children, with whom he lived.

In subsequent cases, the Court strongly reaffirmed the federalization of the "all eligible individuals" clause. It consistently ruled that any persons eligible for AFDC under the terms of the Social Security Act must be granted benefits, unless it was clear from the language or history of the provisions in question that Congress intended to give states the option whether to make a particular group eligible. Any unclear intent was to be construed in favor of expansive eligibility. It is important to recognize, in considering the future implications of this first phase, that the courts were undoubtedly influenced by the political movement for expanding "welfare rights" and the resulting change in public consciousness on welfare issues.

In addition, it is vital to acknowledge the obvious vulnerability of court decisions based on statutory as opposed to constitutional interpretation: the legislature, if it can muster the necessary votes, can change the statute. Thus, in the 1980s, Congress, at the instigation of an extremely conservative, antiwelfare executive branch, has amended the AFDC provisions of the Social Security Act significantly, adding specific statutory restrictions which have drastically cut back on the "available income" principle and the categories of eligible persons. Indeed, these recent amendments have reversed a substantial number of the legal victories of the first phase of welfare litigation.[20]

The Ambivalent Role of the Courts

Resort to the courts on procedural issues has been extremely successful in obtaining declarations of what procedures are fair, and judicial decisions have rarely been undercut by the legislature. However, the value of the declared fair procedures in practice is a more complicated question, due in part to the "bureaucratic contingency": the difficulty of getting wide-ranging changes in procedure adopted by bureaucracies without subversion.

Procedural arguments in welfare cases have two primary bases: the due process clause of the Fourteenth Amendment and the statutory guarantee of the right to a "fair hearing," and statutory and regulatory provisions concerning the provision of benefits with "reasonable promptness." Thus, the concept of fair procedures encompasses more than the notion of the right to adequate notice and hearing. In a program involving subsistence benefits of last resort, delay can be equivalent to denial.

Prior to the onset of welfare litigation in the mid-1960s, there was virtually no notion of "fair procedures" in the welfare system at all. Although the Social Security Act contained a provision requiring states to provide "fair hearings," the term had virtually no content, and almost no hearings had ever been held. For example, in New York, the state with the largest welfare caseload, 14 fair hearings were held in 1964, 16 in 1965, and 20 in 1966. Even in 1971, after the mass use of fair hearings as a strategy by the welfare rights movement, hearings were requested in only about 2 percent of appealable cases, and 54 percent of those appeals were lodged in three states.[21]

Similarly, despite the provision requiring that eligibles receive benefits with "reasonable promptness," no time standards were enforced, and people often had to wait for whole days at the welfare office and come back again and again, just to have their applications taken, well enough acted upon. To many, the primary characteristic of the welfare system was its arbitrary, and often vindictive (and racist) actions against poor families.

The landmark decision in the area of fair procedures is *Goldberg* v. *Kelly*, which involved the right of welfare recipients to a hearing *prior* to having their benefits terminated or reduced. *Goldberg* established the fundamental principle that welfare benefits are an entitlement, or "property," protected by the due process clause, as discussed earlier. From this first step, the Court went on to the balancing test. Here, again, the *Goldberg* decision has remained an untouched high-water mark in welfare rights litigation, for the Court held that the "brutal need" of eligible welfare recipients for the "very means to live" outweighed the government's interest in saving funds by holding hearings only subsequent to the termination or reduction of benefits. Particularly as the Court has backed away from expansive procedural protections in other areas of government benefits, the continuing validity of *Goldberg* has underlined the special legal significance accorded to welfare as the means of subsistence.[22]

How important are hearing rights? Clearly, a hearing prior to termination cannot prevent the termination from happening a few weeks or months later, when that result is required by the substantive eligibility rules. "Fair" procedures cannot guarantee "fair" results when the substantive rules themselves are inequitable. Moreover, relatively few recipients facing adverse action by the welfare system request hearings. Nonetheless, for those individuals who do make use of their hearing rights, especially for those who are able to obtain legal representation, hearings do correct numerous illegal bureaucratic actions. For example, in 1985 there were 138,713 requests for fair hearings in the AFDC program. In March 1985, there were approximately 3.7 million families on AFDC. Not all families have an appealable action taken in the course of the year. But these figures undoubtedly severely under-represent the number of recipients who could have taken merito-rious appeals. Of these, about one-third were probably settled prior to hearing. Of the 37.7 percent which were decided by an agency hearing officer, 60 percent were decided in favor of the claimant. Only 9.6 percent of the claimants had legal counsel.[23] Such corrections have broader effect than just the individual cases, as agencies will often clarify to their workers the need to change the implementation of ambiguous rules to prevent reversal by hearing referees. And perhaps most importantly, hearing rights are the prerequisite to recipients taking the most basic step of questioning authority. Essential to recipient organizing, the right to a prior hearing protects recipients from arbitrary administrative action.

In addition to declaring the more common aspects of due process protections, such as hearing rights, courts have been willing to give content to the "reasonable promptness" requirement, by ordering states to act on requests for benefits within specific time frames. The courts' role, at least in these initial declarations of rights, is similar to the role of the courts in declaring substantive eligibility rights under the federal statutory provisions discussed above: the courts merely state what the governing law requires.

However, declaring the right to timely service, and enforcing that right, are two very different things. Effectuating a court decision requires more than a mere change in rules. It requires significant changes in agency procedures. However, courts are often reluctant to issue the kind of implementing orders that are necessary to really change the way agencies function. As a result, timeliness has been an important issue in welfare litigation, but one in which courts have played a more difficult and ambivalent role than in ensuring the more classic due process rights of notice and an opportunity to be heard. Unless the lawyers representing welfare recipients maintain continual oversight of agency compli-ance with timeliness norms established by the court, and carry through with often very time-consuming legal actions to ensure compliance, court decisions regarding the right to timely service will not in practice be worth much if anything. But with such efforts, courts can, and have, played an extremely significant role in changing agency procedures, so that the right to timely service can become a reality.

Thus, resort to the courts on procedural claims has been and continues to be a positive avenue for change, with the caveats that procedural claims are inherently limited in their effect, and achieving changes which deeply affect bureaucratic functioning are likely to require a lengthy judicial and administrative struggle.

The Limited Powers of the Federal Courts

Despite the initial hopes of the welfare litigation strategists that court actions could result directly or indirectly in the establishment of minimum adequate benefits, equal protection doctrine turned out to be of no use in accomplishing this goal, and of extremely limited use even in expanding the categories of eligibles, as discussed earlier. Perhaps an even more fundamental problem, however, than the limitations of equal protection doctrine, is the nature of our federal system of government. Federalism is relevant here in two respects: the nature of the Social Security Act itself, and the constraints on federal courts in dealing with issues involving state appropriations.

While the Social Security Act never says in so many words that it is up to the states to set their benefit levels, this appears to have been the congressional intent. Nothing in the language of the act itself specifies what needs the states must take into account in setting their "standard of need," well enough their level of benefits.

The only time that Congress has ever legislated on the issue of the level of benefits was in 1967—obviously coinciding with the rise of the welfare rights movement as well as generally increased consciousness about poverty. While the Johnson administration proposed that states be required to pay benefits at the "need" level (which they would still be free to set), all that survived the legislative process was a requirement that states, on a one-time basis, increase their need standards and payment maximums to account for increases in the cost of living. It was possible to argue that Congress, in including the language concerning cost-of-living increases in payment maximums, had also intended to require states which set maximums actually to increase their payments, although clearly Congress did not intend to require states to pay their full need level. In *Rosado* v. *Wyman*,[24] the Supreme Court refused to go this far, ruling that although states had to update their maximums, they could pay even less than their maximum payment amount by switching to a percentage-of-need methodology to determine their payment levels, regardless of family size. Issued the same day as *Dandridge*, the *Rosado* decision was the nail in the coffin of the federal court litigation strategy to increase benefit levels.

Not only did the Social Security Act provide no legal handle to increase overall benefit levels, but the federal courts were also constrained by long-standing principles requiring deference to state sovereignty in issuing any orders which would have the effect of requiring increased state expenditures. Thus, it should have been no surprise that the Supreme Court in *King* v. *Smith*, as well as in every subsequent decision that had the effect of requiring states to increase the number of eligibles, was careful to underline that states retained the overall power to determine how much of their funds to allocate to the program, by reducing payments if necessary to offset the court-ordered expansion in eligibility.

Indeed, viewing this first phase of welfare litigation in retrospect, some welfare rights advocates feared that the ultimate effect of this apparently very successful litigation had been merely to expand eligibility to some previously excluded groups, at the expense of reducing benefits to all. However, with greater hindsight it appears that the subsequent reductions in the real value of AFDC payments were not so much the result of political reaction against the court victories as they were a consequence of the end of the budget surpluses of the 1960s and the onset of the severe inflation and recessions of the 1970s.

Thus, the first phase of federal court welfare litigation met with enormous success in establishing the basic notion of entitlement and reducing arbitrariness, in enforcing the broad norms of the Social Security Act to "federalize" eligibility, and in establishing and at times enforcing fair procedures. However, litigation based on federal law has had limited long-run effect in expanding the groups of eligibles, and could not increase benefit levels. Court decisions based on the Social Security Act, as most were, rather than on constitutional principles, could not withstand legislative assault when political winds changed. Retaining net gain from these court-ordered changes required the political muscle at the state level in order to increase overall AFDC appropriations, rather than adjusting for increased eligibles by decreasing benefits. The history of the first phase of welfare litigation shows that in order for effective, long-term, court-ordered changes in the welfare system to occur and be sustained, the importance of a social movement cannot be overlooked, to provide the necessary climate for expansive decisions in the first instance, and to defend those decisions against legislative and administrative retrenchment.

Expanding Welfare Benefits Through the State Courts

Until recently, very few cases challenging some aspect of a state AFDC program based on state, as opposed to federal, law have been brought. As the federal doors for expanding welfare eligibility or benefits have closed, advocates have looked increasingly to their state statutes and constitutions to see if these hold any basis for relief. Because state as well as federal funds are required to operate an AFDC program, states generally have state statutes which govern the operation of their state AFDC program, although these statutes vary from very lengthy and detailed, to the briefest of statutory authorizations to operate a program in conformity with federal law. In addition, because many states had related programs for widows and their families prior to AFDC, state AFDC laws may contain provisions which predated the federal AFDC program.

Although they vary by state, state laws today carry a potential as a tool for benefit expansion similar to the first-phase experience with the federal Social Security Act: they are often framed in broad, normative terms, and courts may respond positively to a claim to apply the statutory provisions literally to require an expansion of rights. In addition, state court actions to enforce state law rights hold far greater potential than prior federal court efforts for actually increasing benefit levels for two reasons: first, it is the states which set their AFDC benefit levels, and state laws, unlike the Social Security Act, may contain language relevant to the level of benefits; and second, state courts have less, although still significant, constraints than federal courts in issuing orders bearing on appropriations. Of course, potentially beneficial state laws are of little or no value if the state's courts are unremittingly hostile to claims by welfare recipients. But courts in states that have not been traditionally liberal have been receptive to welfare cases.[25] However, as was true in the first phase of welfare litigation, successful state court litigation to expand eligibility and particularly to increase benefits probably requires concurrent political support, through a grass-roots movement or coalition of groups. Their role is necessary to lay the groundwork of general perception of need, to prevent a legislative reaction undercutting the legal basis of the court decision, and to obtain the appropriations necessary to implement any court decision achieved.

Case Study: The Massachusetts Welfare Benefits/ Homeless Case

These principles are well-illustrated by the August 18, 1987, decision of the Massachusetts Supreme Judicial Court in the case entitled *Massachusetts Coalition for the Homeless* v. *Secretary of*

Human Services.[26] A unanimous five-member panel of the state's highest court held that the language in a 1913 state law, requiring that AFDC benefits be sufficient to enable families to bring up their children in their own homes, meant what it said, and entitled AFDC families to a permanent home, and not merely to temporary accommodations in hotels, motels, or shelters. The court gave full effect to the broad statutory terms, despite the defendant's arguments that the language stated merely a hortatory goal. Further, the court held that the statute imposed certain duties on the executive branch defendants, both to seek to prevent the homelessness of AFDC families by providing sufficient AFDC benefits or by other means, and to alleviate it as soon as reasonably possible, by seeking the necessary appropriations from the legislature when its current funds were inadequate to fulfill these duties. Given the dismal record of benefit level litigation in the past, the victorious high court decision in this case is particularly noteworthy, and perhaps holds some lessons for other states.

Background of the Case

This lawsuit was brought in December 1985 as an outgrowth of, and a part of the strategy in, a broad-based campaign to increase welfare benefit levels in Massachusetts: the Up to the Poverty Level campaign. The driving force in the Up to Poverty campaign was the statewide welfare rights organization, the Coalition for Basic Human Needs (CBHN), which originated in the late 1970s. CBHN, along with other allied groups and human service organizations, joined together in mid-1984 around a campaign to raise AFDC and related subsistence benefits to the federal poverty line. The federal poverty line is a uniform, national figure, varying only by family size, which purports to represent the cost of minimum subsistence. It was originally formulated in the mid-1960s, based on two key, and most observers now believe faulty, assumptions: that the cost of food represented one-third of a family's minimum subsistence expenditures, and that the cost of food was adequately represented by the cost of the U.S. Department of Agriculture's Economy (now Thrifty) Food Plan, which is only designed to prevent severe nutritional deficiency for an emergency period. Consequently, not only does the federal poverty line not take into account regional variations in the cost of living, but it is totally insensitive to the possibility (and likelihood) that as shelter costs have escalated in many regions of the country, the multiplier of three has become sorely inadequate. Despite all these defects, however, the federal poverty level has the advantage of being a commonly used indicator of poverty which has broad public credibility.

CBHN had been waging annual legislative campaigns for cost-of-living increases (as well as other benefit improvements), but had become increasingly frustrated with the narrow range of apparently possible gains. The hope was that changing the framework of the debate from how much of an annual increase should there be, to how great was the gap between benefit level and need, would be both a more effective force for organizing welfare recipients and for persuading legislators and other opinion makers.

Underlying the campaign was the fundamental fact that in Massachusetts, as in most other states, the value of AFDC benefits had been severely eroded by the inflation of the 1970s and early 1980s; while benefits had been 15 percent above the poverty line in 1973, by 1984 (after the 4 percent increase enacted that year) they were 46 percent below the poverty line. A family of three received $396/month, or $4,752/year, while the poverty level was officially set at $8,280. The campaign called for closing the gap in three years, which would have required 25 percent increases per year. In fact, in the first year of the campaign, which culminated in June of 1985 with the enactment of the budget for fiscal year 1986, the legislature enacted a 9 percent increase in AFDC benefits, despite the governor's proposal of 5 percent. From the perspective of the past, this increase was substantial, and the Up to Poverty campaign deserved the credit for it, but by the end of the 1985 legislative session the activists in the campaign were seriously frustrated by the remaining huge gulf between their goal and their actual accomplishments. From their perspective there were limited financial gains. However, the campaign had succeeded in making a major inroad on public opinion, so that the extent of increases in AFDC benefits had become one of the primary, if not the major, tests of how the administration and the legislature were performing on a basic decency agenda.

At the same time as the Up to Poverty campaign was being waged, there was increasing consciousness in Massachusetts about the growing crisis of family homelessness. In fact, the data on homeless families showed that the two issues were inextricably intertwined: 80 percent of homeless families relied on AFDC as their sole source of income, and 90 percent were single-parent families and thus probably eligible for or receiving some AFDC. In response to the growing problem, the legislature in late 1983 had enacted a "Homelessness Bill," which, among other provisions, substantially liberalized emergency assistance benefits, including the right to emergency shelter.[27] Consequently, by late

1985, there was a large, growing, visible, and expansive population of homeless AFDC families being put up at state expense (of approximately $2,000/month for a family of three) in hotels, motels, and shelters.

The Legal Strategy

Against this backdrop, activists in the campaign began to look for a handle, in addition to political organizing, which would help shift the terms of the public debate to make genuinely significant and substantial AFDC increases appear more credible. At the request of the director of the Massachusetts Coalition for the Homeless, who was herself a former welfare recipient and leader of CBHN, legal services lawyers early in the fall of 1985 began to look into the possibility of litigation based on the state law which provided that AFDC benefits "shall be sufficient to enable such parent to bring up such child or children properly in his or her own home" (*Massachusetts General Laws*, ch. 118, §2). Her hope was that such a suit could be a vehicle to heighten public attention on the inadequacy of AFDC benefits, as well as to accomplish tangible orders from the court.

After considerable research, the working group, which had been expanded to include representatives of the Coalition for Basic Human Needs and additional lawyers,[28] concluded that a lawsuit should be brought not only under ch. 118, §2, but also under a related provision (ch. 118, §2[B][g]) which required that the state Department of Public Welfare (DPW) annually review the adequacy of its "standard budget of assistance." The theory was that the two statutes could be tied together to require the DPW first, to set a standard which was adequate in light of the cost of housing, among other needs, and second, to pay, or seek the funds necessary to pay, benefits at the DPW-determined level of adequacy. Structuring the case in this way had the advantage of including an easier to win tangible goal—the revised standard of adequacy— and of playing into the court's likely desire to defer to agency expertise in the determination of adequacy or sufficiency, rather than having to make the complex factual determinations itself.

In addition, the working group made the basic decision that although a key goal was to raise the overall level of AFDC benefits, both to avoid the possible problem of the statutes sounding merely like vague, unenforceable goals, and to structure a more politically sympathetic case, the focus of the lawsuit would be on the nexus between AFDC benefits and homelessness. To highlight this nexus, and hopefully to arouse the court's emotional sympathy, the decision was made to build a thorough record on the factual connection between inadequate AFDC benefits and increasing homelessness, and on the harm which homelessness caused to AFDC families, through the life stories of the individual plaintiffs, voluminous supporting affidavits from other homeless families, and a range of experts.

For example, included as initial plaintiffs in the case, in addition to the two organizations, were three homeless AFDC families, whose circumstances well illustrated how families, through no fault of their own, became homeless if they had no source of income other than AFDC. All three original plaintiff families had very young children. One family was homeless because the husband walked out just before the birth of the second child, leaving the family without any support in an apartment in which the rent was only $8 less than the family's AFDC grant, when it finally came. Another was homeless because the mother had to flee from her husband who was threatening to kill her. She and her two young children could no longer stay with the grandparents, one of whom had a very serious heart condition. The third was homeless because the mother had lost her job after her baby's ill health required her constant attention. Like the others, she could not find an apartment she could afford on her AFDC grant when her mother, with whom she had lived, was evicted because the landlord wanted to rehabilitate the apartment to raise the rent.

Prior to requesting preliminary injunctive relief from the court, the plaintiffs filed supporting affidavits of 52 other homeless families (obtained through the Mass. Coalition for the Homeless [MCH] network of shelters, the welfare rights groups, and legal services offices), making graphically real the appalling circumstances in which families were forced to live in the hotels and motels in which the state mostly accommodated them. Affidavits were also filed from a psychiatrist, public health and nutrition experts, and a housing economist, on the effects of homelessness, the overall consequences of inadequate AFDC benefits, and the relation between AFDC benefits and the housing market.

Initial Court Action

From the first public act of filing the lawsuit, which the plaintiff groups announced at a well-attended press conference, the significant and generally favorable publicity which the case received exceeded the plaintiff organizations' best hopes. But the administration, the legislature, and the press did not take the mere filing of the case very seriously, as the 1913 law which was the legal crux of the case was considered a dusty piece of ancient history, and the level of AFDC benefits was considered a political question in which the courts had no proper role to play. However, it is probable that the filing of the suit, timed in part to affect the final formulation of the governor's budget, had resulted in the governor's increasing his proposed AFDC increase from 4 to 10 percent.

Despite the skepticism of the defendants and others, in late June 1986, the superior court ruled in favor of the plaintiffs. The court rejected all of the defendants' procedural arguments against the court ruling on the case, and found wholly in the plaintiffs' favor on the meaning of the statutes that were the basis of the plaintiffs' claim. The court also ruled, based on the factual record the plaintiffs had compiled from the DPW's own documents and officials, that the current level of AFDC benefits (then $432/month, or $5,184/year, for a family of three) was legally inadequate to keep families in their homes. It further ruled that DPW had violated its legal duty to review the adequacy of its standards of assistance by only comparing AFDC benefits to various indices, like the federal poverty line, the consumer price index, and the increase in housing costs, rather than setting its own figure of adequacy.

While the declarations of law were all in the plaintiffs' favor, the court was restrained in its relief: It granted only the narrowest part of the injunction requested by the plaintiffs, ordering the welfare commissioner to develop a standard of assistance that was sufficient to enable AFDC families to bring up their children in their own homes, reserving judgment on the request for an order to pay or take all steps necessary to enable it to pay benefits at the increased level. The court stated that such an order would be "premature," because it could not "anticipate what the reactions of the Secretary of the Executive Office of Human Services, the Governor, or the Legislature will be when confronted with a specific dollar amount."[29]

The timing of the decision and the lack of an order regarding payment prevented the decision from having an impact on that year's AFDC appropriation, which had to be finalized within a few days and had already been voted on by both houses of the legislature. But whether merely from the efforts of the Up to Poverty campaign, or in addition from the pressure and publicity which the lawsuit had already yielded, the legislature in June 1986 enacted not only the 10 percent increase in AFDC benefits which the governor had proposed, but in addition a $25 per child increase in the annual clothing allowance and a $15/month rent supplement. In effect, this was 4 percent more than the governor had proposed for the 70 percent of recipients in private housing.

Despite the advocates' disappointment that the remarkably victorious superior court decision could have no immediate financial impact, there was a stunning result from the court's clear ruling in plaintiffs' favor while exercising restraint in its granting of relief: the administration decided to comply with the order to develop a new standard of adequacy, instead of appealing the superior court's decision. Two months later, the administration announced its new figures. It acknowledged that a family of three in private housing needed $11,117/year for minimal subsistence in Massachusetts— nearly $2,000 above the federal poverty line and approximately $5,000 above the then current level of AFDC benefits of $491/ month for a family of three in private housing! They also acknowledged that even this figure was inadequate for a family already homeless; obtaining new housing in the extremely tight Massachusetts housing market would require far more than the $474/month they were assuming for rent and utility costs.[30]

A new standard of adequacy was not the same as money in the pocket. But there was enormous hope that with this official acknowledgment that minimum subsistence in Massachusetts required even more than Up to Poverty, that executive and legislative action would follow. And at the least, it appeared that plaintiffs had gained the fuel of increased legitimacy for their political campaign.

Subsequent Court Action

At the same time at which defendants were appearing to give the nod of legitimacy to the plaintiffs' claims of the inadequacy of AFDC benefits and their causal link to family homelessness, however, the defendants concluded their report with the caveat that "Cash assistance is only one approach to meeting the basic needs of poor families, particularly their housing needs, and may not be as effective in the long run as other strategies." They made no promise to request an increase in benefits, and as the months went by, it appeared that despite the apparent potential of their report, the administration was not going to change its restrictive approach to AFDC benefit increases. By December 1986, no public figure had been announced for a proposed FY-1988 AFDC increase (to begin July 1, 1987), and the rumor was that the governor was planning to propose 4 percent—in complete disregard of the administration's own standard of adequacy.

In the face of this official stonewalling, the plaintiffs decided to seek further relief from the court. It asked the court to order the defendants to develop a plan for legislative appropriation requests sufficient at least to raise AFDC grants to the level of the standard budgets of assistance, and to ask the governor to submit a request for a supplemental appropriation for the current fiscal year, so that still another year would not go by without the court decision having some tangible impact on AFDC grants. The plaintiffs pointed out to the court that the defendants had failed to make any request yet for an increase based on their own report, and that the incidence of homeless families was continuing to increase at an alarming rate.

Once again, the defendants failed to take the court action very seriously. They believed that the court would not dare to tackle the difficult legal and political questions which would inevitably be raised by an order so directly impacting on appropriations. Once again, they were wrong. They failed to consider the extent to which Judge Charles M. Grabau was convinced of the harm that homelessness does to children—he termed the consequences "catastrophic"—and the degree to which he believed it was appropriate for the court to require the executive branch defendants to do their duty. As he later stated: "There is no more compelling statutory policy in need of enforcement than protecting families from homelessness—a phenomenon increasing in severity and frequency, largely due to inadequate public assistance."[31]

In his order on Plaintiffs' Motion for Further Relief, Judge Grabau went further than plaintiffs had even requested. He ordered the defendants to make their revised standards the new standard of need for AFDC and to increase benefits in an amount to be determined in their discretion "in accordance with" their revised standards. He also fashioned specific relief for homeless families, ordering that DPW provide sufficient financial assistance to enable families who had been in hotels, motels, or shelters more than 90 days to obtain nontransient housing.[32]

When the relief order was first issued, the governor and the press took the position that the order required the immediate expenditure of an additional $750 million (of which approximately half would be state funds) to increase AFDC benefits to the full amount of the revised standards. Although the plaintiffs argued that this was not what the order meant (as Judge Grabau later clarified), the inflammatory interpretation was in some ways the best public relations agent the plaintiffs could have had. The order got substantial local as well as national news coverage and led to numerous media requests to have spokespeople from the plaintiff organizations or the legal team on various talk shows and interview programs, with the attendant opportunity to do some significant public education on welfare issues.

However, there was a down side to all of this media attention, court victories, and revised standards. Legislators reported that they were getting substantial adverse constituent reaction to the idea of welfare families "deserving" to have more than $11,000 per year. Some legislators were extremely antagonized at what they saw as a court telling them what to do with regard to AFDC appropriations, and perhaps perversely, the energy of the Up to Poverty campaign was in some ways undercut, as people looked to the court to solve what seemed an intractable problem of persuading the legislature to enact increases at the 25 percent level to which the campaign was committed.

As the superior court enforcement order was stayed pending review by the state's highest court on defendants' appeal, another budget cycle passed without an effective order from the court. However, it is reasonably likely that just the bringing of the Motion for Further Relief resulted in raising the governor's requested AFDC increase for FY 1988 from the rumored 4 percent to the 6 percent increase he actually proposed. Whether due to the state's clearly identifying the additional costs faced by families in private housing, or just the constant emphasis on the unmet needs of AFDC families, of which the lawsuit was a part along with the broader campaign, the legislature raised the AFDC increase to 7 percent and added a further $25/month increase for families in private housing. Thus, AFDC benefits for the approximately 70 percent of the caseload in private housing went from $491/month for a family of three to $550/month, an increase of 12 percent. In addition, additional resources were targeted specifically at homeless families. For example, shortly after the superior court issued its January 5th order, the governor proposed allocating an additional $7.2 million for housing subsidies for homeless AFDC families, a recommendation which the legislature largely adopted in the FY 1988 budget. The state housing agency also obtained from the federal government 500 housing vouchers, all of which, contrary to the agency's initial intention, were directed for use by homeless AFDC families. Significantly, these increases occurred in a climate of much-restricted revenues compared with prior years.

The decision of the Massachusetts Supreme Judicial Court (SJC), largely upholding the decisions of the superior court in the case, although not the judge's orders for relief, was only announced one month prior to the writing of this chapter. Thus, it is still too soon to tell what its effect will be. However, certain things are clear.

The SJC has put its considerable prestige, in a unanimous opinion, behind a sweeping interpretation of the state laws relied upon by the plaintiffs, calling the 1913 law "seminal legislation," and stating, "Today's emergency shelters may have more than a casual resemblance to almshouses whose use for needy families with children our remedial legislation was designed to end." Further, the court established the "acute problem" of homelessness as an indisputable fact. It included lengthy statements in its opinion about the "devastating effects" of homelessness on AFDC families, and about the particular harmful effects of life in hotels, motels, and shelters. The court also came down squarely against the legal validity of the current level of AFDC benefits, as had the superior court. It ruled that not only was the benefit level legally inadequate, but also that as a matter of fact, inadequate AFDC benefits cause homelessness, and that DPW has a duty to set a dollar standard of adequacy which is sufficient to keep families in their homes.[33]

With regard to relief, the SJC decision declares three obligations of DPW: (1) to update the standards of adequacy annually; (2) if there is any shortfall between current grants and the legally required standard of adequacy—i.e., the amount necessary to keep families in their own homes—to ask the legislature "for an adequate appropriation or for some other solution to the problem"; and (3) "to prevent, as far as reasonably possible, the use of transient housing by AFDC families." The updating of the standards is unlikely to be controversial, at least after this first year, and thus will provide a regular, easily enforceable means of obtaining an indisputable target for increases in assistance. While this order does not have the immediate consequence of expanding the number of families eligible for AFDC which upholding the Superior Court's order on the standard of need would have had, it has the same hoped-for political effect. It regularly requires the legislature to pay attention to a tangible figure expressing actual need, and should result over time in more substantial and rapid increases in benefit levels.

On the appropriations request and homeless relief issues, the SJC decision empowers the superior court to take further steps in terms of injunctive relief if defendants do not comply with their duties as declared in the opinion. It is premature to determine whether such further steps will be necessary, and if so, how far the court will go. However, it is clear that while the SJC was mindful of the constitutional prerogative of the legislature in determining the level of appropriations, it has already taken a very strong stand on the duties of the executive branch and the power

of the judiciary to enforce those duties, notwithstanding the ultimate determination of appropriations by the legislature.

Thus, the court's strong command to the executive branch was
an enormous defeat for the defendants' basic legal and political
position in the case: that they were absolved of any responsibility
for the nexus between inadequate AFDC benefits and homelessness, as only the legislature set the level of benefits.

Implications of the Court's Actions

Although an order to the executive branch to seek appropriations
is still a large step removed from the ultimate desired result of
increasing AFDC benefits, it is probably the only relief that a
court could constitutionally order consistent with separation of
powers principles, as a court cannot generally order the legislature
to appropriate funds. While an executive request is no guarantee
of legislative success, there is generally sufficient legislative deference to executive ordering of priorities that the higher the executive request for an AFDC increase, the higher the likely result.
Thus, the relief ordered by the court holds enormous potential for
assisting in accomplishing the aims which plaintiffs originally
sought, as well as being even a more potent tool for immediate
relief for homeless families than plaintiffs had anticipated.

Furthermore, there are positive consequences of the court's
relief being framed as an order to the executive to seek appropriations, rather than a direct order to pay. The legislature's sensitivity
to any breach of its prerogatives should be assuaged, making it
more possible for the court decision to act as a forceful lobbying
tool with the legislature about the long-standing public policies at
issue. Furthermore, it makes clear to members of the Up to
Poverty campaign that the lawsuit does not eliminate the need for
a forceful lobbying and grass-roots campaign. Indeed, the court
decision focuses attention again on the ultimate need to persuade
the legislature, both to increase funding, and to preserve the law,
as the plaintiffs' newly declared "rights" are wholly vulnerable to
legislative rescission. (However, we believe that the spotlight and
legitimacy cast on the statutes relied on by plaintiffs by the SJC
decision will, as a practical matter, make it politically unfeasible to
rescind the statutes.) Thus, the Up to Poverty campaign should be
strengthened by the increased legitimacy it should be able to
derive from the SJC decision. At the same time the campaign will
hopefully have its momentum reinvigorated. It is clear that where
increased welfare benefits are concerned, an "elite" legal strategy

can only be an accompaniment to, and not a substitute for, a broad-based movement.

Finally, the Massachusetts SJC decision illustrates the greater potential which state courts may hold, in contrast to federal courts, for issuing orders which relate directly to appropriations. State statutes may contain normative, need-related language, unlike the federal Social Security Act. State courts do not suffer from the further hindrance of federalism concerns and are more likely to be able and willing to give full force and effect to such broad statutory norms, at least to the extent of orders to the executive to seek sufficient appropriations. While federal courts issuing decisions expanding benefits eligibility were always careful to remind states that they need not increase their total expenditures, the state courts can at least exert significant pressure in the struggle to create a true, net expansion of benefits.

Thus, the state courts are the most likely avenue to "welfare reform" through the courts in areas where the state courts are reasonably responsive to the claims of the nonprivileged, where state laws contain broad, normative language concerning need, and where legal advocates can work jointly with grass-roots movements or coalitions.

Conclusion

In the first phase of welfare litigation in the mid-1960s to mid-1970s, the courts played a very significant role in expanding eligibility for welfare benefits and reducing arbitrariness, by creating the concept of entitlement to certain forms of public assistance and by subjecting government programs for the poor to the rule of law. While the broad, normative language which characterized the federal Social Security Act made these expansive interpretations possible, although by no means inevitable, the accommodations of the Social Security Act and the federal courts to the states' sovereign interests in limiting and controlling their expenditures limited the ability of welfare advocates in this first phase to use the courts to increase the level of benefits. As the welfare rights movement and the broad-based political support for expanded welfare benefits waned by the mid-1970s, the judicial gains were significantly undercut, though not entirely reversed, by substantive amendments to the Social Security Act and the erosion of the value of AFDC benefits by inflation.

In litigation based on broadly framed, need-oriented provisions of state law, the state, rather than federal courts, is likely to be the advantageous forum for expanding and increasing welfare benefits through the courts, although such opportunities are likely only to exist in some states. To be successful, and to actually obtain the increased funds which courts may declare are required, such efforts are likely to require the support of organized groups or coalitions. Thus, the courts have in the past, and can in the future, play a significant role in "welfare reform," but only if court actions are one element of a multipronged effort.

Endnotes

1. See, e.g., Joel Handler, *Social Movements and the Legal System: A Theory of Law Reform and Social Change* (New York: Academic Press, 1978); and Handler, "Continuing Relationships and the Administrative Process: Social Welfare," *Wisconsin Law Review* (1985): 687.

2. See Frances Fox Piven and Richard Cloward, *Regulating the Poor: The Functions of Public Welfare* (New York: Vintage Books, 1971), pp. 290–92.

3. See Edward V. Sparer, "Social Welfare Law Testing," *The Practical Lawyer* 12, no. 4 (April 1966); Charles A. Reich, "Individual Rights and Social Welfare: The Emerging Legal Issues," *Yale Law Journal* 74 (1965): 1245; Reich, "Midnight Welfare Searches and Social Security Act," *Yale Law Journal* 72 (1963): 1347; Jacobus ten Broek, *California's Dual System of Family Law: Its Origin, Development, and Present Status* (Berkeley, University of California, Department of Political Science, 1965), Reprint Series No. 23.

4. For materials on the welfare rights movement, see Nick Kotz and Mary Lynn Kotz, *A Passion for Equality: George A. Wiley and the Movement* (New York: W. W. Norton, 1977), pp. 181–328; Piven and Cloward, *Regulating the Poor*, pp. 285–340; and Piven and Cloward, *Poor People's Movements: Why They Succeed, How They Fail* (New York: Pantheon Books, 1977), pp. 264–362. The discussion in this chapter is drawn from all three sources.

5. Sylvia A. Law, "Women, Work, Welfare, and the Preservation of Patriarchy," *University of Pennsylvania Law Review* 131 (1983): 1249, 1268.

6. Piven and Cloward, *Regulating the Poor*, pp. 306–34.

7. Excerpt from transcript of hearing in *Smith* v. *Board*, 259 F.Supp. 423 (D.D.C. 1966), quoted in Edward V. Sparer, "Welfare Reform: Which Way Is Forward," *NLADA Briefcase* 35 (Sept. 1978): 110, 113.

8. Charles Reich, "The New Property," *Yale Law Journal* 73 (1964): 773; Reich, "Individual Rights and Social Welfare," *Yale Law Journal* (1965): 1255.

9. Ibid., 1256.

10. *Goldberg* v. *Kelly*, 397 U.S. 254, 262 (1970).

11. For example, in *Brown* v. *Board of Education*, 347 U.S. 483 (1954), the Supreme Court held that segregated public schools violate the right of black and other minority children to equal protection of the laws under the Fourteenth Amendment to the U.S. Constitution. In 1963, in *Gideon* v.

Wainwright, 372 U.S. 335, the Supreme Court held that the Sixth Amendment required the appointment of counsel for indigent defendants in state court criminal cases. Criminal defendants won expanded rights under the Fifth Amendment guarantee against self-incrimination in *Miranda* v. *Arizona,* 384 U.S. 436 (1966). The right of privacy found constitutional protection in *Griswold* v. *Connecticut,* 381 U.S. 479 (1965), which was then the basis of *Roe* v. *Wade,* 410 U.S. 113 (1973), which legalized abortion.

12. See *Bowen* v. *Gilliard,* 107 S. Ct. 3008, 3018 (1987); *Brown* v. *Board of Education,* 347 U.S. 483 (1954); *Graham* v. *Richardson,* 403 U.S. 365 (1971); *Westcott* v. *Califano,* 443 U.S. 76, 89 (1979) (women as quasi-suspect class); *Mills* v. *Habluetzel,* 456 U.S. 91, 99 (1982) (illegitimacy).

13. *Bowen* v. *Gilliard,* 107 S. Ct. at 3017, quoting from *Dandridge* v. *Williams.* This decision, rejecting an equal protection challenge to the 1984 amendment to the AFDC statute which added the "sibling deeming" rule, requiring all siblings and half-siblings living in the same house to be in the AFDC unit, even if they have sufficient independent income from child support or another source, is the Court's most recent refusal to apply the equal protection clause to invalidate an aspect of the AFDC program. In his dissent, Justice Brennan based his reasoning in large part on the increasing prevalence of single-parent families in American society. In the social welfare area, the minimal scrutiny equal protection doctrine is rooted in *Dandridge* v. *Williams,* 397 U.S. 471, 485 (1970).

14. *King* v. *Smith,* 277 F. Supp. 31, 39 (M.D. Ala. 1967).

15. *Shapiro* v. *Thompson,* 394 U.S. at 633 (1969).

16. *Dandridge* v. *Williams,* 397 U.S. at 485–6 (1970).

17. *Jefferson* v. *Hackney,* 406 U.S. 535 (1971). Nationally, as of 1979, slightly over half of AFDC families were white. U.S. House of Representatives, Committee on Ways and Means, *Children in Poverty,* 1985, 473. Based on data drawn from a quality control sample rather than individual surveys, in 1983, 43 percent of AFDC families were black, 41 percent were white non-Hispanic, and 13 percent were Hispanic. William P. O'Hare, *America's Welfare Population: Who Gets What?* (Washington, D.C.: Population Reference Bureau, 1987), p. 7.

18. *Westcott* v. *Califano,* 443 U.S. 89 (1979).

19. *King* v. *Smith,* 392 U.S. at 316 (1968).

20. In 1981, as part of wholesale revisions in the AFDC statute proposed by President Reagan and enacted in the first Omnibus Budget Reconciliation Act, Congress eliminated the broadly framed work-related expense prescription, and substituted the narrow requirement that states "disregard from . . . earned income . . . the first $75 of total of such earned income" per month. 42 U.S.C. §602(a)(8)(A)(ii). In *Heckler* v. *Turner,* 470 U.S. 184 (1985), the Court ruled that by enacting this language, Congress intended to depart from the available income principle, and therefore that taxes and other mandatory withholding were encompassed within the $75 disregard, regardless of its inadequacy in fact. Congress has also altered the available income and resources rule in recent years by adding specific language concerning what resources are to be counted and how, and requiring the deeming of income, regardless of actual availability, from a stepparent in the home.

21. Jerry L. Mashaw, "The Management Side of Due Process," *Cornell Law Review* 59 (1974): 772, 784.

22. *Goldberg v. Kelly*, 397 U.S. 254 (1970).

23. HHS, Quarterly Public Assistance Statistics, Jan.–Mar. 1985, "Requests for Hearings in AFDC, Fiscal Year 1985," pp. 26–34.

24. *Rosado v. Wyman*, 397 U.S. 397 (1970).

25. State statutes, particularly in the general assistance area, often incorporate broadly framed state or local duties to "relieve and support" the indigent, or to provide aid which is "sufficient for decency and health," which state courts have been willing to enforce to require increases in benefits. See, e.g., *City and County of San Francisco v. Superior Court*, 57 Cal. App. 44, 128 Cal. Rptr. 712 (1976), *enforced by* 78 Cal. App. 3d 51, 144 Cal. Rptr. 64 (1978) (there has been substantial subsequent litigation in California concerning general assistance benefit levels, which are set by counties); *State ex. rel. Ventrone v. Birkel*, 54 Ohio St.2d 461 (1978); *Villa v. Arrizabalaga*, 86 Nev. 137, 466 P.2d 663, 665 (1970). The West Virginia Supreme Court has interpreted a state law concerning adult protective services to prohibit the state from excluding the homeless from eligibility for these services, regardless of insufficient appropriations. *Hodge v. Ginsberg*, 303 S.E.2d 245 (W.Va. 1983).

26. 400 Mass. 806 (1987). I have been one of the lawyers for the plaintiffs in this case since its inception, and have been lead counsel in all direct litigation. In addition, in my role leading the welfare law work for Greater Boston Legal Services since 1978, I have personal knowledge of the recipient groups and the surrounding political circumstances. Unless otherwise specified, the material which follows is drawn from my personal experience and files, and/ or the record of the case.

27. The Emergency Assistance program is authorized by 42 U.S.C. §606(e). States which opt to participate in this 50 percent federally reimbursable program are substantially free to determine what types of emergencies they will cover. See *Quern v. Mandley*, 436 U.S. 725 (1978). States can only receive federal reimbursement for expenditures authorized within one 30-day period in any 12 months, but in Massachusetts federal reimbursement has been obtained for up to 90 days of emergency shelter authorized within a 30-day period.

28. My co-lead attorney in the case since the beginning has been Lucy A. Williams of the Massachusetts Law Reform Institute. Also actively involved have been Karen Slaney, Belle Soloway, Lauren Curry, and Marjorie Heins. (All the attorneys worked for legal services programs in the Boston area except Ms. Heins, who is a staff counsel with the Civil Liberties Union of Massachusetts.)

29. Findings, Rulings and Order dated June 26, 1986, at 15, Suffolk Superior Court Civil No. 80109. The original defendants in the case were the Governor, the Secretary of Human Services, and the Commissioner of DPW. The Court granted the defendants' motion to dismiss the Governor on technical grounds, but rejected their other challenges of lack of jurisdiction.

30. See Defendants' Report of Standard Budgets of Assistance, filed August 29, 1986. In addition to the standard for families living in private housing in

metropolitan Boston, there was a middle standard for families living in private housing in nonmetropolitan Boston of $10,373 per year, and a lowest standard of $7,745 per year for families living in public or subsidized housing. In 1987, the standards were increased to account for inflation, and the public housing figure was brought up to slightly in excess of the poverty line.

31. Memorandum of Decision and Interim Order of Judgment on Plaintiffs' Motion for Further Relief, January 5, 1987 at 5. It is fair to say that Judge Grabau had no prior judicial reputation on social welfare issues. He had initially been appointed to the bench by the prior, conservative governor, after having worked in the public defender's office. He was promoted to the superior court by the current Governor Dukakis. He was, however, the first Hispanic judge appointed in Massachusetts (he is from Cuba) and had a history of working on issues of importance to the Hispanic community. It was pure chance that he was the judge who heard the original preliminary injunction motion on the case.

32. Judge Grabau set the starting period for relief for homeless families at 90 days because that was the period of federal reimbursement for emergency shelter, not because he thought it was acceptable that families live under the conditions he found "catastrophic" for that period.

33. The one issue on which the plaintiffs could be considered to have lost in the SJC was on whether the defendants' new standards of adequacy also had to operate as the official standard of need for AFDC, as Judge Grabau had ordered. While the SJC acknowledged that this had been the intended result under the substantive laws at issue, the court ruled that the legislature had lawfully superseded these statutes by setting the standard of need in the budget in the past several years. To have ruled for plaintiffs on this issue would have precipitated at least a minor budget crisis, as the added cost of the increased standard of need was estimated to be between $15 and $150 million annually, depending on how the state chose to treat families' outside income in determining their benefit amount. There was no appropriation for such an additional sum.

Chapter 8

FEDERAL POLICY-MAKING AND FAMILY ISSUES

Anne L. Radigan

In the preceding chapters the case has been made for instituting measures to aid single-parent mothers. This chapter will look at how the federal policy-making process works, or fails to work, to improve women's lives. An examination of the tensions that affect this process—the tug and pull of opposing viewpoints and political forces—is followed by two case studies of the making of national policies for women. Drawing on these examples, the conclusion suggests that while various factors frustrate large-scale policy-making, incremental policy steps for women do add up to significant net gains.

Fragmentation and Incremental Gains

The actions of the federal government, when dealing with women's issues (the heading under which single-parent mothers fall), tend to be both fragmented and sporadic. The policies that result, at least in recent years, are generally modest in scope.

There are two practical reasons for fragmentation in policy-making for women. First, the breadth of the feminist agenda is such that piecemeal and seemingly random attention to it is inevitable: decisionmakers, overwhelmed by the volume of proposals, often take blind stabs at it, while the groups that support the agenda often have different priorities within their broad boundaries. Second, the policy-making process, frequently bogged down in the ongoing operation of the government, does not lend itself to a systematic consideration of wholesale agendas.

The sporadic nature of policy-making has intensified during this decade as decisionmakers respond to the ups and downs of women's electoral power. Women's issues seem to go in and out of fashion with remarkable speed in Washington. When the government does act, the effort is usually modest and the scope narrow. The incremental pattern[1] of gains for the women's agenda, established in the 1980s, can be traced to several factors.

Foremost, hostility toward the feminist agenda by the Reagan administration has made it difficult for policymakers to reach consensus on the individual recommendations. Absent a general declaration of support from the executive branch, the work of establishing policies for women has been largely left to individual members of the legislative branch. These members were initially hampered in their efforts, not only by the lack of unifying purpose but also by a Senate in control of Republicans mostly sympathetic to the administration's priorities. To avoid provoking large demonstrations of opposition to its work, feminists purposefully promote small-scale issues in order to keep the agenda progressing. With each incremental victory, a path toward more large-scale policy-making is prepared.

Second, the budget deficit greatly inhibits measures that would create or expand federally supported programs. Those legislators who attempt to establish new services face the difficulty of locating the scant federal resources to finance them. The choices are limited: siphoning funds from other programs—from the domestic, not the military, arena—or raising taxes. A matter of priorities comes into play, as legislators resist new proposals in order to defend the status quo or resuscitate those programs that have fallen victim to the budget ax.

The third factor contributing to the incremental progress of the women's agenda is antifederalism. This notion basically rejects government solutions to social problems. The antigovernment spirit is less pervasive now than at the beginning of the 1980s, when President Reagan announced in his inaugural address, "Government is not the solution to our problem; it is the problem." All the same, the laissez-faire attitude planted a lingering doubt and discomfort in the minds of many policymakers toward instituting new federal authority.

These influences have a conservative impact on an already conservative process. Nevertheless, women's issues do make progress in Washington. The national women's groups have identified and defined important issues for the attention of policymakers. These groups further provide both expert information and a critical perspective on major national issues, such as the budget and tax code. Whether their objectives succeed or not, feminists are an indispensable part of the policy-making process today.

How Policies Are Established

Civil Rights Era and the Moral Crusade

The first strike against gender-based discrimination came during the civil rights crusade and directly from the executive branch, unlike the rule today. In fact, the government acted before the modern women's movement was even organized. It is true that the initial policies represented only a glancing commitment to equal opportunity for women, since the Equal Pay Act and Title VII of the Civil Rights Act were not conceived with women's interests foremost in mind.[2] Nonetheless, the federal government was in a righteous frame of mind: discrimination against minorities, and women, was immoral. The government went on record in support of women's rights and large-scale efforts to secure them.

From that point on, the drive to make policy switched to the emerging women's movement. Discrimination against women was so pervasive, particularly in the work force, that subsequent federal provisions were necessary, and so an agenda was drafted. By the early 1970s, polls show that public opinion generally approved of the new feminist agenda and broad government authority to remedy past wrongs.

As a consequence, in the space of just 15 years, the federal government instituted a remarkable series of wide-ranging policies for women:

- The Equal Pay Act of 1963 stated that men and women who perform the same jobs must be paid the same wages.
- Title VII of the Civil Rights Act of 1964 outlawed employment discrimination against persons on the basis of race, color, religion, national origin, or sex.
- In 1972, the Equal Employment Opportunity Commission (EEOC) was given new power to enforce the Equal Pay Act and Title VII. By the beginning of the 1970s, it became clear that the civil rights statutes were meaningless without special enforcement authority.
- Title IX of the Education Amendments of 1972 prohibited discrimination against women and girls in education.

- The Equal Rights Amendment (ERA), also approved by Congress in 1972 and sent to the states for ratification, declares that equal rights under the law shall not be denied nor abridged by the United States or any state on account of sex. Seven years later, when the ERA was only three states shy of becoming the 27th Amendment to the Constitution, Congress acted to extend the ratification period another five years. (This measure, endorsed by President Carter, was in many ways more controversial than the ERA itself.)
- The Equal Credit Opportunity Act of 1974 prohibited discrimination in consumer and business credit on the basis of sex or marital status.
- Finally, the Pregnancy Discrimination Act of 1978 amended the Civil Rights Act to outlaw employment discrimination based on pregnancy.

Not to diminish the efforts of the feminist lobby, it is safe to say that these achievements owe a great deal to the activist climate of the times. However, the times were not without serious contention and defeat. Probably the biggest failure of the era was President Nixon's veto of the Comprehensive Child Development Act of 1971. This landmark legislation would have provided day care for all children, but the chief executive rejected this "communal" approach to child care in favor of "family-centered" care.

Still, during much of the 1960s and 1970s, the executive and legislative branches of government shared a moral vision for improving women's status in the United States. This sense of purpose issued in bits and pieces still added up to a coherent national policy. Except for some notable spottiness during the Nixon years, the premise of feminism and the women's platform was generally accepted and progressed during Democratic and Republican administrations alike.

President Nixon, when vetoing the day care bill, echoed a grave concern of conservatives: government policies that "encourage" women, especially mothers, to work outside the home threaten the traditional family model. Traditional families perpetuate traditional values or morals. Therefore, government action that hastens the decline of the family hastens moral breakdown as well. A movement took shape to argue this view and burst into flower with the success of the Equal Rights Amendment and the 1973 *Roe* v. *Wade* decision upholding abortion rights. This countermovement identified these two issues, and feminism in general, as concrete evidence of moral corruption.

By the mid-1970s, Eagle Forum founder Phyllis Schlafly took

the fight to Washington, where she announced that the federal government should be in the business of promoting only those initiatives aimed at preserving the traditional family unit. Alleging that feminism is antifamily, antihomemaker, and antimale, the Eagle Forum roused a vocal constituency to fight abortion, day care, domestic violence prevention, and a number of other issues viewed as contrary to traditional values. Thus, policymakers faced a moral backlash against their policies for women. The majority of these bureaucrats and legislators were not persuaded by the countermovement's call for a return to traditional roles and values. But the conservative tenor of this call comported with a growing air of conservatism across the nation.

The antifeminist movement did not succeed in thwarting the last of the large-scale government policies for women—the ERA extension and the Pregnancy Discrimination Act—but it did inject its moral view into other issues of the time. By 1980, the competing values of equality and traditionalism created something of a policy impasse. The larger initiatives, obviously, were bigger targets. For instance, a six-year battle by feminists to establish a national strategy for protecting against family violence—wife battering, mostly—failed at the 11th hour to win congressional approval. Conservatives charged that government had no business to intrude on private matters of the family, nor certainly to spend the proposed $65 million for three years to do so. The proposal died.

On the other hand, at this time, the concept of marriage as an economic partnership achieved a measure of legal recognition. The pension programs of foreign service officers and CIA operatives were amended to entitle divorced spouses to a pro-rata share. While these particular pension-sharing laws may serve a small proportion of American women, the underlying theory has gained a foothold in national policy-making: the contributions of nonearning spouses have an economic valuation. Many feminists have been pushing this theory further, so that the work of homemakers may be computed as part of the nation's gross national product (GNP).

Fragmentation of government policies for women intensified from about this point, not merely because of one setback for feminists, but because a new administration came to power and renounced government activism on behalf of equal opportunity.

Policy-making in an Adversarial Era

By the beginning of this decade, America was in the throes of what U.S. Rep. Patricia Schroeder (D-Col.) calls a demographic revolution. More than half of all women were working outside the home.

The percentage of women heading families rose dramatically. The nation's general economic pressures increasingly required wives as well as husbands to earn an income to support their households.

As the demographics evolved, so did the feminist agenda. The need for civil rights remedies had been addressed; now the time was ripe for economic remedies, bread and butter issues such as pension rights for former spouses and strengthened child support enforcement. The emphasis on economic equity not only served a practical purpose; it helped to defuse the animus of conservatives toward the agenda. Who can be against fairness, after all? Equity had a softer edge than equality.

The maturation of the women's movement and the broadening of its agenda coincided with the arrival in Washington of the Reagan administration. The new administration rode into power on a platform—every bit as radical as it perceived the women's agenda to be—which decried government involvement in domestic matters. It charged the Great Society with great failure.

The administration, capitalizing on the resurgence of conservatism in the country, moved quickly to alienate the human interest community. While it did not make an official declaration per se regarding women's issues, its attitude was clear: feminists were a pernicious special interest, a fringe movement, bent on securing government setasides for a "rowdy minority."[3] The general public appears all too willing to see special interests as their enemies, yet individual citizens are likely to share concerns with any number of special interest organizations. The President, however, made these groups—at least the ones he disagreed with—appear inimical to the political process. In reality, they are essential to the process, providing a voice for a population that is not otherwise represented. Chief executives, less pervious to special interest politics than legislators, tend to take a dim view of these organizations. President Wilson remarked in 1912 that "The Government of the United States is the foster-child of the special interests."

The administration's vision of a drastically reduced centralized government was implicit in the federal budget and other official directives. The 1981 budget request, sent to Congress for action, proposed to eliminate or weaken every social program on the lawbooks. Women's support services were especially hard hit, from legal services to maternal and child health. Appropriations for enforcement agencies were reduced. Regulations, such as affirmative action, came under fire. The courts were petitioned to strike down or limit previous broad-based decisions for women and minorities.

Although Congress resisted rubber-stamping the budget policy in total, the President's message was understood: the federal government was no longer to be the instigator of social reforms. That would be left to the discretion of the states or the private sector. The moral vision of the administration was that of laissez faire. Any source but the government or the federal courts would best serve the social interests of the nation.

With the federal government now framed as the nation's problem rather than its salvation, women's groups could not expect the executive branch to formulate policies on their behalf. Out of necessity, they focused their attentions on the legislative branch.[4] However, the U.S. Congress is not uniquely situated to carry out broad policy statements. It is comprised of 535 individuals with regional concerns foremost in mind. Unlike the political homogeneity of an administration, Congress is divided by partisanship, and then further divided into two separate houses. These divisions were greatly exacerbated by the fact that the Reagan election severely deepened partisan rivalries, and the Senate fell into Republican control (the House has held a Democratic majority in all but four years since the New Deal).

The climate in Washington, then, would appear very cool for progressing the feminist agenda, regardless of its toned-down message of economic equity. Unable to pursue its broader proposals through executive branch avenues, feminists entered the labyrinth of the legislative process. The fragmented fashion in which this process operates necessarily imposed fragmentation on the agenda.

Shifting Sands of Electoral Politics. This apparently aimless, motiveless process is really anything but. Legislators respond to electoral heft much more readily than bureaucrats. This is true particularly in the House of Representatives, where 435 members must campaign for reelection every two years. A member's voting record must be defended every two years. This tends to make them shun acting on legislative proposals that elicit large outpourings of organized opposition. In the case of the women's agenda, many of its individual recommendations drew serious fire from the business community and moral indignation from the far right. Without a supportive administration to lean back on when their votes were challenged, members took a grave risk in promoting the feminist agenda. It should be noted, nevertheless, that many liberal Democrats and Republicans did take the risk.

The Gender Gap. By 1982, pollsters had identified a phenomenon called the "gender gap"—the difference between the issues that count with men and women voters—which favored Democratic over GOP contenders. The perceived electoral power of women emboldened legislators to look at the agenda for proposals that would win feminist favor back home. Even the Reagan administration sought to make amends for its initial hostility.

There was a great deal to choose from on the agenda and federal decisionmakers did not respond to any particular sense of priority. Rather, they chose to act on those items that could develop consensus the quickest (in time for the next round of elections). This is why, during the 98th Congress, strengthened child support enforcement and private pension reform led the list of 17 new laws for women. The administration threw its weight behind both.

Feminist Priorities. Child support and pension issues are certainly matters of urgency, but the priorities of the feminist community at the time were passage of the newly reintroduced Equal Rights Amendment and a bill to overturn the Supreme Court's ruling that limited enforcement of Title IX. Both failed, although by poignantly close margins. Had these two issues been made unequivocally clear to legislators as the priorities of voting women, perhaps they would have succeeded. The receptive 98th Congress was certainly the best opportunity to move these issues—although the President would have vetoed them.

But perhaps this was an impossible situation. The executive branch wields enormous influence with partisans belonging to the legislative branch, and it strenuously opposed the ERA and the Title IX bill (known today as the Civil Rights Restoration Act). Both garnered less GOP support than Democratic. Women's issues became more politically polarized than ever due to this fact.

The crushing defeat of Walter Mondale and Geraldine Ferraro in 1984 appeared to be a national repudiation of the ticket's supporters. Thus ended, for the time being, the meteoric rise of the women's vote. Even many Democrats pulled away from special interest groups, pilloried by sympathetic and unsympathetic observers alike as to the cause of the Mondale/Ferraro downfall.

Expertise in Policy-making. Events of the 98th Congress, with its almost frantic attention to the feminist agenda, may not be experienced again, but feminists nonetheless made a lasting connection with policymakers. They proved to be a reliable source of expert information and an effective promoter of ideas. In other words, women's groups are an institution, indispensable to the process of making national policies.

Reform of the federal tax code, for instance, which reduced by as much as 60 percent the tax burden on low-income earners, owed a great deal to the efforts of the women's groups and its allies. Single heads-of-household, in particular, won new recognition from policymakers as having special economic concerns. This notice would not have occurred without the perspective provided by the Coalition on Women and Taxes, a consortium of women's groups. It should be noted that policymakers did not embrace the entire perspective of the coalition, and as a result the overall results for women under the tax reform were somewhat mixed.[5] So in this single example of policy-making for women, fragmentation and incrementalism are graphically evident.

Policy-making Strategies Today

The less-government philosophy of the Reagan administration may be losing ground, as the administration itself winds down, but it has left an imprint on policymakers of all political stripes. The massive federal deficit also haunts would-be champions of new federal programs. Together, these two factors have dampened the enthusiasm of many legislators to the federally run social programs so popular just ten years ago.

This is a tentative time for legislators, who are trying to fathom the temper of the public in the dawning post-Reagan era. Already, child care appears to be breaking through members' reserve, as striking new proposals have been introduced recently to support and increase day care services. However, the possibility that these bills will become law immediately is remote. Differences over spending allocations on day care have yet to be resolved.

The significant fact is that these bills have been introduced in the Senate—the deliberative, reactive body—and by the individuals most likely to get the proposals passed. The more striking proposal, known as the ABC bill (the Act for Better Child Care Services), has bipartisan co-sponsorship, led by Senators Christopher Dodd (D-Conn.) and John Chafee (R-R.I.); a companion bill pends in the House. The ABC bill would authorize $2.5 billion per year, with state matching fundings of 20 percent, to subsidize day care for poor families and improve the quality of child care for all families. Senator Ted Kennedy (D-Mass.), a leading spokesman of congressional Democrats, recently introduced a bill providing $4.25 billion over 3 years to finance nationwide day care for all 4-year-olds. The legislation also requires matching funds from states. Most significantly, conservative Senator Orrin Hatch (R-Utah) has sponsored a third day care measure directing that $875 million over 3 years in incentive money be directed to states to establish local child care programs.

Even last year these proposals would have appeared unlikely—unlikely to have been introduced by their sponsors in the first place, and unlikely to gather serious attention. Day care, however, is emerging as a campaign issue dear to grown baby boomers.

Interestingly, the dominant characteristic of the day care proposals is the emphasis on state sharing of program costs, an acknowledgment of the limitations of federal resources. The price tags are high, regardless, but one must keep in mind that the legislation merely authorizes the spending of these sums. Actual appropriations, should any of these bills become law, are apt to be much lower.

The imprint of the Reagan years is easily discernible in these and other social policy recommendations with serious pretentions. Even staunch liberals have turned away, over the last few years, from new social welfare proposals that would create or expand government bureaucracy. The *Washington Post* reported in 1987 on this trend:

> *[But] Reagan's concept of a more limited federal government, reinforced by continuously high federal deficits, has been embraced by Democrats to a degree that would seem unimaginable only a decade ago. Many of the broad themes that Reagan articulated, especially in his most successful years, have become part of the mainstream of American politics—for Democrats no less than Republicans. [March 9, 1987]*

Beside cost-sharing, the other dominant strategy of policy-minded lawmakers in the looming post-Reagan era is the "marketplace" solution. This strategy directs the private sector to provide certain benefits, such as health insurance or parental leave. The new "low-cost social justice" envisions a central role for the government, but without government spending. As Sen. Kennedy noted in 1987, "America does not have to spend more to do more."

This vision has won considerable approval among congressional sources, but the "marketplace solutions" are not without organized opposition. Business interests are vehemently against government-mandated benefits for employees, in principle as well as practice. With American companies facing a grave threat from overseas competition, new burdens to their competitive edge are viewed harshly by the U.S. Chamber of Commerce and its allies.

Women's issues are not only women's issues anymore, and this reality will help to deflect criticism from businesses, conservatives, or others. The women's agenda reflects this fact. It is populated by proposals that would affect a range of individuals, women and men alike. Mandated health insurance, for example, benefits all workers regardless of gender. It is especially important to women, many of whom work for small businesses that do not offer such benefits.

Factors Contributing to Successful Family Bills

The strategies and dynamics of the last eight years reveal several points about how policies for women succeed today.

Role Equity and Role Change. Political scientist Marian Lief Palley identified the tension between "role equity" and "role change" in feminist legislation:

> *Role equity calls for the extension to women of rights that are now enjoyed only by men. Issues relating to this are presented as relatively narrow in their implications; they permit policymakers to seek uncontroversial, low-cost advantage with feminist groups and voters. . . . By contrast, role change issues appear to alter the dependent roles of women as wives, mothers, and homemakers. This, in turn, raises for some people the possibility of greater sexual freedom, independence, and the transformation of existing values.*[6]

Private pension reform is an example of role equity, the ERA of role change.

Palley's definition of role equity underscores separate factors that deserve additional mention. Low cost proposals are central to success, unless a major demonstration of public support overcomes fiscal reservations. The Senate day care bills will need just such a sign of approval. Noncontroversial proposals also beg the obvious, but the point is that legislation requires momentum to make it through the law-making process. If momentum is impeded by organized displays of opposition, then the legislation is in jeopardy. Finally, the limited scope or narrow focus of a proposal helps to keep the matter well defined in the minds of lawmakers. It also suggests that the matter will be low cost and noncontroversial.

So, while legislators may be guilty of choosing modest initiatives for action, feminists are equally culpable for providing them with plenty of bite-sized morsels. However, small gains are preferable to no gains at all, and they keep moving the general momentum behind the women's agenda.

A Champion to Walk the Labyrinth. One last point must be observed. As already mentioned, the legislative process is labyrinthian. Potentially, 535 individuals have a chance to put their imprint on a single bill. Several committees in both houses will scour the issue. And then, voting may be held up for weeks or months as other, more essential business crowds the congressional schedule. What this means is this: a successful family bill must have a champion, usually its sponsor, who will make a thorough commitment to promote the proposal through every turn of the maze. The sponsor and the organizations that endorse the bill must stay the course, no matter how long the course may run.

When they do, the progress of the issue at hand takes on an inexorable quality, and success is, if not assured, at least more promising.

Case Studies in the Policy-making Process

In taking a closer look at how feminist policy recommendations have, or have not, become law, the 98th and 99th Congresses (1983–84, 1985–86) offer fertile territory. During the former period, more was achieved for women's equity than in any other two-year period of our government save the 92nd Congress (1971–72). The latter period witnessed the generally chilly aftermath of the 1984 elections.

For this examination, the Child Support Enforcement Amendments of 1984 (P.L. 98-378) and the Equitable Pay Practices Act are good representations of the tensions that surround women's issues and policy-making. The Child Support Enforcement Amendments achieved universal acclaim, championed by politicians across the philosophical spectrum. The Federal Equitable Pay Practices Act, on the other hand, suffered the extremes of political controversy, passing the House of Representatives twice, only to die from inattention in the Republican-controlled Senate.

There is one generic point about congressional lawmaking to be made. Demonstrable merit, coalition building, and the involvement of strategically key players are all part of any measure's triumph. The institutional process itself, however, may play the biggest part. Often, potentially explosive proposals are appended to other innocuous or must-pass measures and thereby win passage. In the House, rules of germaneness require that the grafted material bear some relation to the host legislation; the Senate is not constrained by such rules.

Child Support Enforcement Amendments of 1984 (P.L. 98-378)

A combination of well-marshalled, persuasive data and an easy to despise villain—the deadbeat dad—made strengthened child support enforcement legislation immensely popular on Capitol Hill. The fact that the initiative at hand amended an already existing federal mandate in the area of court-awarded support subverted any question over the proper role of government in this regard.[7]

The existing program was administered by state child support enforcement agencies with the preponderance of its funding from the federal government; its mission was to establish paternity and obtain overdue support. But the program fell far short of its goal to serve all eligible children. Many states primarily served AFDC families, because the support collected went directly to the state to offset welfare payments. The lack of uniformity among the states' collection procedures made the program very difficult to enforce.

So appealing was the notion of shoring up the child support system that 13 bills were introduced on the subject, including a version submitted on behalf of President Reagan. The introduction of Rep. Marge Roukema's (R-N.J.) bill coincided with Father's Day, indicating the stinging disapproval of members to nonsupporting dads. The consensus bill forged from the different proposals—H.R. 4325—articulated the theme that every child, whether served by the AFDC program or not, has a right to court-awarded support. Certain procedures were mandated to secure a more effective system, including wage withholding and state and federal income tax interception. And, the federal matching rate was reduced, to be offset by a new financial incentive for states that recover on behalf of nonwelfare as well as welfare clients.

Virtually no objections were voiced about the principle of H.R. 4325 (differences arose over matching ratios and similar details, but these were ironed out to everyone's general satisfaction). The bill's coalition of supporters was diverse, including the traditional human interest organizations as well as the National Conference of State Legislatures and administrators of state support agencies. These latter groups served not only to bring the message from the homefront, dispelling any notion of the bill as an inside-Washington issue, but also to dramatize the support of actual service providers for better enforcement tools. With the active support of the administration's Health and Human Services Secretary Margaret Heckler, the success of H.R. 4325 was assured.

Were there no opponents to the measure? Actually there were, but they were victims of negative publicity, were unorganized, and vastly outnumbered. These were the representatives of fathers' groups who made the point that many noncustodial parents withheld child support because they were denied their court-ordered visitation rights. The validity of this claim received scant consideration, an indication that members and the public at large disregarded the claim and desired to act. The Child Support Enforcement Amendments of 1984 entered the lawbooks without a single dissenting vote. The consensus among public officials created such an atmosphere of bonhomie that this writer, then the director of the Congressional Caucus for Women's Issues, was invited to the presidential signing ceremony—a first for the staff of the organization.

H.R. 4325 had a little bit of something for all observers. It was a "feel-good" bill. Members felt purposeful supporting it, believing they were really accomplishing some good for "abandoned" women and children, while at the same time whittling away the welfare rolls. It was a "get-tough" measure. It was a "no cost" bill, requiring minute federal expenditures in the relative terms of government spending. Perhaps most importantly, the Child Support Enforcement Amendments had the aura of a moral crusade, both against irresponsible parents and reliance on increased federal bureaucracy.

When the President signed the legislation, he was careful to hit every one of these popular themes:

> *This legislation represents a significant break from the tradition of simply throwing tax money at a problem. Instead of creating more dependency on government, we're requiring responsible behavior by our citizens. And this is the kind of innovative and principled approach to problem-solving that will make a difference. It will not only make a difference in the lives of our children, but for so many women who have been forced through no fault of their own onto welfare rolls due to abandonment.*

White House support for a bill cannot be overemphasized when the chief executive is popular and a masterful communicator. It is probable that H.R. 4325 would have won the hearts and minds of Congress without administration involvement, but the extra presidential boost gave the Child Support Enforcement Amendments an air of unassailable respectability. Rep. Barbara Kennelly, under whose name the consensus bill was drafted, observed that H.R. 4325 had a "halo around it."

Given the White House's generally negative record on women's issues, and the incremental one of Congress, an observer might wonder whether the bill carried any actual weight. In fact, Rep. Kennelly and the feminist community warned that the new law was not a panacea or an instant answer to the feminization of poverty. For black women especially, only 36 percent of whom are awarded child support by the courts, the drawback of the law is obvious: male unemployment precludes wage garnishment, the major thrust of the child support enforcement amendments of 1984.

It is too early, even now, to evaluate the effectiveness of the law. The most recent data collected by the Census Bureau show a discouraging 12 percent drop in the average amount of child support payments made in 1985, but experts caution that P.L. 98-378 has only recently become fully operational across the nation. Because the program is a joint federal-state effort, and turns on individual court decisions, expectations about an immediate hike in child support payments may be disappointing. Still, the improvements in the law are necessary and will make the system, inadequate as it is, a better one.

If the feminist movement demanded an equity measure, the Child Support Enforcement Amendments were an easy one for Congress to undertake. The title of the act alone points to its fundamental strength—the perception was that this was a children's initiative, not a women's one. Even the most conservative, antifeminist member in the Congress could therefore help advance the feminist agenda and not lose any standing with his or her natural constituency.

The Federal Equitable Pay Practices Act

As the last remark about child support indicates, a bill's title, formal or informal, has a lot to do with its reception. In the case of the Federal Equitable Pay Practices Act, the informal tag of "comparable worth" proved an albatross, and name-calling marked the terms of the resulting debate.

Pay equity is a means of correcting a vastly complex problem—the wage differential between men and women's pay. Women earn 68 percent of what men earn, a figure that remains little changed by either the passage of time or equal employment laws. This persistent earnings gap has been attributed to a number of factors—about which most of today's debate rages—but the major culprit is the occupational segregation of women that results in the undervaluation of their work.[8]

The National Academy of Sciences reported in 1981 that

> *the wage rates of women's jobs are depressed because women do them. Women are concentrated in low-paying jobs, not solely out of choice—though choice may play some role—and not because these jobs would be low paying regardless of who did them, but rather as a result of earlier traditions of discrimination against women that have become institutionalized—as well as, possibly, current intentional discrimination.*[9]

It is the institutional nature of the wage gap, the pervasive, systemwide phenomenon of women's depressed earnings, that caused feminists and labor organizations to seek the broad remedy of pay equity. Under this policy, the job classifications of a single employer would be studied. Jobs predominately performed by men would be compared to those done mostly by women on the basis of skill, effort, responsibility, and working conditions. Women's occupations determined on this basis to be equivalent to men's would then be compensated at an equivalent level.

Because pay equity calls for comparing men and women's jobs, the issue is also known as *comparable worth* (equal pay for work of comparable value). Proponents of this strategy for closing the wage gap say that two-thirds of all employees today work for firms that use some type of job evaluation that compares dissimilar jobs to establish pay scales. Opponents charge that comparing jobs is a hopelessly subjective exercise; the free market is the only correct arbiter of wage scales. How can one compare apples and oranges, poets and plumbers? Furthermore, the critics assert, not only is the remedy of comparable worth faulty, but the reasons identified for the wage gap are insupportable as well. Rather than discrimination and employer-directed occupational segregation, pay equity opponents say that the career choices and personal preferences of women account for their lower wages. Market factors such as the number of women entering the work force and their turnover rate are also at the roots of the issue.

Perhaps at the heart of opponents' antagonism toward pay equity is the assumption that women are not victims of the system, but have consciously chosen their low-wage predicament. Given the lack of a victim or valid assumptions about the wage gap and its proposed remedy, pay equity critics say, the entire issue is groundless and therefore open to ridicule. When the federal debate began, these forces practiced the "deride and conquer," rather than the divide and conquer, strategy to great effect.

As this discussion of the issue indicates, pay equity did not arrive on Capitol Hill as a readily understandable or universally acclaimed proposal. An issue that requires this much walking through before one gets to the terms of the bill itself is in trouble.

The legislation that caused this intense debate pertained solely to the work force of the federal government. Male civil servants earn an average of $12,000 more per year than female civil servants, according to a report by the General Accounting Office (GAO).[10] The job and wage classification systems of the federal government were established in 1923 and have not been reevaluated since then. Eighty percent of women who work for the federal government remain concentrated in grades 7 and below, while 85 percent of the men are employed in the higher grades of 10 through 15.

Introduced during the 98th Congress as H.R. 5680, the Federal

Pay Equity and Management Improvement Act would have required an independent consultant to study the federal wage scales and report back to Congress with recommendations for correcting any discriminatory pay practices identified. The pay equity study was one part of a larger and noncontroversial federal employee initiative, which passed the House of Representatives in June 1984 with only six dissenting votes. The Senate refused to take action on the pay equity portion of the package, but a bipartisan group of senators did go so far as to seek a GAO study on different methods of conducting a pay equity evaluation.

Strong objections were lodged against H.R. 5680, from the Chamber of Commerce to Phyllis Schlafly, but a full campaign against the federal pay equity study did not materialize until after the House action. With the Senate under Republican control, opponents probably thought that they could wait out the House's inevitably futile activity and then let the issue pend forever. But the margin of victory in the House, coupled with enthusiasm about the power of the gender gap, may have convinced hostile observers to strangle the pay equity infant while still in its cradle. The rhetoric used by pay equity boosters made it clear that the federal study was envisioned as a model for private sector emulation. The business community and its supporters were stung into action.

By the time the 99th Congress convened, pay equity critics had made it clear that the legislation was detrimental to the well-being of the business world. The Chamber of Commerce and the National Association of Manufacturers led the private sector assault on the newly introduced H.R. 3008, the Federal Equitable Pay Practices Act. But the administration was weighing in heavily against a federal pay study, as well. The U.S. Civil Rights Commission fired the first official salvo when Chairman Clarence Pendleton labeled pay equity a "looney tunes" idea. The Equal Employment Opportunity Commission (EEOC) repudiated pay equity shortly thereafter, creating a sense of public momentum against the issue.

Public attention was hardly riveted on the federal bill, however. The national legislature was actually behind the times on pay equity, following the lead of state and local governments in coming to terms with the wage gap among their own job pools. Public employee unions had already won pay equity adjustments through collective bargaining and other means. National attention was turned more to activity in the courts than in Congress; a highly publicized case involving the Washington state government was under appeal before the Ninth Circuit Court at the time.[11] The court's awaited decision created much more anticipation than the Federal Equitable Pay Practices Act.

All the same, the business community needed to stem the pay equity tide by ensuring no such proposal made it through the Congress. Feminists, on the other hand, wanted a federal imprimatur to keep the momentum forward. Charge and countercharge were leveled against the bill.

H.R. 3008 was primarily attacked as setting a precedent for government-mandated wage scales. Even though the measure pertained solely to the federal government's work force, opponents claimed that it was "the camel's nose under the tent," or only the beginning of federal action in this arena, and that intrusion into the private sphere would surely follow. Rep. Richard Armey (R-Tex.), a first-term former economics professor, warned that H.R. 3008 would "bring about a decline in productivity, social chaos, and a loss of individual liberty."

The grimmest and probably most persuasive argument against H.R. 3008 was this: a study that turned up rampant discrimination in the federal workplace would put a potent weapon into the hands of the federal employee unions. This, opponents alleged, would lead in turn to automatic lawsuits against the government and ultimately force federal appropriations to pay for wage adjustments. The cost issue was sobering. Congress was about to put its own head in the noose, critics warned.

One of the greatest assets of H.R. 3008, on the other hand, was its sponsor, Rep. Mary Rose Oakar. As secretary of the Democratic Caucus, Rep. Oakar was both a highly visible party regular and a close associate of the House leadership. A gifted strategist, she manipulated the legislative process to discredit her foes; after the Civil Rights Commission's action, for instance, Rep. Oakar ordered an investigation by the General Accounting Office (GAO) that found many "inconsistencies and errors" in the commission's report. Finally, her warm personal style helped Rep. Oakar build a coalition in support of what she called her "little bill." Assisting in this effort was a united front of feminist and labor organizations, ranging from the American Nurses Association and B'nai Brith Women to the American Federation of State, County, and Municipal Employees (AFSCME) and the National Treasury Employees Union.

When H.R. 3008 was finally scheduled for full House debate, more than 160 amendments were filed, a dozen of which proposed to change the bill's name to such titles as "the Sexist Socialism Act," "Feminist Folly," and "This Is What Happens When the Democrats Are in Control." The amendments served the purpose of delaying consideration of H.R. 3008 until more calendar time could be scheduled.

In the interim, as anticipated by H.R. 3008 opponents, the Ninth Circuit Court of Appeals finally handed down its opinion on the Washington State case, overturning the original 1983 ruling in favor of pay equity for state employees. This should have been the final stroke against the federal bill. The judicial branch had ended this particular legal flirtation with comparable worth. Members of Congress are not obliged to rubber-stamp judgments of the federal courts, since the three branches of government were designed as equal powers. But a legal decision that harmonizes with a legislative viewpoint can be very influential to legislators. Pay equity critics seized on the Ninth Circuit Court's ruling, while the proponents hastened to separate H.R. 3008 from the perimeters of the decision.

The damage control effort ultimately proved successful, for on October 9, 1985, the House of Representatives approved H.R. 3008 by the wide margin of 259 to 162. A coalition of liberal Republicans joined with a majority of Democrats to overwhelm opposition from GOP regulars and southern Democrats.

The victory hinged on a number of factors. First, members voiced a strong sense of responsibility for "getting its own house in order" by ridding the federal work force of wage discrimination.[12] "We cannot shrink from our responsibility to develop information and to develop a fair compensation system," Rep. Nancy Johnson (R-Conn.) said on the floor. "We must do what is right and just for our employees."

Second, most members were unconvinced that economic chaos could possibly follow a government study of its own work force. H.R. 3008's proponents were careful to separate Congress's responsibility to act on the report from its responsibility to undertake the study. Congress would retain authority to act or not act on the study's findings, as it saw fit in the future.

Finally, the cost question, which normally drives the debate on legislation, was mitigated by two facts: H.R. 3008 itself cost next to nothing in bureaucratic terms, and the example of local governments which had implemented pay equity adjustments showed that, when phased in, their costs were relatively modest.

In the final analysis, the practical aspects of this measure have always been eclipsed by what it stands for: a government endorsement of pay equity. While the House of Representatives has gone on record twice in support of a federal pay equity study, the issue remains volatile there. The Senate may act on a federal pay equity measure during the 100th Congress, the first time that chamber has faced going on record on pay equity, but passage is by no means assured, even under resumed Democratic control. Perhaps the least divisive and most direct path pay equity supporters can take is to focus on the pervasive state and local activity on equal pay for work of comparable value and await a Democratic administration more sympathetic to taking executive action on behalf of federal equitable pay practices.

Summary

Legislation often seems to go when it will, moving according to its own whim, but the reality is that behind the scenes all activity is carefully orchestrated. Yet there is a sense of timing that is all important.

The child support bill met with success because it was viewed as a role equity measure and contained the attractive ingredients of a small price tag, narrow focus, and noncontroversial subject matter. The timing of this bill could not have been more propitious, however. The gender gap fueled a sense of urgency among policymakers to establish a record for women's rights. Had the legislation not been enacted at this juncture, and the matter raised at a later date, it is possible that the passions of policymakers would have cooled and the interests of noncustodial parents given greater heed. A different, weaker policy might well have emerged altogether.

The pay equity bill passed the House of Representatives with little debate while the gender-gap fuel ran strong. However, it ran into considerable resistance during its second outing: the timing was no longer conducive to easy passage of this measure. The vehement, organized opposition to the pay equity bill obliterated any notion that it was merely a matter of role equity. Although the bill itself fit the definition, the bill itself was not really in question. Rather, at issue was transforming the way employers do business. The business community, at least that part represented by the U.S. Chamber of Commerce, remains bitterly opposed to the federal government directing the transformation.

Conclusion

In this decade, virtually all policies to improve the lives of women have originated from the U.S. Congress. This body, the first branch of government, possesses all the procedures but little of the unifying perspective to declare a coherent, wide-scale policy for women. All the same, a deeply committed bloc of legislators share a vision of equal opportunity for women, and they have managed moderately well to advance the feminist agenda. Contrary to the popular adage, the President has not proposed, yet the Congress has disposed of many new policies to enrich the lives of American women.

Congress has worked against an adverse backdrop, all the same, and as a result its efforts have been modest. The opposition of the Reagan administration to most of the women's agenda has injected partisanship to the debate, making it difficult to build consensus in Congress for individual proposals. The negative estimation in which the White House holds "special interests" has created a sense of public suspicion about the feminist agenda. Dwindling federal resources compound the problem. As a result, lawmakers tend to respond conservatively to feminist policy recommendations, seeking a path of least resistance. Conservative policy-making makes for conservative, or small-scale, policies.

Historian Arthur Schlesinger observed that there are cycles in American politics, lasting about 30 years. In Washington, there are minicycles that barely last three years. In 1985, after the Mondale/Ferraro defeat, it appeared that women's issues were buried. Now, the opposite seems possible.

Policymakers may be catching up to the new demographics, marked by more single-parent and dual-income households. Several leading legislators are ready, at least, to push for large-scale antidotes to the stresses of modern life. Feminists are recasting their objectives to reflect these stresses, so that women's issues become working people's issues, older people's issues, and disabled people's issues. Increasingly, women's issues are being relabeled as family issues.

Problems affecting women affect their families, and discussing the political agenda in "family" terms instead of as "women's" issues broadens its appeal. Liberals and conservatives, feminists hope, can join together to enhance family stability. Indeed, lawmakers are starting to confront today's social demographics, and indications point to greater success for the new family strategy.

Rep. Schroeder has launched a nationwide "Great American Family Tour" to "inform parents, as well as teenagers and grandparents, on a range of family concerns—from child development to family policies." Included are policies related to parental leave, child care, pay equity, housing, and health care. Presidential candidates are including some of these issues in their campaign themes, and it is not unthinkable that the new chief executive will announce a national family policy.

Would such a declaration alter the pattern of fragmentation and incrementalism for the women's agenda? Not necessarily. An executive branch policy, in order to have some balance, would have to address the needs of all women or all families, including the traditional form. Due to the polarization of feminists and traditionalists, who define family issues in very different ways, it is hard to imagine these forces working together to promote an all-inclusive family policy. Where do controversial issues such as abortion and the Equal Rights Amendment fall under a family policy? In order to avoid division from the very start, wouldn't a White House policy have to be very general, vague and weak? That would leave individual policymakers, cabinet heads, and legislators to fill in the details of a family policy. And a fragmentary, incremental pattern would surely follow. In other words, this is the nature of the policy-making process. The narrowly drawn measures are the sleek ones, capable of making it through the process within a reasonable time span. Unless we wake up tomorrow and find a vocal, demonstrable majority of Americans beating on the doors of government to perform grand feats, the slow, conservative pattern will continue. However, as slow as the progress is on family issues, it is also steady, and the gains made along the way do add up.

Endnotes

1. "Incremental," used in this chapter, refers to the small steps by which policies for women are achieved—in other words, the end result of the policy-making process. Political scientist Charles Lindblom identifies incremental-ism as a model of policy-making, which "considers existing policies, programs, and expenditures as a base. It concentrates attention on newly proposed policies and programs and on increases, decreases, or other modifications of existing programs. Incrementalism is conservative in that policymakers generally accept the legitimacy of established policies and programs. The focus of attention is on proposed *changes* in these policies and programs. This narrows the attention of policymakers to a limited number of new initiatives, increases or decreases in the budget" (Diana DiNitto and Thomas Dye, *Social Welfare: Politics and Public Policy*, Englewood Cliffs, N.J.: Prentice Hall 1983.) This model does indeed fit the manner by which women's issues are considered by Washington decisionmakers. The process is incremental and the results are incremental.
2. The Equal Pay Act, an idea almost a century old at the time of enactment, was promoted by unions as a way of ensuring that the wages of men were not deflated due to the cheaper wages paid women. "Sex" was included in Title VII only after a plan to defeat the entire measure backfired. Southern lawmakers in the Senate amended "sex" to the legislation hoping to make Title VII appear ridiculous and insupportable, but their colleagues refused to balk at this maneuver.

3. Columnist Ellen Goodman quoted Sarah Harder, president of the American Association of University Women, as warning presidential candidates, "Don't think of women's issues as a tiny handful of setasides that will satisfy a rowdy minority" (*Boston Globe*, February 2, 1988).

4. It should be noted that feminists did not always work hand in glove with the executive branch to promote the agenda. The current administration created extreme dislike among feminist groups, but the Democratic Carter administration was often condemned also. The difference is that earlier administrations were receptive to women's rights activists.

5. Perhaps the tax code reform's disposition of family issues reflects the difficulty of enacting a general family policy. Some types of families were better served than others, under the reform measure. The priority of reform-minded legislators was to lessen the tax burden on poor families, and in this effort they met with success. For instance, under the previous tax code, single heads-of-household—who generally have lower incomes than two-parent households—could claim a standard deduction (a minimum amount of tax-free income for basic living expenses) equal to that of single taxpayers with no dependents, while married couples filing jointly could claim a substantially higher standard deduction. The tax reform package that became law in 1986 raises the standard deduction for single heads-of-household, although married couples still earn a higher deduction.

On the other hand, the law eliminated the two-earner deduction that offset the so-called marriage penalty, which causes working couples filing jointly to pay higher taxes than if they had been able to file separately as single taxpayers. Individual retirement accounts (IRAs) were restricted. And the dependent care tax credit, which provides little relief for low-income and higher-income families alike, was not expanded.

Moreover, the tax code reform contained very important private pension program revisions that will allow many more women to gain access to the private pension system, primarily by cutting the vesting requirements—the period of continuous years of service with a company before an employee is guaranteed pension benefits—from ten to five years. Because women tend to stay in jobs for shorter durations than men, this shorter vesting requirement will be very helpful to them.

So, the entire tax code reform sends some mixed messages on families. It was weighted toward lower-income taxpayers, and given the finite resources with which policymakers had to work, this priority is a fair one.

6. Marian Lief Palley, "The Women's Movement in Recent American Politics," *The American Woman 1987-88, A Report in Depth*, ed. Sara E. Rix (New York: W. W. Norton Co., 1987).

7. The original child support and paternity establishment law, Title IV-D of the Social Security Act, met with initial hostility from Congress and the White House. President Ford signed it into law, but expressed reservations about provisions that "go too far by injecting the Federal Government into domestic relations."

8. Refer to Teresa Amott, "Working for Less: Single Mothers in the Workplace," Chapter 5 this volume, for a fuller discussion of this point.

9. Donald J. Treiman and Heidi I. Hartmann, "Women, Work, and Wages: Equal Pay for Jobs of Equal Value," National Research Council, 1981.

10. General Accounting Office, "Options for Conducting a Pay Equity Study by the Federal Pay and Classification System" (Washington, D.C., 1985).

11. *AFSCME* v. *the State of Washington* was first decided by a federal district court in 1983, when Judge Jack Tanner ruled that Washington State committed discrimination against women by paying them lower wages than men who were performing jobs determined by the state itself to be equivalent in skill, effort, responsibility, and working conditions. Judge Tanner found the evidence of intentional discrimination "overwhelming" and ordered the state to pay back-wages to the female employees.

12. Actually, the issue of putting the House itself in order, by performing a pay equity study of the legislative branch, was gingerly sidestepped during debate. No lack of legislative remedies have been proposed, however: Rep. Olympia Snowe (R-Maine) drafted a bill to authorize such a study, and Reps. Lynn Martin (R-Ill.) and Patricia Schroeder (D-Col.) have long sought equal employment protections for congressional staff, who are not covered by Title VII of the Civil Rights Act. Because enforcement of congressional coverage raises questions about the separation of powers, the issue of equal employment protections for legislative branch workers has been controversial. The current system of nondiscrimination is one of voluntary compliance with the federal statute, a great irony from the body of government which otherwise spurns solely voluntary efforts from the private sector.

Chapter 9

SINGLE-PARENT FAMILIES AND A RIGHT TO HOUSING

Frank I. Smizik and Michael E. Stone

As the housing crisis continues to worsen across the country, single-parent families are among those suffering most and whose needs require new approaches to addressing the crisis. Despite housing's importance to the very existence of a family and housing's direct relationship to health, safety, and the quality of life, as a society we still have not committed our abundant resources to truly meeting this need for all families. We will argue in Chapter 9 that this continuing failure to meet housing needs is due in part to the failure to establish a legally enforceable "right to housing." We therefore suggest a constitutional "right to housing" as an innovative step toward solving the housing crisis. While growing out of an actual campaign to amend the Massachusetts Constitution, most of the ideas are equally relevant to other states and even the federal arena. In addition, in developing the arguments, we give particular attention to the housing needs of single-parent families and the implications that establishment of a right to housing would have for such families.

The legal issues are complex but not without precedent. Our purpose is not to show how a constitutional right to housing would

The authors would like to acknowledge the support of Florence Roisman, Peter Marcuse, Laura Monroe, Sue Marsh, and Tom Spriggs for reviewing the draft of this chapter, and we thank the Advisory Board of the "Massachusetts Right To Housing Project" for the opportunity to work with them.

make a state legally liable for the failure to provide adequate housing, but to show how such a constitutional right would give the government more clout to solve both the immediate crisis and the long-term problem. Not all of the legal issues are raised in Chapter 9 because they are too numerous. However, we do know that right to housing would strengthen existing housing laws by giving greater protections to tenants and owner occupants. We also know that a constitutional right to housing would support freedom-of-choice statutes and give legal efficacy to long-term tenure strategies.

In the last section of Chapter 9 we present some practical measures that state and local officials might use in the furtherance of the right to housing focused on the needs of single-parent families. While some of the measures are already being utilized, they would be easier and more coherently and comprehensively implemented if a right to housing were a fundamental right in a state's Constitution. It is time for state governments and the federal government not only to provide more funds to solve the housing crisis, but also to protect the existing housing supply; protect long-term affordability; develop protections against speculation and gentrification; and recognize finally that *affordable, habitable, nontransient housing* is not a privilege but a fundamental right for all.

Housing Needs of Single-Parent Families

Why should attention be directed particularly to establishing a right to housing when single-parent families have such a multiplicity of needs, of which housing is only one, that are not presently being adequately met? The answer is that housing has unique economic, social, psychological, and symbolic significance, which results in housing having a profound and pervasive impact on the quality of life far beyond just the provision of shelter. For example, as co-author Stone has explained in distinguishing housing from other necessities such as food, clothing and medical care:

> Housing is a bulky, immobile and durable good that rarely can be purchased in amounts other than whole dwelling units and usually is used over a considerable period of time. These characteristics make it extremely difficult, at least in the short run, for a family to alter the quantity, quality, or amount spent for the housing they consume. Sudden changes in the income of a household, especially downward changes, are generally reflected immediately in other expenditures, including food, but not in the amount spent for

shelter. Increases in housing costs usually must be offset by reductions in other expenditures, rather than reductions or substitutions in housing consumption. When the rent or property taxes go up, a family cannot readily give up its living room or switch to a cheaper brand of bathroom to offset the increase.

The second way in which the cost of housing uniquely affects the overall standard of living of a family is through its determination of where they can live. This relationship influences the physical quality of the housing people are able to obtain, the amount of dwelling space they have, and the type of community and neighborhood they live in. The influence over locational choice means that the amount a household can pay for housing affects its access to commercial facilities, the quality of schools and other social services, the character of the immediate physical and social environment, and the availability of transportation networks to jobs and other services elsewhere in the metropolitan area. No other consumption item is nearly as pervasive in its effects.[1]

Furthermore, on the extraordinary psychological significance of housing, psychiatrist Matthew Dumont has recently testified, specifically with regard to the experience of homelessness among single mothers and children:

Is there a specific effect of losing one's home in the whirlpool of powerlessness and poverty? Yes. Of all life's grating events, of all the stressors which drive people crazy, the loss of one's home ranks at the top. Erich Lindemann's studies of the people who used to live in Boston's West End concluded that the incidence rate, the number of people who became psychiatrically ill, doubled when they were moved against their will to homes elsewhere. This was true even though they were moved to stable homes, as opposed to over-crowded, unstable temporary accommodations, as is now usually the case, at best.

Conversely, there is no evidence that those families who become homeless are, prior to their homelessness, suffering any more from mental illness than families of similar income and social composition. . . .

The fear of losing one's home of being "on the streets," . . . is not merely the threat of exposure to the elements. The biological need for protection from intemperate weather can be satisfied by public shelters, waiting rooms, and even doorways. What gives the experience its particular horror, particularly among mothers of young children, is a whole ecology of stressed realities. At some deep and central level of our emotional lives we all carry a sense of dread that we will someday be alone and abandoned in the world, like atoms in the void. . . .

The existence of a "home," an address, a place where someone we know can always be found, where we belong, is the only source of solace for that universal dread. Every homeless mother and child carries within them an empty space where the solace can be found in the rest of us. It affects the way they will deal with every subsequent experience, giving the anxieties that most of us carry with us a whole new dimension of depth. . . .

Homeless children are subjected to the interruption of their schooling, the loss of their friends, malnutrition and infection. The loss of a child's home is nothing less than an invitation to chronic illness.[2]

Homeless families on public assistance have been placed in family shelters or in state-paid motels and hotels when the family shelters are full. During 1985 over 4,000 such families were forced to reside in motel and hotel rooms, usually without cooking facilities, and at a cost to the state of thousands of dollars per month per family.

The most pervasive and deep-seated of housing problems is that of affordability, the squeeze between incomes on the one hand and housing costs on the other. Indeed, most familiar aspects of the housing problem—including problems of physical condition and space; security of tenure; community viability; the amount, type, and location of new construction; and the allocation of public and private resources to housing—not just the obvious cost problems of rents, utilities, taxes, interest rates, and sales prices—have their roots primarily in the interaction between incomes and housing costs. Single-parent families of course experience this squeeze to an extraordinary degree because of their disproportionately low incomes.

Yet not all housing problems are reducible to the affordability squeeze. Discrimination in housing, for example, has a dynamic of its own. Restricted housing opportunity for various groups is in part an affordability problem resulting from lower income caused by discrimination in education and employment, but clearly housing discrimination has long occurred quite apart from any ability to pay. Denial of equal opportunity in housing for single parents occurs in many instances simply due to the lack of a spouse, more often due to the presence of children. In addition, as shown in Chapter 6, single parents on AFDC face discrimination on the basis of source of income; single parents who are employed are disproportionately recipients of state or federal rental assistance certificates or vouchers due to their low incomes, and they face housing discrimination because of landlord resistance to accepting certificates. Furthermore, the relatively higher incidence of single parenthood among people of color permits racial discrimination against them to be masked by other factors, because federal law does not prohibit discrimination on the basis of family status, presence of children, or source of income. While state law in a number of states does prohibit housing discrimination on these other bases, such discrimination is extraordinarily hard to prove.

There are also dimensions of housing need associated with or growing out of the design and location of housing. Such problems are the result of certain assumptions and conventions about household structure and composition, which fail adequately to consider changing needs through the life cycle, special-needs populations, and diverse life-styles.

Housing design and location conventions have been recognized increasingly as being insensitive to and indeed oppressive of women in general and female-headed and single-parent families in particular: in terms of geographical isolation and inaccessibility; in terms of site plans that do not facilitate neighboring, mutual aid, and child supervision; in terms of development and management that fail to provide adequately, if at all, for child care, shared or provided food preparation, security from crime; and in terms of interior designs that are insensitive to single parents' particular needs to be able to handle child supervision, food preparation and home maintenance most efficiently.[3] Single-parent families disproportionately are forced to live in inappropriate, unsupportive, or inaccessible settings, because proper housing does not exist—even in the absence of affordability constraints or explicit discrimination.

In the broadest sense, a right to housing must mean the commitment to meet housing needs along all of these dimensions. In practice, the process will, of course, be evolutionary. With a constitutional right to housing, the dimensions of need will become more fully recognized and addressed, and the existing partial and piecemeal responses will give way to a more comprehensive approach to meeting the needs. Single-parent families facing an extraordinary set of unmet housing needs along these various dimensions would thus be among the major beneficiaries of a constitutional right to housing.

How Much Can Single-Parent Families Afford for Housing?

The traditional "rule of thumb" regarding housing affordability was that people supposedly can afford to spend up to 25 percent of their incomes for housing; in recent years this standard has been raised to 30 percent. But for all low-income families and many moderate-income families, paying 25 percent for shelter does not leave them with enough money to meet their other needs. On the other hand, many high-income households actually can afford to pay more than 25 percent for housing. So the "rule of thumb" is not a very good rule at all.

A better way to figure out how much a family can afford for shelter is to take the difference between their disposable income (i.e., income after taxes) and the cost of meeting their *nonshelter* needs at an adequate level. The Lower Standard Budget developed by the U.S. Bureau of Labor Statistics (BLS) gives the cost of basic necessities for a minimum adequate standard of living in urban areas all over the country. While the BLS budgets have not been computed by the federal government since 1981, the 1981 figures are easily updated by using components of the consumer price index (CPI) for a particular urban area. It is also possible to adjust the standard budgets for various household sizes and compositions and to take into account food stamps, Medicaid, and other noncash benefits received by some families.[4]

Using this approach yields a sliding scale of how much people can afford for shelter: higher-income families can afford to pay a higher percentage of their income than can lower-income families; smaller households can afford to pay a higher percentage than larger households with the same income. People paying more than they can afford on this basis are "shelter poor"—the squeeze between inadequate incomes and excessive housing costs leaves them with not enough money to meet their nonshelter needs at the minimum level of the BLS Lower Budget.

Figures 9–1 and 9–2 summarize the shelter poverty affordability scale for wage-earning single-adult families in Massachusetts in 1985. They reveal that a family of four (single parent and three children) with a gross income (before taxes) of under $23,500 could not have afforded as much as 25 percent of their income for housing if they wanted to be able to meet their other needs at a minimum level of adequacy. If their income was under $18,000, they could have afforded about $150 a month for housing (including utilities), which is just 10 percent of their income.

For single parents receiving AFDC, the scale would be some-what different, since their incomes are not taxable and they are eligible for noncash benefits, most particularly Medicaid, plus in many instances food stamps, and in Massachusetts a small clothing allowance. Table 9–1 summarizes the affordability scale for the model three-person AFDC family in Massachusetts in 1985; it is a function of actual housing costs as well as income, because food stamp benefits are affected by actual housing costs.[5] A single parent with two children receiving public assistance of $510 a month cannot afford to pay anything for housing and still meet their other

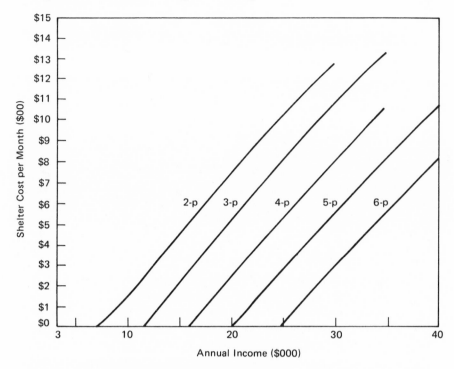

Figure 9-1 Maximum Affordable Shelter Cost per Month for Single Adult
Plus Children in Massachusetts, 1985.

needs at a minimally adequate level. Even with food stamps and
Medicaid they cannot afford to pay anything for shelter.

The Housing Market

The shelter poverty affordability scale reveals that for low- and
moderate-income families finding affordable housing would be a
serious problem, even without the housing inflation that began in
the 1960s and has accelerated in the 1980s. For single-parent
families the crisis is particularly acute, due to the interaction
between their disproportionately low incomes, on the one hand,
and the patterns of housing discrimination and inappropriate housing on top of high housing costs, on the other.

Worsening supply problems have only exacerbated the affordability crisis. In Massachusetts, for example, vacancy rates for
private market apartments hover at approximately 1 to 2 percent,
while economists estimate that a vacancy rate of at least 5 percent
is necessary to avoid runaway price increases in an unregulated

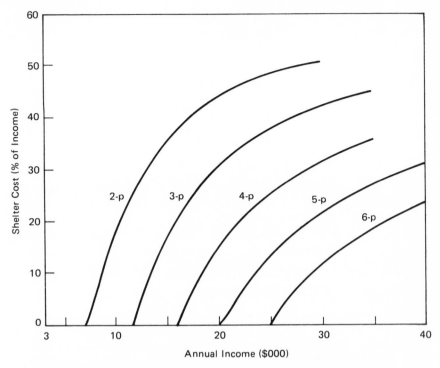

Figure 9-2 Maximum Affordable Shelter Cost as a Percentage of Income
for a Single Adult Plus Children in Massachusetts, 1985.

market. Further depleting this low supply of housing is the continuing conversion of apartments to condominiums, the removal of rental housing to facilitate commercial or luxury-residential development, and incidents of arson.

Between 1970 and 1986 the median price of existing single-family homes for the entire Northeast increased from about $25,000 to about $125,000—a 400 percent increase. Nationally, according to the Census Bureau, the increase was 249 percent, compared with a 183 percent increase in median family income. Since 1980, the percentage of families owning homes has declined each year, contrasted with the preceding 40 years of increasing home ownership. While very few single-parent families could afford to buy a home even before this rampant speculation, diminishing home ownership opportunities for the overall population has resulted in intensified competition for available rental units, with single-parent families near the end of the line as landlords generally have plenty of other potential tenants with greater purchasing power and more appealing social characteristics.

Table 9–1 Maximum Affordable Shelter Cost ($ per month) for Three-Person AFDC Households in Massachusetts, Fiscal Year 1986

| Actual Shelter Cost/Mo. | Grant Levels | | | | | | | |
| | Max AFDC $432 | +10% $476 | +25% $540 | +50% $650 | Poverty Level $760 | Grant Levels to Afford Private Housing | | |
						$900	$1000	$1100
$ 0	-3	28	73	150	227	355	455	555
50	-3	28	73	150	227	355	455	555
100	-3	28	73	150	227	355	455	555
150	-3	28	73	150	227	355	455	555
200	7	31	73	150	227	355	455	555
250	22	46	82	150	227	355	455	555
300	37	61	97	157	227	355	455	555
350	39	70	112	172	233	355	455	555
400	39	70	115	187	248	355	455	555
450	39	70	115	192	263	355	455	555
500	39	70	115	192	269	355	455	555
550	39	70	115	192	269	367	455	555
600	39	70	115	192	269	367	455	555

Note: Shelter cost was calculated by taking the grant level and subtracting the cash needs for nonshelter items.

Small-scale efforts to create "affordable home ownership" offer a little opportunity to middle-income families, but none for the low- and moderate-income, who are disproportionately single-parent families. Some municipal governments and community development corporations with heavy subsidies in the form of donated land, public grants, and volunteer labor have managed to produce some housing for as low as about $50,000, and some condo developers, under heavy public pressure, are providing a few "affordable" units at about $100,000. Consider, though, the best case: a family manages to make a $10,000 down payment on a $50,000 unit, taking out a mortgage for $40,000; with a 30-year loan at 10 percent interest, the monthly mortgage payment is about $350; property taxes are about $100 a month; fuel, utilities, and maintenance add at least another $100, bringing the monthly outlay minimally to $550. With below-market financing and minimal tax benefits under the new tax law, perhaps the net cost can be brought down to $500 a month. Thus, with heavy subsidies, the cheapest home ownership costs $500 a month. Who can afford it? Based upon 25 percent of income, a family would need an income of at least $24,000, which in this case happens to be just the same as the shelter poverty standard; at an unrealistic 35 percent of income, families at $17,000 would have to stretch to make it. And of course at "affordable" prices of $100,000, twice as much income is needed. Thus the traditional right to housing of middle-income Americans—conventional home ownership—is gone; only with heavy subsidies can families in the $15,000 to 40,000 income range achieve this "right."

But what of those with lower incomes, who are inevitably relegated to the rental market? As discussed in Chapter 6, market rents are pricing low-income households out of the private rental market. Meanwhile, public housing, the traditional fallback for the low- and moderate-income single-parent population, has become increasingly scarce, with new construction not offsetting the loss of units due to deterioration and neglect, and in some instances, sale to private developers. In some cities, public housing waiting lists are so long that it will take 15-20 years for all those waiting to obtain a unit.

In addition, subsidized privately owned housing is under increasing pressure, as nearly half a million units across the country are near the end of the period that they are profitable to investors as subsidized housing. Simultaneously (in most cases), this housing stock is reaching the point where it is no longer required to be retained for low- and moderate-income use. Much of this housing is located where owners would find it very profitable to convert to market-rate rentals or to condominiums. Such housing has been another major resource for single-parent families, who thus will suffer disproportionately if this housing is converted.

Meeting the Need

The present housing crisis has revealed the fundamental and long-term failure of this society to meet the housing needs of a large portion of its members. Single-parent families, whose housing needs have never been recognized, have increased tremendously in number during the same period that the housing crisis has developed. Yet, over the past half century, for all the various elements that are offered as a housing policy, there has never been a systematic, sustained commitment because housing has never been recognized as a basic right.

Establishment of a constitutional right to housing is thus a logical step. In and of itself a state constitutional amendment will not meet the housing needs, but it will oblige the legislative and executive branches of states, cities, and towns to place housing action permanently on their agendas and to act affirmatively to meet the needs of all citizens, with the most vulnerable finally beginning to receive the attention they deserve.

The Foundation for the Right to Housing

A Right to Housing Amendment Codifies a Moral Principle

Any political, economic, or social system is legitimized by the moral principles on which the system is based. Constitutions create structures for codifying the broad social expression of the common morality and common good. The moral principle involved in a right to housing amendment is that the society views housing as a basic human need and believes it should institutionalize the provision of such a basic need. The process of amending the Constitution is the method of examining that question. Once established in the Constitution, the amendment codifies and protects this common morality in a body of law and no longer leaves the issue for ad hoc governmental and private responses.

We find declarations of this moral principle from many of our religious leaders. The Episcopal City Mission, for example, has stated in its policy statement, "Housing: a Basic Human Right":

> *Shelter in decent, affordable housing is not a luxury. It is a necessity upon which access to other necessities and the development of*

healthy, productive families and communities most often depend.
Nothing is more essential to the welfare of men, women and children.
Nothing is tied more directly to the recognition of the dignity, worth
and values of persons. Because housing is so closely related to the
welfare of persons and to recognition of their value as persons
nothing is a more basic right than the opportunity, regardless of
income or class, to live in that kind of housing which supports the
welfare of the family and community.[6]

Recently, the U.S. Catholic Bishops asserted the right to housing
in their pastoral letter, "Catholic Social Teaching and the U.S.
Economy":

. . . the rights to life, food, clothing, shelter, rest and medical care
. . . are absolutely basic to the protection of human dignity. . . .
These economic rights are essential to human dignity as are the
political and civil freedoms granted by pride of place in the Bill of
Rights of the U.S. Constitution.

Indeed, protection of these economic minimums is crucial to the
growth of freedom within our borders and throughout the world.
Nothing will threaten the cause of freedom in the world more surely
than the notion that political democracy and economic justice for
the poor are incompatible. We believe, therefore, that these eco-
nomic rights should be granted a status in the cultural and legal
traditions of this nation analogous to that held by the civil and
political rights to freedom of religion, speech and assembly.[7]

In the Old Testament it is said that in order to be considered
righteous one should share his bread with the hungry and bring
the homeless into his house (Isaiah 58.6-8). Brandeis University
history teacher David Scobey expressed a modern Jewish perspective when he wrote:

Housing is a compelling Jewish issue because of our historic experi-
ence of homelessness and insecurity. Each year at Sukkot, we re-
enact that experience, in part to remind ourselves not to take our
security for granted. . . . The Jewish Coalition for the Right to
Housing has been formed in the same spirit: to make this ethical
commitment a constitutional one as well.[8]

Rabbi Frank Waldorf, another leading Jewish spokesperson, has
declared:

. . . [W]e recognize how vulnerable we would be as homeless
Americans. Without a home address, we would be unable to vote, to
receive food stamps or welfare, home health aides or friendly
visitors. As a homeless person we would be bereft of the support
that normally comes from community.[9]

The Universal Declaration of Human Rights adopted by the United
Nations in 1948 states:

It's difficult to imagine a more basic human need. Throughout
history, housing has been recognized as a necessity of life in society.
It is essential to a person's human development and dignity. Without
housing, a person's and/or family's life, health, safety, opportunity,
welfare and happiness are all in jeopardy. Every person has the
right to a standard of living adequate for the health and well-being
of himself [sic] and his [sic] family, including . . . housing.

Basic Needs Should Be Constitutional Rights

Both the U.S. Supreme Court and the highest state courts view
the Constitution as the infrastructure on which to build public
policy:

The Constitution is a frame of government for a sovereign power. It
was designed by the framers and accepted by the people as an
enduring instrument, so comprehensive and general in its terms that
a free, intelligent and moral body of citizens might govern them-
selves under its beneficient provisions through radical changes in
social, economic and industrial conditions. It declares only funda-
mental principles to the form of government and the mode in which
it will be exercised.[10]

Article I of the Massachusetts Constitution, for example, reflects
the fundamental rights in the Commonwealth, including enjoying
one's life and liberties free from discrimination and abridgment;
including the *acquiring, possessing* and *protecting* of property.
"[T]hese rights can be regulated by the legislature only in the
interest of public health, safety or morals, and in a restricted sense
in the interest of the public welfare." If the ownership of property
and the right to possess that property are protected, so should the
right to affordable, habitable and nontransient housing. Persons
who lose their residences without fault because of arbitrary decisions by owners, or because of the speculative nature of the
housing market, or even because of loss of their jobs should have
some protections provided by the Commonwealth. The protection
of an individual's place to live is "essential" within the meaning of
Article I, i.e., to "have certain natural, *essential* and unalienable
rights."

As the prominent psychiatrist Abraham Maslow has pointed out,
there is a hierarchy of human needs. If the basic physiological
survival needs are not met, a person becomes so preoccupied with
attempting to meet these needs that he or she is unconcerned with
the social needs of belonging, participation, esteem, and self-
fulfillment. Maslow's theory is, in some sense, a modern statement
of Jefferson's premises for an effective democracy, namely that

citizens must have a basic measure of material security in order to be able to participate fully and responsibly in the affairs of the community. If one doesn't have a home, one cannot vote. A person who is worried about paying the rent is unlikely to go to a candidates' night or to participate in community affairs. Without stable housing, a family is unable to exercise most of its other rights: the right to privacy, the right to vote, to go to school, to drive a car, and to receive certain government benefits. Most basically, the right to the pursuit of happiness is but a distant dream for a family living in a car or on the street. A family who cannot afford to live near other family members and friends in the neighborhood where they grew up because of increased costs loses the proximity and access to an important support group. A family who has to live in overcrowded conditions with other family members or friends cannot easily thrive and grow as well as those who have the security of living in their own home.

It is difficult for low-income persons to have their voices heard in the legislature. No matter how vocal, they cannot compete with other interest groups. They are neither powerful nor in the majority, and thus without constitutional sanction they have an especially difficult time convincing legislators that their needs are legitimate. If housing were a right, it would reflect a consensus that a state as a whole is concerned about providing housing for every vulnerable member of the community.

Society's Social Obligation Toward the Homeless and Inadequately Housed

Law Professor Charles L. Black, Jr. has declared there is a social nexus between society and those ill-housed:

> Shelters and soup lines do not offer those who are presently home-less or the many citizens who are in jeopardy of falling through the "safety net" to the streets a basis for recreating their lives. At best, these services temporarily halt the physical, emotional and intellectual deterioration of the homeless person. . . . Clearly, if the needs of the homeless, chronically unemployed or temporarily employed are to be met, then economic entitlements must be expanded or advanced, not diminished. This expansion or redefinition must begin with the economic right of citizens to housing and a job at a living wage.[11]

Judge J. Skelly Wright has stated that the law must recognize the evolutionary nature of the landlord-tenant relationship. He found that it was no longer possible to ignore the responsibility of the landlord for the conditions of the premises. Judge Wright stated that modern society required that a warranty of habitability be implied to the contract terms between the parties. This case is a practical example of the courts finding a social obligation in the law:

> *Even beyond the rationale of traditional products liability law, the relationship of landlord and tenant suggests further compelling reasons for the protections of the tenant's legitimate expectations of quality. The inequality in bargaining power between landlord and tenant has been well documented. Tenants have very little leverage to enforce demands for better housing. Various impediments to competition in the rental housing market, such as racial and class discrimination and standardized form leases, mean that landlords place tenants in a take it or leave it situation. The increasingly severe shortage of adequate housing further increases the landlord's bargaining power and escalates the need for maintaining and improving the housing stock. Finally, the findings of various studies of the social impact of bad housing have led to the realization that poor housing is detrimental to the whole society, not merely to the unlucky ones who must suffer the daily indignity of living in a slum.*[12]

Why a Constitutional Response?

Statutes: More Tenuous Than Constitutional Rights

> *Lack of a perfected constitutional right to be housed would be immaterial during any period when a like right prevailed by force of statute. But despite the great volume of housing legislation, it probably cannot now be said that there is a statutory right to be housed. . . . [W]hen duly appropriated rent-supplement or public housing money runs out, lawsuits do not pry loose more money— despite unappropriated authorizations or unfilled need.*[13]

Recent political changes have shown how tenuous statutes can be when a new administration attempts to dismantle existing laws. The Reagan administration has virtually put a halt to all housing programs designed to produce and preserve affordable housing. While a few states have expanded or created housing programs, there is no guarantee that elected officials in the future will be so committed. And despite the present efforts, the housing crisis worsens. A constitutional amendment would create a continuing institutional responsibility to reach solutions to the housing crisis. With the enactment of a constitutional right to housing, housing will always have to be on the agenda of a state legislature and as a requirement of the Constitution it will remain a priority, even with shifts in the political climate.

Just as any state constitution provides that each year resources must be appropriated for the legislature, the executive branch, the judiciary and the constitutional offices, it is implicit with a right to housing that resources be provided for housing on a continuing, ongoing basis. The passage of an amendment would assure local communities of state assistance, both technical and financial, to meet the housing needs of their residents.

With an amendment to the state constitution or a court-created right, the housing industry, the legislature, and the executive branch would have to focus primarily on housing needs rather than tax shelters and industry profits. The housing sector would be directed primarily toward preserving and providing as much affordable housing in as many ways as possible, and to a lesser extent toward expanding employment opportunities.

Housing: Never Recognized as a Right

The 19th-century growth of cities and of industrialization in the United States led to severe housing problems, especially for the immigrant workers in the manufacturing, textiles and garment industries. Whether it was Lowell, Massachusetts, or New York City, housing conditions were intolerable.

The Tenement Housing Act of 1867, the very first law to address housing conditions, was enacted in 1867 in New York City, but it was riddled with loopholes. Essentially, the law required the construction of fire escapes in New York City tenements. Characteristically, insufficient funds were made available for enforcement. This law and other early laws show the meager beginnings of statutory and regulatory attempts to establish certain rights based on evolving community standards of housing adequacy. Later tenement laws proved more effective and established minimal housing standards. However, following the passage of a Tenement Act in New York in 1901, no major housing law was enacted until after World War I.

The first major federal effort to establish the semblance of a housing policy occurred in 1933 as part of the National Industrial Recovery Act. However, the federal district court held there was not a sufficient public purpose involved to justify the exercise of eminent domain.[14] Reflecting the values of the day, the judge held that a federal housing program for private citizens, even if the citizens were poor, was not a valid public purpose. As a result of this type of opposition, a new method of public financing was enacted in the Wagner-Steagall Act of 1937. The law provided federal financing for state-chartered public housing authorities and withstood anticipated legal challenges. These authorities were creatures of the state law; local entities and the localities would decide which developments would get built and who would get to live there.

The wall of resistance to federal support of housing had been breached. In the years since, public housing has become a familiar aspect of the urban landscape. Yet in 1937 the country was suffering in the throes of the Great Depression. Twenty-five percent of the work force was unemployed during the worst days of the depression. In the spring of 1933, 13 to 15 million people were unemployed. Millions of families were barely making a living. It was this latter group that Freidman called "the submerged middle class":

> It would be a mistake to suppose (if anyone did) that the Wagner-Steagall Act arose solely out of a gradual persuasion of decent minded people that the slums were odious, crowded and evil, and that the federal government had a duty to relieve the sufferings of the poor. The social and economic conditions in the slums provided the opportunity, the background and much of the emotive power of the law. Yet reformers had long dreamed in vain of public housing, and the slums were surely no worse than they had been in the nineteenth century, though possibly they were larger.
>
> The potential of public housing was enhanced because the potential clientele was enormous, composed of millions of relatively articulate citizens angry and dispirited at their unjust descent into poverty. . . . a discontented army of men and women of high demands and high expectations stood ready to insist on decent housing from government or at least stood ready to approve and defend it.[15]

The Wagner-Steagall Act was thus shaped by the force of concrete social conditions; what emerged was a program geared to the needs of the submerged middle class, tied to slum clearance, and purged of any element of possible competition with business.[16] Indeed, the major elements of federal housing policy from the 1930s to the present have not been addressed to the needs of the poor at all, but to the support of the mortgage-lending and construction industries and the promotion of middle-class home ownership. In essence, federal housing policy in the decades after World War II created a right to housing for white middle-class Americans who were easily able to buy single-family suburban tract houses because of federal mortgage insurance and guarantees plus generous income tax benefits.

Yet, as housing conditions worsened in the cities for both the growing minority populations and the remaining white working class, Congress felt compelled to give at least rhetorical recognition to the fundamental needs of the entire nation. Thus, in the landmark Housing Act of 1949, Congress declared a national housing goal of "a decent home in a suitable living environment for every American family." But while this goal was reaffirmed in the subsequent Housing Act of 1968 and remains the rhetorical cornerstone of federal housing policy as a statutory declaration and not a Constitutional stricture, it continues to be unrealized and elusive.

When the government intervened into the housing market more than 50 years ago, it marked a recognition that the private housing market couldn't address the problems of low- and moderate-income persons. Yet all the programs the government has tried have fallen short of solving the housing problem. According to housing experts Achtenberg and Marcuse:

> *The overall pattern of federal housing and neighborhood subsidies in the post war period has been highly regressive, reinforcing the unequal distribution of income and wealth. Direct federal budget outlays for housing and community development, currently totaling about $10 billion, have been severely cut by the Reagan administration with Congressional acquiescence. But, housing related tax expenditures (revenues lost through homeowner and investor tax deductions) have more than doubled since 1979 (and are now about $50 billion a year). These hidden subsidies primarily benefit those in the top 10 per cent of the income distribution.*[17]

Thus, more and more, it is the richest members of society who are assured of a right to housing through regressive and even cynical public policies, rather than all members of society and especially the poorest. A constitutional right to housing would provide a basis for beginning to redress this injustice.

Housing: Not a Federal Constitutional Right

It is clear from the Supreme Court's opinion in *Lindsey* v. *Normet* that the U.S. Supreme Court holds housing to be of fundamental importance. In that case, the court was asked to rule on the constitutionality of an appeal system used in landlord-tenant cases that placed an onerous burden (bonding requirement) on those of limited means. Arguing that it lacked constitutional authority, the court deferred to legislative action:

> *We do not denigrate the importance of decent, safe and sanitary housing. But . . . we are unable to perceive in the Constitution any constitutional guarantee of access to dwellings of a particular quality. . . . Absent constitutional mandate, the assurance of adequate housing is a legislative and not a judicial function. [p. 874]*[18]

The concurring opinion of Justice Douglas went further in explaining how fundamental he felt the right to housing was:

The home—whether rented or owned—is the very heart of privacy in modern America. . . . modern man's place of retreat for quiet and solace is the home. Whether rented or owned it is his sanctuary. Being uprooted and put into the street is a traumatic experience. . . . in the setting of modern urban life, the home is . . . where man's roots are.[19]

In sharp contrast, the Supreme Court of India specifically inferred such a right from its country's constitution, which has in it a right to live. In *Tellis* v. *Bombay*, an action was brought on behalf of slum dwellers and other homeless persons, leading to the following court determination:

Their [plaintiffs] contention is that they have a right to live, a right which cannot be exercised without the means of livelihood. They have no option but to flock to big cities like Bombay, which provide the means of bare subsistence. They only choose a pavement of a slum which is nearest to their place of work. In a word, their plea is that the right to life is illusory without a right to protection of the means by which alone life can be lived. And the right to live can only be taken away or abridged by a procedure established by law, which has to be fair and reasonable, not fanciful or arbitrary such as is prescribed by the Bombay Police Act. [This act gave the police the authority to clear the streets and the pavements.] They also rely upon their right to reside and settle in any part of the country which is guaranteed by Art.19(1)(e). [AIR 1986 Supreme Court 180, p. 190]

The Supreme Court of India explained the rationale for inferring the "right to be free from eviction" aspect of a "right to housing" from India's already explicit right to live:

The sweep of the right to life conferred by Art. 21 is wide and far reaching. It does not mean only that life cannot be extinguished or taken away as, for example, by the imposition and execution of the death sentence, except according to the procedure established by law. That is but one aspect of the right to life. An equally important facet of the right is the right to livelihood because, no person can live without the means of living, that is, the means of livelihood. If the right to livelihood is not treated as part of the constitutional right to life, the easiest way of depriving a person of his right to life would be to deprive him of his means of livelihood to the point of abrogation [p. 193]. . . . That the eviction of a person from a pavement or slum will inevitably lead to the deprivation of his means of livelihood, is a proposition which does not have to be established in each case. [p. 195]

Thus, because the right to live requires the ability to earn a livelihood, and the right to housing is also necessity in order for one to work, one therefore must have housing in order to live. However, the Supreme Court of India was in actuality protecting the tenants' right to live in a slum or on the sidewalk without interference, not the right to adequate dwelling.

In 1970, Harvard law professor Frank Michelman argued that the right to housing should mean more than "housing will be made available as the market can produce it." In his article he outlines some elements of such a right, including the right not to be tendered substandard housing:

> *Suggestion of a right to be adequately housed will immediately suggest to some a duty not to furnish or place on the market, housing of substandard quality. If a person has a claim on society to be decently housed despite a lack of personal means, it may seem a natural inference that no one is free to take advantage of another's income shortage by inducing him through low rents to accept substandard housing.*[20]

Michelman also pointed out that a right to housing also means free choice in housing:

> *. . . [f]ull freedom to choose housing suited to one's particular needs and tastes may not as a short run goal, be in all respects compatible with that of securing "adequate" housing for all. Yet free choice is in its own right a prime goal. . . . Currently the greatest threat to free choice stems from racial discrimination. A good deal of other ethnic and social class discrimination also occurs. There is a right not to be forced to live in a racially segregated area. . . . Unreasonable land use restrictions are struck down because they restrict freedom of choice on the grounds of one's socio-economic status. There is also the right to use the home as you wish, including protections against censorship of tenant activities. A right not to be uprooted. If a house becomes a home only through its occupants' settling in and making it so, then a society's recognition of a right to housing must encompass some receptivity to claims not to be involuntarily removed from housing already occupied. Some examples of the right to not be uprooted include antieviction safeguards in both public and subsidized housing.*[21]

Several legal writers in the United States have argued that there is a constitutional right to housing, implicit in the Third, Fourth, Fifth, and Fourteenth amendments to the Constitution.[22] Because the home and the privacy of an individual are so intertwined throughout the Constitution, these authors believe the courts could infer a right to housing to protect and give meaning to these other fundamental rights.

The lack of explicit constitutional obligation contrasts with the provisions of some other state constitutions which, for example, make the care of the needy a right. Unique to the New York State Constitution is a provision that "[the] aid, care and support of the needy are public concerns and shall be provided for by the state and by such means as the legislature may from time to time determine" (NYS Const. Art XVII, §1). This provision supported the right-to-shelter suit in New York, which was brought on behalf of homeless men in New York City.[23]

Present Rights in Government and Private Housing

While the courts have not yet said that society must provide housing for all, the courts have agreed that when government does provide housing it creates a sufficient property interest for the occupants that the government cannot take away without constitutional due process. Additionally, if housing is offered as a resource, it must be available in a fair and nonarbitrary manner. Every public and subsidized housing tenant presently has the right to tenancies subject to termination only if there is "good cause." Further, they cannot be refused housing without good and sufficient reason based on objective standards.[24]

Many of the early cases were brought because of blatant discrimination against single-parent families. For instance, the Little Rock, Arkansas, Housing Authority discriminated against unwed mothers; the Yonkers, New York, Housing Authority was found to discriminate because of welfare status; Kansas City, Missouri, discriminated on the basis of student status; unmarried cohabitation was an illegal classification created by Kern County, California; separated but not divorced applicants were discriminated against by the Indianapolis Housing Authority; and even inadequate income was the basis for denying persons housing by several housing authorities.[25] Because of these court decisions, the federal government has now embodied these constitutional protections into its housing program regulations.[26]

There are also cases holding that a leasehold interest, even in private property, entitles the tenant to constitutional protections. In other words, a tenant with a lease is entitled to similar protections against state interference with that lease interest as a resident in public housing. In *Devines* v. *Maier*, the court found that plaintiffs, a class of tenants who were displaced by the city of Milwaukee's housing code enforcement activities, had a constitutionally protected property interest.[27]

This line of cases and the other cases providing a right of compensation for governmental interference with ownership rights are consistent with a societal obligation to provide housing. The right to be free from public interference and the right to housing are not at odds. If there is a fundamental right to housing, states will have to determine how all members of the community are entitled to benefit from this right. If a local government fails to create housing opportunities, rules and regulations will emerge from the executive and legislative branches requiring the creation of new opportunities for development or by requiring protections for existing residents. By the same token, those restrictions enacted in order to implement a "Right to Housing" that have an impact on private ownership will be limited by the right of an owner to receive a "fair return on investment" or "fair compensation for a taking."[28]

Freedom of choice has also been made a priority in existing housing discrimination laws. It is against the law to refuse to rent or sell housing to someone because of that person's race, creed, or national origin. This right has been determined by the federal government to be more important than even individual ownership rights. The right is given a high enough priority that the federal courts have jurisdiction to hear almost any discrimination case.[29] Additionally, the federal government has an affirmative duty to further fair housing opportunities in those communities receiving federal funds.[30] A constitutional right to housing amendment would embody this existing federal statutory right and give greater efficacy to the goal of increasing housing opportunities for minority residents.

Analogy to Other Affirmative Rights

Right to Counsel. The judiciary's interpretation of the right to counsel is an example of how courts may give meaning to constitutional rights. Even if the right to housing were to be a fundamental right, it would not be absolute and would be subject to reasonable limitations.[31] By analogy, the right to counsel cases indicate that if the right to housing were a fundamental right under a state constitution, plaintiffs seeking to enforce that right would be entitled to housing that meets code standards but would not necessarily be able to designate choice or location.

Right to Be Free from Cruel and Unusual Punishment. Courts have consistently held that lack of money is no excuse for maintaining prisons that violate the cruel and unusual punishment standard. In those cases, the court is able to threaten to close the prison and let the prisoners out. Even with the general proposition that there is no money available, courts generally make allowance by increasing the time limit in which the state or municipality must meet its obligations. The courts balance the prisoners' right to be free of cruel and unusual punishment with the public interest in having criminals locked up.[32] If this rationale were applied to the right to housing amendment, municipalities would have to look at all alternatives to state funding for providing housing opportunities, including private sector and zoning regulations to increase housing opportunities, and would have reasonable time to implement such programs (see pages 257–258).

Right to Education. There is a difference in the way citizens look at education and the way they look at housing. In the 1840s the battle over education was between local control of the schools versus a strong state system. The Whigs felt positive governance was necessary and a useful means of improving the quality of public schools. Democrats felt state interference in local educational matters gave potential for a centralized state school system that would dictate too much how children were to be educated. Despite the differences, there was undoubtedly a consensus for upgrading education in every community.

While the battle for local control is still going on today, we nevertheless have decided not to rely on the private market to ensure equality of opportunity in education. In sharp contrast, we treat housing as a speculative commodity, to be bought, sold, and resold and mortgaged. We would not think of building schools only for the rich; nor would we allow an increase in tuition to force families from the schools. Yet we permit that to occur with the housing supply. The irony is that children cannot even get an education unless they have housing to prove where they reside.

Some states have made education a right under their constitutions. The Connecticut Constitution was amended in 1965 to provide in Article 8, §1, that "there shall always be free public elementary and secondary schools in the state. The general assembly shall implement this principle by appropriate legislation." The court decisions make it clear that school systems must provide sufficient monies to meet the constitutional guarantee, but do not support a suit for claims that are not directly tied to the constitutional guarantee. In 1977, the Connecticut Supreme Court used the constitutional language to hold unconstitutional the state system of financing public schools, which relied primarily on the property tax without regard to the disparity in wealth in various communities. The court found that public education was a fundamental right and subject to strict scrutiny. The court did not devise an alternative method of financing, but left this to the legislature.[33]

In Arizona, where the right to education has been in the constitution since statehood, a challenge to the property tax as a funding mechanism failed. The Arizona Supreme Court held that as long as the school financing system meets the educational mandate of the Arizona Constitution (i.e., is uniform, free, available to all persons aged 6 to 21 and open a minimum of 6 months per year), it need otherwise be only rational, reasonable, and neither discriminatory nor capricious.[34]

The lessons we learn from analogizing a right to housing and education are twofold. First, once it is determined to be a primary right, the state must assure that financing is provided in a reasonable, nonarbitrary, noncapricious manner; when localities fail, the state must assume responsibility. Second, if it were a fundamental right, housing would no longer be viewed as an incident of the marketplace.

Expansion of Constitutional Rights

There are those who claim that enacting a constitutional right to housing would lead to attempts to amend the Constitution to add a whole panoply of other social and economic rights. We would argue, though, that none of these other rights, while important to a free society, are necessarily as crucial as the right to housing. Citizens are entitled to seek to amend their constitution in ways they deem appropriate, all the while considering each proposed amendment on its own merits.

Those who question whether a right to housing should be in their state constitution, or even in the statutes, should consider what other rights and entitlements are already part of those laws. The Massachusetts Constitution, for instance, contains in parts other than Article I many rights which are important; nevertheless, one is hard put to consider an amendment as important as the right to housing. In Article XLIX, for example, adopted in 1972, the people are given "the right to clean air and water, freedom from excessive and unnecessary noise, and the natural, scenic, historic, and esthetic qualities of their environment." Massachusetts citizens also enjoy rights in the state constitution that are also contained in the Bill of Rights of the U.S. Constitution. These include the right to hold public officials accountable (Article V); the right to compensation for a public taking (Article X); the right to a criminal trial in the location where the crime occurred (Article XIII); the right to a jury trial in certain civil cases (Article XV); the right to keep and bear arms (Article XVII); the right not to have excessive bail or to be subject to cruel or unusual punishment (Article XXVI); and the right to receive justice "as free, impartial and independent as the lot of humanity will admit" (Article XXIX).

While most would agree that these are among the fundamental rights which we should enjoy, it is difficult to make a serious case that a right to housing is less critical.

In order for housing to be a fundamental right it should be made a part of the basic rights section of a state constitution which generally contains language providing for the right of "acquiring, possessing and protecting property." It is not a startling extension of the right to obtain and retain property to provide the right to affordable housing. Article I of the Massachusetts Constitution and similiar articles in other state constitutions have been interpreted to require the provision of legal counsel and free access to court on the part of those who cannot afford to pay for these rights. Is the right to a decent home any less important or noble?

Statutes and State Constitutions

There is an argument that a right to housing is implicit in existing state laws. Various statutes provide a patchwork tapestry of rights to demonstrate threads of recognition for a right to housing throughout state law. For instance, Mass. General Law (M.G.L.) Ch. 118, §2 provides the basis for a public welfare benefit structure adequate for parents to raise children properly in their "own home." In addition, M.G.L. Ch. 18, §2(d) provides for emergency assistance to women for the prevention of homelessness and the provision of temporary shelter. M.G.L. Ch. 18B, §2 further expands welfare assistance to "women in transition" due to homelessness, and an equal protection argument would probably include coverage under this act for homeless men. There is also the existing lofty constitutional mandate that "it shall be the duty of legislatures and magistrates . . . to countenance and inculcate the principles of humanity and general benevolence [and] public and private charity." However, such humanity includes no obligation on the part of the state to care for its indigent or needy in any way: "[We] are aware of no Constitutional obligation on the state to provide financial assistance to all of its needy residents."[35]

In Massachusetts there is currently a law governing local communities requiring municipalities to support the provision of low- and moderate-income housing, the so-called Anti-Snob Zoning Law.[36] Towns may meet the obligation of this section by addressing either a land area or a dwelling unit standard. The land area standard is met "if land comprising more than (one and one half per cent) of the total area in the town zoned for either residential, commercial or industrial use has been used for low income housing." The dwelling standard is met if low- and moderate-income units comprise more than 10 percent of the total number of units.

On the other hand, the New Jersey Supreme Court, basing its rationale solely upon the New Jersey Constitution, demonstrated how a state court may implicitly establish a right to housing for low-income persons in developing communities in the so-called Mt. Laurel case.[37] The court held that a municipal zoning ordinance prohibiting townhouses, apartments, and mobile homes, and excluding low- and moderate-income housing violated the state's due process and equal protection clauses. Developing a basis to determine a compelling state interest, the court found, "it is plain beyond dispute the proper provision for adequate housing of all categories of people is certainly an absolute essential promotion of the general welfare required in all land use regulation." Although the *Mount Laurel* decision dealt specifically with exclusionary zoning practices in developing its reasoning, it has broader implications. The nexus between housing and the promotion of general welfare is equally apparent in other contexts. The court went on to discuss the adverse effects on a community caused by an inadequate supply of housing due, in part, to governmental action or inaction.

Because this was a constitutional right emanating from a court decision, not a legislative enactment, there was substantial difficulty in implementing the right, a problem that had to be addressed in a later opinion. In the later case the court recognized that exclusionary zoning practices affect not only the offending community but have a regional impact. Thus, in the second *Mount Laurel* decision, the court not only held that the community obligation goes beyond the failure to remedy discrimination against multi-family housing, but required affirmative provision of housing opportunities to satisfy the constitutional mandate. As a result of the court decision, the legislature finally enacted a statute creating planning criteria for developing communities and attempted to balance the need for increased housing opportunities with the financial and environmental concerns of the locality. However, "The specific location of such housing will of course continue to depend on sound municipal land planning."[38]

A constitutional right to housing would require an extension of the holding in the *Mount Laurel* case as well as modifications in the operation of the Massachusetts Anti-Snob Zoning Act. Although many of the provisions in the Anti-Snob Zoning Act could remain intact, an amendment guaranteeing habitable housing would provide state government with adequate leverage to get municipalities to reach their statutory limit of housing and additionally make land available for construction.

Interpretation of the Right to Housing

A State Supreme Judicial Court: The Final Interpreter of the Constitution and Any Amendments

If a constitutional amendment were enacted, it would be in the power of the legislature to establish programs and guidelines. However, it is within the jurisdiction of the courts to interpret the constitutionality of the legislation. Interpretation is within the authority of the highest state court under powers granted by the state constitution. This does not mean that there will be an automatic right to sue for every individual.

Standards

The constitution is the infrastructure for government—the amendments set the parameters. The courts are expected to interpret an amendment to a state's constitution in the broadest sense. "A word in an amendment to the constitution is not to be given a constricted meaning but the sense most obvious to the common understanding."[39] Amendments to the state constitution should be interpreted by the courts in the context of the history behind their adoption and the common understanding of the language at the time of adoption. The interpretation of an amendment is no different than the meaning given to the constitution as a whole. A constitution states general terms, not specific details.

Advisory Opinions

In interpreting an amendment, the court may issue two types of opinions. A state's highest court will often issue advisory opinions. These opinions begin to give shape and meaning to a new amendment. An example of how a state may issue an advisory opinion can be seen following the 1975 passage of the State Equal Rights Amendment, Article 106 of the Amendments to the Constitution of Massachusetts. In 1977, the court was asked to review a proposed bill prohibiting women from participating with men in certain contact sports. The proposed bill presented an outright prohibition on female participation in male sports. The court responded that under Art. 106 of the constitution the prohibition in the bill is subject to the same strict scrutiny standard as applied previously in equal protection challenges. Thus, legislation based on disparate treatment of the sexes would be upheld only when there exists a compelling state interest. The language, the court found, would not survive the strict scrutiny test. In 1977 the court evaluated another bill pending before the legislature restricting participation in an extracurricular activity to female students. The court examined the facts supporting the bill and failed to find even a "fair and substantial relationship" to a state objective. The result in both cases was that legislation was not enacted.

These advisory opinions of the justices are merely legal opinions of the court on various matters and are only guidelines for subsequent litigants. If a bill is enacted, it will be open to future litigants to attempt to demonstrate a legitimate governmental purpose furthered by the legislation that is sufficient to overcome the claim of unconstitutionality.[40] Thus, legislation concerning housing could very well be presented before the court to be tested for constitutionality in light of the amendment. An opinion issued by the court would become an advisory guideline for all future challenges based upon the newly adopted amendment.

Specific Controversies

The other type of opinion issued by a state's highest court involves specific controversies. Such controversies permit the court to further refine interpretations of an amendment. In the 1977 advisory opinion on the Massachusetts equal rights amendment above, the court refused to express its view on whether different wording would change the constitutionality of a proposed statute prohibiting women from participating with men in certain contact sports:

> An individual case involves a real, rather than a hypothetical complainant; it furnishes specific facts on which effective constitutional analysis may be based; and it provides a vehicle for the presentation of circumstances and argument in support of the constitutionality of a statute, rule or requirement.[41]

Following this guidance from the court, interpretations of a state constitutional right to housing amendment may be best presented in the context of specific controversies in which the constitutional rights of a party are in question. For example, a party may claim a violation of state constitutional rights under the housing amendment for the failure by a local government to provide secure adequate housing for that party. By examining the facts of the case, the court will develop a legal interpretation of the amendment applicable to that case in particular and to other similar situations in the future.

The original *Mt. Laurel* case began with a specific controversy over zoning restrictions in certain New Jersey communities that excluded multi-family housing. The court received much criticism for its "activist" decision in finding that municipalities did not have the right to exclude multi-family housing. The court responded in the second decision:

> We act first and foremost because the Constitution of our state requires protection of the interests involved and the Legislature has not protected them. We recognize the social and economic controversy (and its political consequences) that has resulted in relatively little legislative action in this field. We understand the enormous difficulty of achieving a political consensus that might lead to significant legislation enforcing the constitutional mandate better than we can, legislation that might completely remove this court from those controversies. But enforcement of Constitutional Rights cannot await a supporting political consensus. So while we have always preferred legislative to judicial action in this field, we shall continue—until the Legislature acts—to do our best to uphold the Constitutional obligation that underlies the Mount Laurel doctrine. That is our duty. We may not build houses, but we do enforce the Constitution.[42]

As a general rule, the judicial role could decrease as a result of legislative and executive action, but necessarily will expand to the extent that the court remains alone in the field. In the absence of adequate legislative and executive help, the New Jersey court felt compelled to give meaning to the constitutional doctrine in the cases before it through the court's own devices, even if they are relatively less suitable.

Enforcement of an Amendment

The language of an amendment, either explicitly or through interpretation, may require the violations to be through the actions of the state. A constitutional amendment should be read as a prohibition against state actions denying the constitutional rights of its individuals to adequate and affordable housing. For example, the construction of a state's equal rights amendment protects the constitutional rights of the individual against state actions. In other words, a state may be sued by a citizen who claims her state constitutional rights have been violated by discriminatory actions of the state.[43]

Strict Scrutiny Standard

With a constitutional amendment, existing protections for residents living in state and federal public or subsidized housing will not change dramatically. Some of the protections which a right to housing amendment will extend to all tenants have already been provided for subsidized housing tenants because housing offered by a governmental entity has been held by the courts to be an "entitlement." If the right to housing were enacted, the notion that housing is an entitlement would be expanded. Laws that conflicted with this principle would be subject to a "strict scrutiny" standard in the courts. In order for these laws to be upheld there would have to be a "compelling state interest."

A constitutional right to housing would have an impact upon other aspects of housing and even family law. Generally, controls on rental housing have been held to be constitutional so long as the restrictions do not constitute a taking of the property without compensation.[44] Rent and condominium control regulations are generally based on the health and welfare powers given to local communities to protect their citizens. These restrictions, while they have been mostly upheld as a valid exercise of government power, have come under some attack. For example, in a recent Ninth Circuit Court of Appeals case, the court held that a rent control ordinance limiting the amount of rent mobile home parks could charge and restricting the park owner's ability to evict tenants or to remove their mobile home from the park upon sale, constituted a taking. According to the court it caused the landlord to lose forever a fundamental aspect of fee simple ownership; the right to control who will occupy his property and on what terms. The court found this was a violation of the landlord's liberty interest. A right to housing would provide more support for the tenant's property interest and permit possibly more comprehensive regulation. These regulations would help to provide more affordable housing opportunities, thus helping our most vulnerable citizens.[45]

A right to housing would also create a property interest for tenants, requiring good or just cause before termination. Those tenants who are living in areas subject to speculation and gentrification would have a defense to an attempted eviction so long as they paid their rent and didn't violate any material terms of their lease. A similar argument could be used for many groups subject to discrimination under the law, including single-parent families.

As in public housing, any right to housing would give new life to a state statute that prohibits discrimination against persons solely on the basis of their source of income.[46] This statute suffered a setback in Massachusetts when the Supreme Judicial Court held that there was a business reason defense available to a landlord who discriminated against Section 8 tenants. The landlord claimed he couldn't use his regular leases, couldn't collect a security deposit and last month's rent from section 8 tenants, and thus had to alter his regular practices for these applicants. The statute is unclear because it merely states that a landlord cannot discriminate "solely because the individual is a recipient." Thus, as the *Brown* case indicates, if the discrimination is not solely for the purpose of denying someone housing because the source of income is public assistance, it appears the landlord may do so. Laws designed clearly to protect families of limited means could be strengthened with the implementation of a right to housing.

A particularly difficult problem for single parents is distribution of realty following a divorce or separation. A right to housing could alter the distribution of property if the state assumes that, when possible, individuals who are presently providing shelter for themselves should continue to do so. Such an assumption would be supported by the courts by distributing property in favor of the best interests of the family. In a Missouri case the court argued that it is given the power to decide who gets the shelter because it may consider the economic circumstances of each spouse. The court found the lower court erred when it ignored the difficulty the wife would experience in trying to find shelter for herself and her children. A similar result was reached in a Florida case. The appellate court failed to award the primary residence to the custodial parent, the wife, until the youngest child reached the age of majority. Thus, a constitutional amendment could help combat some of the problems women face in seeking shelter by encouraging courts to award residential property in ways that will assist family members who are most in need of a primary residence.[47]

Single-Parent Families and Implementation of the Right to Housing

Implementation of a constitutional right to housing would inevitably occur over a period of many years, not all at once. Furthermore, establishment of such a constitutional right would not mandate a specific program or policy, but rather will create an affirmative obligation to act—in ways that state policymakers and local communities determine to be the most appropriate and efficacious.

It is reasonable to expect that implementation of a state right to housing would involve increased public expenditures for this necessity, because of the very small proportion of the state budget now devoted to housing. However, enactment of such a constitutional amendment would not primarily impel a substantial increase in public dollars for housing, but rather an evolution of our concept of housing and the nature of the housing market; single-parent families are likely to be major beneficiaries of such an evolution, since the private housing market and traditional public policies have been so unresponsive to their needs.

Achievement of a right to housing will actually lead to a far more cost-effective use of those public dollars which are appropriated for housing, as it will require a more rational, integrated and comprehensive approach to meeting housing needs than the ad hoc and piecemeal approach we have had heretofore. The right to housing would no doubt result, for example, in much more systematic and coordinated efforts to preserve existing affordable housing and reduce displacement of single-parent families and other vulnerable groups, thereby minimizing the need for costly new construction of subsidized housing. Indeed, emphasis on new construction has precluded a serious public commitment to halting and reversing the loss of affordable units that has been occurring in the absence of a right to housing.

Much of the actual responsibility for implementation of a right to housing would be on local governments, as communities differ in their housing situations and much of established housing regulation and delivery already exists at the local level. Thus the obligations of the state government would primarily be to establish standards and provide various types of assistance to localities and, only as a last resort if localities fail to act, compel and/or override local action.

Many different types of housing action and policy affecting single-parent families could be expected following establishment of a constitutional right to housing. Some measures would grow out of and respond to the special needs of such families, while other more general policies could also particularly benefit single-parent families. In what follows we consider both targeted programs and broader policies that would be especially beneficial to single-parent families.

State Government Action

Implementation of a right to housing would necessitate an affirmation, extension and strengthening of the responsibilities and power of statewide housing agencies. It would involve, as well, some clarification by the legislature of the mandates of other state-sponsored agencies involved with housing such as commissions against discrimination to ensure that their activities affirmatively further the realization of the right to housing.

Some of the types of state government actions which could be initiated to implement the right to housing are as follows:

1. The legislature and the statewide housing agency could create a framework of guidelines and procedures for communities to carry out housing needs assessment, goal-setting, policy development, and implementation aimed at achieving the right to housing for all through the preservation and extension of housing affordability and security of tenure and the affirmative promotion of fair housing and equal opportunity. Such a framework would ensure that the needs of single-parent families are explicitly recognized and incorporated into local and state planning. The housing agency would be mandated and funded adequately to provide technical assistance to localities to develop and implement their housing plans, including support for intergovernmental and regional cooperation in furtherance of the right to housing. (Massachusetts Executive Office of Communities and Development affordable housing initiatives grants are an example, on a modest scale, of this type of assistance.)

2. A state agency would be given the authority to ensure affirmative local action to preserve and strengthen the right to housing (including, e.g., local participation in regional fair share housing opportunity programs) through a mixture of financial and legal incentives and disincentives, including, as a legal stick, state overrides and acting as houser of last resort. Such authority would, for example, pressure localities and provide state governments with the power to provide emergency/immediate shelter, transitional/short-term shelter, and permanent/long-term housing for single-parent families.

3. A state legislature could enact enabling laws providing local governments with a set of tools to be used as localities deemed appropriate for affirmative housing action in furtherance of the right to housing. These might include, for example, enabling legislation for localities to adopt linkage programs and real estate transfer or antispeculation taxes with proceeds earmarked for affordable, nonprofit housing (presumably exempt from tax cap), or a state-assessed but locally collected real estate transfer or antispeculation tax. This would also include enabling legislation for local condominium conversion and rent controls, and inclusionary zoning to ensure that neighborhoods and developers incorporate a

reasonable proportion of short-term and transitional housing for displaced and at-risk single-parent families, as well as affordable long-term housing.

4. A state legislature could provide state resources from special mechanisms in order for communities to carry out appropriately phased implementation of their housing policies and plans. For example, it would be possible for the state to channel unearned interest on property tax and insurance escrows held by lenders, excess interest on security deposits, and other nontax sources to local right to housing programs. (For example, in Massachusetts there are also new state trust funds, such as the Housing Partnership Revolving Fund ($35 million) and the Government Land Bank Thrift Fund ($100 million) which could be earmarked for developing and acquiring affordable housing for nonspeculative ownership.)

5. A state legislature could commit a specific minimum fraction of the state budget annually to existing and new state and local policies and programs in furtherance of a right to housing, just as a permanent minimum level of funding is now provided for the various constitutional officers, the judiciary, and the legislature itself. This would assure stable funding and thus permit long-range and comprehensive planning with assurance of resources for implementation.

6. A state legislature could reform various existing laws and programs which directly or indirectly affect housing affordability and accessibility, but which are not as cost-effective as they could be or are actually counterproductive. One such area would involve altering the subsidy formulas in state-aided housing (public housing and rental assistance programs) to a sliding scale based on income and housing cost that more realistically reflects true ability to pay; single-parent families would be the primary beneficiaries of such reform, since even those in subsidized housing are generally paying more than they can afford. A second area would be fire insurance reform to take the profit out of arson; the law would require that insurance proceeds be used to rebuild for existing residents, with the municipality as additional loss payee to ensure proper use of insurance proceeds. A third area of such reform might apply to a state housing finance agency, mandating greater attention to housing for the neediest populations and requiring limited-equity resale stipulations in their home ownership programs.

7. Another major state action in support of a right to housing would be to increase public assistance grant levels to prevent and overcome homelessness and shelter poverty among recipient fam-

ilies. Such action would most directly and dramatically improve the affordability situations of single-parent families on AFDC.

8. Codifying a state housing bill of rights, including existing laws and expanded statutory rights, would do a great deal to begin to move toward the notion of affordable and accessible housing as an entitlement. The major tenets of such a codification could be the following:

- Statutory life tenure for all tenants who continue to pay their rent and do not interfere with the rights of other tenants (just cause for eviction).
- Life estate security for low- and moderate-income elderly home owners under equity conversion and foreclosure relief programs.
- Stronger enforcement provisions of state sanitary codes, with mandated community and resident participation, and strengthened receivership and condemnation provisions.
- Legislative recognition of the right of tenants to form unions and bargain collectively.
- Strengthened antidiscrimination enforcement powers to state antidiscrimination commissions and local fair housing commissions.
- Funding for public education, outreach, publicity and technical assistance to housing residents and groups on their housing rights and how to exercise them individually and collectively.

Local Actions

Under a right to housing constitutional mandate, each local government would have to develop procedures and undertake actions that demonstrate their good-faith effort to preserve and provide housing opportunities for vulnerable members of the community. The particular mix of policies and programs would vary greatly from one municipality to another, of course, reflecting the local housing market, demographics and types of physical and financial resources available.

There are an extensive variety of possible local policies out of which a locality might craft an appropriate program that is responsive to the findings of their mandated needs assessment and consistent with the goals they establish. The remainder of this section considers such policies with particular relevance directly or indirectly for single-parent families. The policies are organized around the following five broad policy goals:[48]

1. Preserving affordable rental housing
2. Facilitating home ownership without speculation
3. Preserving and upgrading government-assisted housing
4. Producing housing for nonspeculative ownership
5. Generating and channeling financing for social production and ownership

Preserving Affordable Rental Housing. Although many communities have supported the expansion of subsidized housing, most single-parent renters do not receive subsidies and are shelter poor. They are thus in need of measures which can at least limit—if not reduce—the cost of their housing. Some such measures can deal directly with the cost of housing. Others can have the effect of reducing displacement of low- and moderate-income people, as displacement usually results in both the loss of relatively lower-cost units and the displacees paying more for whatever housing they eventually obtain. Still other measures can permanently remove existing private rental housing from the speculative market.

Local actions to protect tenants and enhance the viability and affordability of the private rental stock could include strict enforcement of the elements of a state's housing bill of rights, aggressive seeking and utilizing of available state and federal housing assistance funds, and enactment of strong rent, eviction, and conversion controls.

Private rental housing is increasingly being recognized as an anachronism, at least by those landlords who are converting to condos, abandoning their buildings, or burning them for the insurance money. To the extent that the state and local policies make conversion and arson no longer available or profitable, and to the extent that tenants achieve greater legal protection and municipal enforcement, landlords who wish to bail out should be able to do so in ways that are not harmful to tenants. Therefore, mechanisms must be established—or existing mechanisms more fully utilized—so that private rental housing can be converted to forms of social or nonspeculative ownership, such as nonequity or limited-equity coops, mutual housing associations (i.e., no possibility of speculative resale but assured life tenure), ownership by community trusts, or public ownership. Single-parent families in unsubsidized rental housing would be major beneficiaries of such conversions, and not only in terms of enhanced affordability and security of tenure: such housing creates increased resident control and participation, thereby facilitating mutual aid and the development of shared services, which are important components of the "housing plus" needs of single-parent families.

Facilitating Home Ownership without Speculation. The attractions of home ownership are undeniable: all of us desire the security of tenure and control over our living space which home ownership offers, along with the possibility of relatively stable housing costs, some equity accumulation, income tax benefits, and a sense of full community membership and social status which home ownership may provide.

Yet conventional home ownership is not without problems: high acquisition costs and interest rates have made it virtually impossible for all but the wealthiest to buy their first home; the risks of mortgage foreclosure and tax foreclosure undermine the security that this tenure seems to offer; the popular home owner tax benefits are highly regressive, flowing almost entirely to home owners with incomes of over $30,000; and, sadly, home owners may place the enhancement of property values above the preservation and enhancement of community, developing resentment toward tenants and others they regard of lower social or economic status, and finally, riding the wave of speculative increases in property values which can deprive other members of the community of the possibility of home ownership.

The challenge, then, is to find ways of facilitating the positive aspects of home ownership while overcoming the negative ones. There are a number of feasible local strategies which municipalities could use under the following general categories:

- Increasing opportunities for low- and moderate-income community residents, including single-parent families, to achieve individual or coop home ownership through below-market prices and/or financing.
- Maintaining continued affordability for future owners and ensuring community stability by establishing resale stipulations through deed covenants, liens, or retention of land title by a community land trust.
- Increasing security of tenure and housing affordability for existing low- and moderate-income home owners through foreclosure protection, equity conversion, tax relief, and rehabilitation grants.

While most single-parent families cannot afford conventional home ownership, even with existing price and mortgage reduction programs, as discussed earlier, policies to implement a right to housing would increase opportunities for shared ownership arrangements: these include limited-equity and nonequity coops and mutual housing associations, mentioned in the previous section, and also joint ownership of resale-restricted, below-market single-family homes by several single-parent families.

In addition, a right to housing could increase security of tenure and affordability for those single parents who are home owners, by providing them with property tax relief, rehabilitation grants, and foreclosure protection in return for their giving up the right to sell in the speculative market.

With a right to housing, divorce would be less likely to result in the loss of the existing home by the parent with custody of the children. As mentioned earlier, a right to housing would result in modifications of family law in this regard. Also, when a divorce included a property division involving an owner-occupied home, nonprofit entities might be mandated to buy out the departing spouse's interest, according the single parent and children the right to stay in the home and at an affordable cost but with limited-equity resale restrictions.

Preserving and Upgrading Government-Assisted Housing. Most larger cities and some smaller communities have a considerable amount of housing under subsidy, either through the local housing authority or privately owned but government-assisted, with single-parent families among the greatest beneficiaries, as already indicated. Nevertheless, the extent of shelter poverty and homelessness reveals the need both for more subsidized units and for subsidies more appropriate to need. Yet at the same time, there are factors working to reduce the amount of assisted housing—factors which localities will need to oppose if the housing affordability problem is not to worsen and single-parent family homelessness not to increase. Municipalities themselves have limited control over most subsidized housing, but it is possible to establish a policy of support for the preservation and improvement of this vital resource. The elements could encompass the following:

- Preserving the existing supply of publicly owned housing and state and federally subsidized housing for lower-income people, by preventing private resale of public housing and conversion of subsidized housing to market-rate rentals or condominiums and requiring one-for-one replacement of assisted units which must be removed from the housing stock for socially necessary reasons.
- Protecting tenants in government-assisted housing and enhancing its affordability and viability, by upgrading existing public housing, supporting changes in rent formulas for public and subsidized housing, plus adequate operating subsidies and strictly enforcing a state's housing bill of rights.

- Increasing nonspeculative ownership of government-assisted housing, by pushing for foreclosure by HUD and the state housing finance agency on irresponsible owners, and using local discretionary benefits and leverage to encourage conversion to limited-equity resident-controlled coops or nonprofit community ownership.

Producing Housing for Nonspeculative Ownership. It is all too easy to say that there ought to be more federal and state funds for the production of subsidized housing. The reality, of course, is that drastic federal cutbacks continue, while state aid for subsidized housing production will not come close to offsetting the federal cuts. Local communities obviously should actively work to restore and increase funding, especially for state and federally aided public housing, while aggressively seeking and utilizing whatever funds are available. There are some types of local initiative, though, which are possible and which also could be pursued aggressively, rather than placing all hope and blame on the state and federal coffers. Single-parent families would benefit both directly and indirectly from localities being mandated to pursue the following housing production policies:

- Increasing public and community control over land for housing, through establishment and support for community land trusts, maintaining existing public ownership of land suitable for housing, and discouraging land speculation through taxation and incentives.
- Increasing public and community control over housing development to encourage development of affordable housing, including emergency shelters and transitional housing, as well as permanent housing, through site control, design review, permit approval, tax incentives, etc.
- Supporting development for nonspeculative ownership, through encouragement of public housing development, assistance to nonprofit community development corporations and housing partnerships, joint ventures between developers and social agencies, and requiring deed restrictions to ensure affordable resale.

Generating and Channeling Funds for Social Production and Ownership. Although the possibilities for generating substantial amounts of social capital at the local level for acquisition, rehabilitation, and construction of housing are, of course, severely limited, there are a number of intriguing possibilities for raising funds and many opportunities to target better the funds which are available. Local policies in this area could encompass the following:

- Expanding existing resources and developing new funding sources for the production and preservation of affordable housing for nonspeculative ownership, through such measures as a real estate transfer or antispeculation tax, linkage requiring commercial developers to make payments into a housing trust fund, use of municipal pension funds, use of special state trust fund revenues (see above), strengthened Urban Development Action Grant payback terms, and requiring luxury housing developers to contribute to or build lower-income housing and/or emergency and transitional housing (inclusionary zoning), pressing for increased state funding for public and subsidized housing, and the tapping and targeting of private social financing.
- Better utilizing available public funds to increase the production and preservation of affordable housing, by using municipal leverage to direct such funds to projects that are for populations, such as single parents, poorly served by the private market, while also promoting nonspeculative ownership of such housing.

Conclusion

The campaign for a right to housing represents a historic milestone. It is not the first step toward the realization of the right, but rather the crystallization of many efforts over many years to preserve and expand housing opportunity, affordability, and security of tenure. Nor would the adoption of a right to housing be the endpoint of the process, but a new stage. It would constitute a fundamental commitment by a state to the provision of housing opportunities for all its people on a permanent, ongoing basis, now and hereafter, not just today and in response to the crisis of the moment.

Our society has experienced a long historic pattern of housing problems: displacement of tenant farmers, even in colonial times and into the 20th century; tenement conditions and discrimination faced by wave after wave of immigrants, from the Irish in the 1840s to Latino and Asian immigrants today; massive foreclosures and dislocations, rural and urban of the Great Depression of the 1930s; urban "removal" of the 1950s and 1960s; arson and in many areas rapid rent escalation in the 1960s and 1970s; and the homelessness, condo evictions, runaway speculation, and denied home ownership dreams of the 1980s.

In each era, the housing problems have brought public concern, community outcries, government responses; but generally the responses have been ad hoc and the reactions piecemeal (although, as we have indicated, the institutional changes of the 1930s created a virtual right to housing for white, middle-income Americans).

Our society is now at a point, though, where a new public consciousness is emerging about the profound significance of housing in all of our lives—individually and socially. This new public awareness and concern is an instance of yet another more hopeful pattern in our national development—historic shifts in consciousness about our shared rights and obligations.

As our social morality grows to encompass recognition of the pervasive importance of housing—and the consequences of its denial—a right to housing represents the tangible expression of this new consciousness. We realize now that housing is not just an individual problem; it is not just a problem of the few left behind by pervasive prosperity; rather it is a common social need, requiring a common affirmation in that document that embodies our common commitments and purposes.

Endnotes

1. Michael E. Stone, "Housing and the Dynamics of U.S. Capitalism," in *Critical Perspectives on Housing*, ed. Rachel Bratt, Chester Hartman and Ann Meyerson (Philadelphia: Temple University Press, 1986), pp. 44–45.
2. Affidavit of Matthew P. Dumont, M.D., in *Massachusetts Coalition for the Homeless* v. *Dukakis*, Suffolk Superior Court, Civil No. 80109, May 5, 1986, pp. 4–6.
3. See Eugenie Ladner Birch, ed., *The Unsheltered Woman in the 1980s* (Piscataway, N.J.: Center for Urban Policy Research, 1985); Ann R. Markuson, "City Spatial Structure, Women's Household Work, and National Urban Policy," *Signs: Journal of Women in Culture and Society*, vol. 5, no. 3 (Spring 1980) supplement: 23–44; Dolores Hayden, *Redesigning the American Dream: The Future of Housing, Work and Family Life* (New York: W. W. Norton, 1984).
4. For a fuller discussion of the approach see Michael E. Stone, "Shelter Poverty in Boston: Problem and Program," in *Housing Policies in the Eighties: Choices and Outcomes*, ed. Chester Hartman and Sara Rosenberry (New York: Praeger Press, 1987).
5. For detailed adaption of this approach to the situation of AFDC families, see "Sworn Statement of Michael E. Stone, Ph.D.," in *Massachusetts Coalition for the Homeless* v. *Dukakis*, Suffolk Superior Court, Civil No. 80109, May 5, 1986.

6. Episcopal City Mission, "Housing: a Basic Human Right," Boston: (1986), p. 3.

7. U.S. Catholic Bishops, "Catholic Social Teaching and the U.S. Economy," 2d Draft, October 1985.

8. *The Jewish Advocate*, September 25, 1986.

9. Rabbi Frank Waldorf, "Rabbi's column," *Temple Sinai*, vol. 48, No. 2, Brookline, Mass.

10. *Tax Commissioner* v. *Putnam*, 227 Mass. 522 (1917). *Davis* v. *Passman* (1979), 99 S. Ct. 2264, 2275. "The Constitution, on the other hand, does not partake of the prolixity of a legal code [cite omitted]. It speaks instead with a majestic simplicity. One of its important objects [cite omitted] is the designation of rights."

11. Law Professor Charles L. Black, Jr., Rubin Lectures, The Columbia School of Law, March 26, 1986.

12. *Javins* v. *First National Realty Corporation*, 428 F2d 1071, 1079-1080 (D.C. Cir. 1970).

13. Frank I. Michelman, "The Advent of a Right to Housing," *Harvard Civil Rights-Civil Liberties Law Review* 5 (April 1970): 207, 212.

14. *United States* v. *Certain Lands in the City of Louisville*, 9 F. Supp. 137 (1935).

15. Lawrence M. Friedman, "Public Housing and the Poor: An Overview," *California Law Review* 54 (1954): 642, 646.

16. Ibid.; pp. 652, 653.

17. Emily Achtenberg and Peter Marcuse, "The Causes of the Housing Problem," in *America's Housing Crisis, What Is to Be Done*, ed. Chester Hartman (Boston: Routledge and Kegan Paul, 1983), p. 100.

18. *Lindsey* v. *Normet*, 405 U.S. 56 (1972).

19. *Ibid.*, p. 879.

20. Michelman, "The Advent of a Right to Housing," p. 207.

21. *Ibid;* pp. 211–25.

22. *See* Steinberg, "Adequate Housing for All: Myth or Reality?" *University of Pittsburgh Law Review* 37 (1974): 63, 68. Comment, "Towards a Recognition of a Constitutional Right to Housing," *University of Missouri at Kansas City Law Review* 42 (1974): 362. Mathews, "The Right to Housing," *Black Law Journal* 6 (1983): 247. Notes: "Building a House of Legal Rights: A Plea For the Homeless:" *St. Johns Law Review* 59 (1985): 530.

23. *Callahan* v. *Casey*, N.Y.L.J., Dec. 11, 1979 at 10.

24. *Joy* v. *Daniels*, 479 F.2d 1236 (4th Cir. 1973); *Holmes* v. *New York City Housing Authority*, 398 F.2d 262 (2d Cir. 1968).

25. *Thomas* v. *Housing Authority of Little Rock*, 282 F.Supp. 575 (E.D.Ark. 1967); *Battle* v. *Municipal Housing Authority of Yonkers*, 53 F.R.D. 423 (S.D. New York 1971); *Hill* v. *Housing Authority of Kansas City Missouri*, Civ. Act. #20 563.2, 2 Pov. L. Rep. (CCH) ¶19, 632 (W.D. Mo. 1974); *Atkisson* v. *Kern County Housing Authority*, 59 Cal. App.3d 89, 130 Cal. Rep. 375(1976); *Nicolas* v. *Housing Authority of Indianapolis*, Civil No IP71-C378 (S.D.Indiana, 1971); *Mandina* v. *Lynn*, 357 F.Supp. 547 (N.D.Cal. 1973), *Fletcher* v. *Housing Authority of Louisville*, 491 F.2d 793 (6th Cir. 1974) *vacated* 419 U.S. 812 (1974), *reinstated on remand*, 525 F.2d 532 (6th Cir.

1975); *Junker* v. *Housing Authority of Milwaukee,* Civ. #68-C-303 (E.D. Wis. 1970).

26. *See* 24 C.F.R. §966, 24 C.F.R. §882.210, and 24 C.F.R. §401.

27. *Devines* v. *Maier,* 665 F.2d 138 (7th Cir. 1981) *rev. in part on other grounds,* 728 F.2d 876 (1984); See also *Ward* v. *Downtown Development Authority,* 786 F.2d 1526 (1986); *Texas, Inc.* v. *Short,* 454 U.S. 516, 526 (1982); *Alamo Land and Cattle Co. Inc.* v. *Arizona,* 424 U.S. 295, 303 (1976); *United States* v. *Petty Motor Co.,* 327 U.S. 818 (1946).

28. See, for example, *Berman* v. *Parker,* 348 U.S. 6, 75 S.Ct. 98 (1954); *Loretto* v. *CATV Corp.* 458 U.S. 450, 102 S. Ct. 3164 (1982); *Birkenfeld* v. *City of Berkeley,* 500 P.2d 1001, 130 Cal. Rptr., 465 (1976); *Flynn* v. *City of Cambridge Rent Control Board,* 383 Mass. 152 (1981); *Marshall House* v. *Rent Control Board of Brookline,* 358 Mass. 703, 705-706 (1970); *Niles* v. *Boston Rent Control Administrator,* 6 Mass. App. Ct. 135 (1979); *Wilson* v. *Brown,* 137 F.2d at 351-52 (1943).

29. 42 U.S.C. §3612, 42 U.S.C. §1982.

30. 42 U.S.C. §3608(d)(5).

31. For example, federal courts have granted relief in cases where courts have failed to provide counsel to indigent defendants. *Tucker* v. *City of Montgomery Board of Com'r,* 410 F.Supp. 494 (D.C. Ala. 1976). But, the courts have not reduced the right to counsel to a superficial right. Persons are entitled to a competent lawyer; counsel that is reasonably diligent, conscientious and competent. *U.S.* v. *Bailey,* 581 F.2d 984 (D.C. Cir. 1978). On the other hand, a defendant is not entitled to choose a particular attorney for court appointment, *Brown* v. *Craven,* 424 F.2d 1166 (9th Cir. 1970). The defendant may accept the court's appointee, and though the defendant may ask for a substitution, it is up to the court's discretion as to whether to grant it, depending upon the reasonableness of the demand. *Raullerson* v. *Patterson,* 272 F.Supp. 495 (D. Colo. 1967).

32. *Michaud* v. *Sheriff of Essex County,* 390 Mass 523,532,534,535(1983).

33. *Waterbury Teachers Assn.* v. *Furlong,* 162 Conn. 390, 399 (1972); *Horton* v. *Meskill,* 172 Conn. 615, 376 A.2d 359 (1977).

34. *Shofstall* v. *Hollins,* 110 Ariz. 88, 515 P.2d 590 (1973).

35. (MA. Const. Pt. 2, c.5, §2); *Opinion of the Justices,* 368 Mass 831, 846 (1975) (Opinion in response to questions submitted by the Mass. House of Representatives on the Constitutionality of a proposed, and subsequently adopted, amendment to M.G.L. Ch. 117 §1 limiting the provision of General Relief.

36. Mass Gen. Laws c.40B, §20-23 the so-called *Anti-Snob Zoning Law.*

37. *Southern Burlington County NAACP* v. *Township of Mount Laurel,* 67 N.J.151, 336 A.2d 713 (1975).

38. *Southern Burlington County N.A.A.C.P.* v. *Township of Mount Laurel,* 456 A.2d 390, 92 N.J. 158 (1983), p. 416.

39. *Opinion of the Justices to the House of Rep.* 262 Mass. 603 (1928); *Oneida Indian Nation of New York* v. *State of New York,* 691 F.2d 1070 (2d Cir. 1982).

40. See *Opinion of the Justices to the House of Rep.* 374 Mass. 836, 371 N.E.2d 426 (1977); *Opinion of the Justices,* 373 Mass. 883, 366 N.E.2d 733 (1977), p. 888.

41. *Opinion of the Justices to the House of Rep.* 371 N.E.2d 426, 430 *supra.*

42. *Mt. Laurel II, supra*, p. 417.

43. The concept of state action as contrasted to private action dates back to the *Civil Rights Cases*, 109 U.S. 3 (1883). In that decision the Supreme Court held that the *individual invasion of individual rights* is not the subject matter of the equal protection clause. See *Shelley* v. *Kraemer, supra* and *King* v. *S. Jersey National Bank*, 66 N.J.161, 330 A.2d 1, 8 (1974). Other states have interpreted their state equal rights amendment specifically to apply to actions by the state against its people. *Schriener* v. *McKensie Tank Lines, Etc*, 408 So. 2d 711 (1982); *Murphy* v. *Harleysville Mut. Ins. Co.*, 282 Pa. Super 244 (1979). Thus, according to these cases sex discrimination violations can only be brought against the state, not against private individuals. However, if there is a symbiotic relationship between the state and a private concern, the line is not so clear. See *Burton* v. *Wilmington Parking Authority*, 365 U.S. 715 (1961). Even if there is a close nexus between the state and the challenged action, the private party may be treated as the state itself. *Jackson* v. *Metropolitan Edison Co*. 419 U.S. 345 (1974). Thus, determining whether a party may challenge the actions of another for violating a constitutional right to housing may depend upon whether the offender is considered "the state."

44. Judson, Victoria, "Defining Property Rights: The Constitutionality of Protecting Tenants from Condominium Conversion." *Harvard Civil Rights and Civil Liberties Law Review* 18 (Winter 1983): 179.

45. *Hall* v. *City of Santa Barbara*, 797 F.2d 1493 (9th Cir. 1986).

46. *Attorney General* v. *Brown*, 400 Mass. 826 (1987).

47. *Gooding* v. *Gooding*, 67 S.W.2d 332 (Mo. App. 1984); *Neustein* v. *Neustein*, 503 So. 2d 439 (Fla. App. 4 Dist. 1987).

48. Michael Stone's "Shelter Poverty in Boston: Problem and Program" (copyright 1986; used with permission).

Chapter 10

SOCIAL REFORM: EXPANDING CHOICES AND INCREASING INSTITUTIONAL RESPONSIVENESS

Elizabeth A. Mulroy

Images of single-parent families begin to emerge from the foregoing analyses of the single-parent phenomenon. Most single-parent families are headed by women; yet they are a heterogeneous group. Single mothers are struggling to put together a manageable package of income, child care, and affordable, safe housing—a struggle made difficult by biases in the courts, the workplace, and the housing market. Such biases are based on gender, race, and class. Institutional biases are reinforced by social welfare policies built on the notion that America can do harm by doing good (generous relief to the poor would encourage laziness and undermine the work incentive) and that investment of the nation's resources to social programs would decrease economic growth by depleting investment capital. Evidence presented in the preceding chapters suggests:

1. Creating equal opportunity does not ensure equal access or equal outcome.
2. Laissez-faire policies which rely on the market to solve social problems fail to achieve their purpose.
3. Implementation of existing policies has been mired by inadequate resources, by attitudes of administrators, by rigidity

of bureaucratic structures, and fragmentation of service delivery systems.

If policy responses recommended by the authors were to be adopted, and suggested institutional changes were implemented, American society would move toward a significant strengthening of single-parent family life. Such investment would have a threefold purpose: first, it would serve to raise the standard of living of the single-parent family unit, creating opportunities and choices where few or none now exist; second, poor mothers and children would have access to active citizenship and democratic participation in the governance of neighborhood and community institutions which affect them; third, the children would subsequently be better prepared for stewardship of the global economy they are about to inherit—an outcome we cannot afford to discount.

This perspective is threatening to many who believe that acceptance of diversity in family form and adoption of responsive public policies portends the demise of the traditional nuclear family structure and threatens dearly held American values of how family life ought to be. It will be argued in this chapter that investment in meeting the needs of single-mother households does not signal impending doom for the traditional family form. Rather, such investment is warranted to counter the cumulative, injurious effects of institutional sexism, racism, and classism. Stereotyped thinking ignores the historical inequities in status, education, employment, and pay between women and men, and between whites and blacks, perpetuating false images on which public policy decisions are left to be made. Ultimately, it is the children, as well as their mothers, who are disadvantaged by it.

This chapter will first make some summary remarks about the realities of single-parent families' lives, an issue initially raised in Chapter 1. Then it will call for social reform in order to expand choices for single-parent families and to increase institutional responsiveness. One concluding theme of this book is that residential instability is a dilemma for single-parent families. Therefore, some final recommendations will be made to address this point.

Reality: The Role Burden Syndrome

Caring and Providing for Children

Recently, attention has been drawn to the problems middle class, dual-career couples have juggling work and family responsibilities. A key problem has been identified as role allocation, wherein father does not equally share the housework and child care, in part because mother is reluctant to relinquish child care responsibilities which she still perceives to be her primary function.[1] This unequal allocation creates an overburdened mother, because strides toward workplace equality have not been matched by equality on the home front.

On the other hand, in households headed by mothers, no other adult is available to whom roles can be re-allocated and responsibilities shared, as discussed in Chapter 4. These single mothers are not only overburdened; they are also role-burdened by carrying the *full* weight of all the roles allocated to them without benefit of the two-earner income, the emotional support, or the household/maintenance tasks many spouses in dual/career households provide. The single mother's jobs have increased and her resources have diminished.

The reality of single mothers' lives is like a puzzle in which each piece represents a family role she must carry out on her own. The puzzle cannot be completed nor the vision of the whole discerned unless all pieces are available, accessible, and properly fit together. For example, motherhood has traditionally been considered a full-time job by society in which child rearing and supervision, housekeeping, cooking, and care giving to extended family members are valued goods and services. Yet such work goes unpaid. Single mothers usually have no choice but to be both the family nurturer and family provider. To accomplish this, two-thirds of them are in the work force; yet dual nurturer/provider roles create conflict. Unpredictability of childhood illness or injury can upset the best of schedules for working mothers. Many working mothers report feelings of guilt in leaving their children in the care of others— guilt which intensifies when children are ill.[2]

Affirmative action and enforcement of equal opportunity laws have helped some women gain access to higher incomes in male-dominated fields of management and the professions. But for many women such strides have been at the expense of waging protracted court battles with resistive employers in both public and private sectors.[3] The preponderance of single mothers are in low-paying, occupationally segregated service and blue-collar jobs, as discussed in Chapter 5. They are confined to below-poverty and near-poverty-level incomes because of low wages, low or no child support awards from disdainful family courts, and low, regulated AFDC benefits.

Implicit in the wage-earner role is the need to first find a job and then to find and pay for quality child care. The trusted grandmother or aunt is no longer available as a child care resource for many single mothers who find themselves living great distances from their own family resources. For the last several decades young families have demonstrated more mobility than families of previous generations. Some moved because employers transferred fathers to new positions; others moved because fathers were lured to better jobs in the expanding economies of the Sunbelt and the West. But after divorce or separation, single mothers who moved with their spouses are then left isolated and removed from familial resources for child care and other supports provided by a nearby kin network. Moreover, the limited availability of publicly supported or private child care facilities further restricts entry into the job market, as analyzed in Chapter 5. The lack of child care stifles other initiatives as well: higher education, job training, and even fundamental tasks like searching for a new place to live, as depicted in Chapter 6, or going to court, as discussed in Chapter 3.

The search for employment, then, begins with the search for quality, affordable child care. Unless child care can be found in the immediate neighborhood, the search for child care and employment may end early. The importance of transportation cannot be underestimated. Use of a car is usually necessary in order to get to the child care centers or jobs for interviews. This basic mode of transportation cannot be financially supported by many single mothers—especially those on public welfare—thus ruling out, in a prosaic way, child care as a resource and wages as a source of income.

Central to caring and providing for children is the parental role of sheltering them in a safe, decent environment. When left to single mothers alone, this responsibility becomes a function of their level of income, resulting in the "affordability squeeze," analyzed in Chapter 9. In the absence of an adequate supply of affordable housing in many urban areas, especially the lack of affordable units in the private rental market, single mothers experience high-rent burdens, leaving less money for other basic household needs. However, when they relieve rent burdens by doubling up with others, they tempt eviction for both households by creating overcrowding, a violation of lease regulations that restrict the number of people who can live in an individual unit.

Those living in suburban single-family homes may be trying to restructure their living arrangements through re-use of their dwellings. Some are building accessory apartments or house sharing with one or two families to generate rental income. Others are establishing home-based employment. Such resourceful initiatives may be a solution to the role burden syndrome by creating new pieces of the puzzle that will fit, but they challenge local zoning ordinances that seek to maintain the character of single-family residential neighborhoods.

The tasks, then, of finding the missing pieces and putting the puzzle together to form a well-functioning whole require more than therapeutic intervention. Counseling and social services are important family resources in the process of adjusting to single-parent status, as recommended in Chapter 4, but other vital resources are external to the family unit, imbedded in the nation's institutional structures. When single mothers tried to access these resources, they encountered resistive barriers, experiences vividly described in the preceding chapters, and a discussion to which we now turn.

Confronting Institutional Barriers

Low-income single mothers who have taken responsibility for improving the well-being of their children's lives by advocating for child support in the courts, for equity in the workplace, for fair housing opportunities, and for higher welfare benefits to stave off homelessness have met intransigent institutional adversaries. For example, when courts disserve children through inadequate child support orders or judicial decisions that award custody of children to the child batterer, some single mothers take on the role of child advocate in an unfamiliar, expensive, and hostile legal environment, as described in Chapter 3. Those whose children have been victims of abuse by the father are more assertively leaving abusive relationships in order to protect the children, yet also creating dire physical, emotional, and legal consequences for themselves. Some mothers hide their children with sympathetic families obtained through a national informal self-help network, then go to jail themselves, rather than reveal the children's whereabouts to the courts.[4]

When AFDC recipients want to realize certain welfare rights intended by the Social Security Act, they have had to become community organizers, and possessors of sophisticated systems skills as described in Chapter 7. The broad purpose of the Social Security Act was a mechanism to give individuals greater freedom in their personal lives when they experience one of "the major vicissitudes of life." It was a way of assuring the dignity and independence of the individual, the integrity of the family, and the stability and purchasing power of the community.[5] But when AFDC recipients are embraced by this definition, the issue of "dependency" gets raised to new heights. In order to bring about any beneficial change, AFDC recipients have had to learn how to form coalitions that could impact the political process.

When the workplace is perceived as antifamily, and female employees seek health care benefits, retirement plans, or comparable pay, single mothers have joined other women's groups to mount congressional lobbying campaigns in order to bring the issues into focus for employers and legislators, as described in Chapter 8.

Other single mothers have tried to improve their living conditions by moving to a safer area with more amenities—behavior the upwardly mobile have modeled for decades. But low-income single mothers meet barriers erected by hostile landlords and barriers erected by communities that resist construction offering both affordable home ownership and rental opportunities. Discrimination based on race, gender, presence of children, and source and amount of income, such as AFDC and the Section 8 Rental Assistance Program, perpetuates segregated housing patterns and serves to exclude low-income single-parent families from the valuable neighborhood and community resources they seek, as outlined in Chapter 6. The confluence of discrimination, the inadequate supply of affordable housing in many urban and suburban areas, and low incomes derived from existing available sources confine many single-parent families to substandard housing and unsafe neighborhood conditions at best, and to homelessness at worst.

In short, single mothers who are individually or collectively challenging the institutional barriers described above are overburdened by a multiplicity of roles that include advocate, organizer and lobbyist, in addition to primary roles of child care provider, nurturer, bread winner and shelterer. Rather than being "shiftless" or "irresponsible," they demonstrate strengths of resourcefulness, commitment, and persistence in their efforts to make a better life for their families.

Directions for the 1990s

Those on the political right and political left have different positions on what policy prescriptions should now be taken with respect to single-parent families. Bruce Jansson suggests that policy positions are influenced by a series of moral principles that guide and help organize social life[6] (see Table 10–1). The differences between those on the right and the left are based on the different relative importance, or weighting, given to these ethical principles. Conservatives place the greatest emphasis on the principle of

Table 10–1   Moral Principles

Autonomy	The right to make critical decisions about one's own destiny.
Freedom	The right to hold and express personal opinions and take personal actions.
Preservation of life	The right to continued existence.
Honesty	The right to correct and accurate information.
Confidentiality	The right to privacy.
Equality	The right of individuals to receive the same services, resources, opportunities, or rights as other persons.
Social Justice	The right of equal access to social resources.
Due Process	The right to procedural safeguards when accused of crimes or when benefits or rights are withdrawn.
Beneficence	The right to receive those treatments, services, or benefits that allow one to establish or maintain a decent standard of well-being.
Societal or collective rights	The right of society to maintain and improve itself by safeguarding the public health and welfare, avoiding unreasonable or unnecessary expenditures, and preserving public order.

Source: Bruce Jansson, *The Reluctant Welfare State* (Belmont, Calif.: Wadsworth, 1988), p. 249. Used with permission of the publisher.

freedom with minimum public regulation and freedom to retain personal wealth. Their interest in societal rights and functions of maintaining public order and morality may lead to favoring policies that limit opportunities of those people perceived to be deviant.

Liberals also emphasize freedom but favor a wide range of policies to protect citizens from the vicissitudes of the market economy. Some on the political left favor expansion of the welfare state, which tempers freedom with social justice and redistributes resources to the less affluent.

The plight of single-parent families has become so serious and so complex that basic changes are needed in social and economic conditions—changes brought about by a combination of social programs, tax policies, and economic policies. For example, these families need "housing, day care, job training, medical, service, and nutritional programs, safe neighborhoods, access to predictable job markets, and an adequate income that derives from some combination of children's allowances, wages, tax rebates, and support payments."[7] In order to meet single parent families' needs, social reform must look beyond traditional concerns of public welfare to economic inequalities and to the institutional arrangements that reinforce these inequities, issues to which the discussion will now turn.

Economic Equality for Women: A Child Welfare Issue

The concept of "family" and of childhood dependency should be re-thought so that economic equality for women can be understood as a child welfare issue. There is a penchant to single out impoverished children as "worthy" of assistance but to separate them out from their "unworthy" mothers on whom society casts a dark shadow. However, burdens from cuts in social programs in the Reagan era and sporadic attention to family issues at the federal and state levels are being borne jointly by impoverished children and their impoverished mothers—the single-parent family unit.

The single-parent family needs to be perceived as a holistic unit measured not by its structure, but as with other families, by its functioning. The integrity of the family will be maintained and the interests of the children enhanced if the family is not further broken into categories of "worthy" children and "unworthy" single mothers. Americans who want to help poor children—those who cannot help themselves—and policymakers who want to strengthen child welfare policies for the 1990s will not continue to stigmatize single mothers as anomalies in a two-parent world. Instead, they will support policies that promote economic and social justice for the children's mothers.

The national goal to "assure the dignity and independence of the individual and the integrity of the family" should apply to all families, including the single-parent family form. With this perspective, policies that expand choices for low-income women and their children can be more clearly seen as mechanisms for independence, not for increasing dependence.

Expanded Choices Increase Independence

Institutional barriers in the courts, the labor market, and the housing market discriminate against single mothers and severely limit their opportunities and choices, as vividly demonstrated in the preceding chapters. Single mothers need the opportunity to support themselves and their children with dignity, and to receive a "family wage" and a decent standard of living in return for hard work.

Fundamental to increasing opportunities and expanding choices are actions taken to eliminate gender bias in the courts, occupational segregation in the workplace, pay inequities between men and women, racial and gender discrimination in housing, and actions to increase family/workplace benefits for health care and child care. These actions taken at federal, state, and local levels focus on mothers themselves rather than on their children. They challenge society's perception of the value of women and men, the roles of women and men, and the realities of their existence. But it is through success of these measures that substantial economic and social gains will be made for the children: higher child support awards that reflect the true cost of child rearing; family wages that improve a household's standard of living; benefits packages that cover children's and wage earners' health care needs; the chance to move out of deteriorating neighborhoods to affordable housing in communities with higher-paying suburban employment. In short, economic and social equality for women will increase opportunities for the whole family. Public responsibility that establishes broad national policy goals for women's equality will create conditions under which private actions of single mothers are then better able to strengthen family life.

Policy Making and Implementation Strategies for Achieving Residential Stability

A main point of this book is that affordable housing is a first line of defense against poverty. Efforts to improve housing and community conditions of low-income families have met with resistance in formulating responsive policies and in designing implementation strategies that could either alleviate or eliminate the social problem they set out to address. The need for access to affordable housing and improved community conditions, then, forms the baseline on which the following broad recommendations are made.

An Interdisciplinary Process

The preceding chapters thread together the interactive nature of public and private decisions: the centrality of affordable shelter as a basic need and the difficulties of achieving it; the impacts of uneven child support awards and enforcement; AFDC benefit levels that are too low to meet a family's basic needs for food, clothing, and shelter; and barriers to attaining a family wage, even with employment and training programs. What is needed is a policy-making process that will consider numerous goals, problems, and programs simultaneously. Defining social problems, conducting policy analyses, recommending solutions, and designing implementation strategies and evaluation studies should be interdisciplinary tasks. Planners and social workers should join economists and lawyers in all phases of policy formulation and in the design of implementation strategies. Social workers and human service planners tend to work only in the implementation phase where services are planned for and delivered. They should bring experiences from this valuable professional vantage point more fully to bear in the policy formulation debate. The next question is which layer of government should be making which decisions?

Local Community Resistance to Single-Mother Households

The unit of government that determines land use decisions may need to expand beyond a city or town's jurisdiction to include a regional point of view. In the 1960s and early 1970s, grave concern for the decaying condition of urban America and its problems of racial inequality in schools, deteriorating neighborhoods, and crime spawned recommendations for cross-town busing to achieve school integration and a metropolitan approach to housing. The federal goal of a metropolitan approach to housing was to deconcentrate central cities, and the method attempted was construction of affordable housing which would "open up the suburbs."[8] Expanded opportunities and choices for all Americans, targeted especially for low-income racial minorities, would be realized. Single mothers and their children would surely benefit. But local communities were threatened by new residential patterns that brought a "mixed" category: affordable housing developments that brought in low-, moderate-, and market-rate tenants, or developments that provided units for both the elderly and for families. These attempts to increase the supply of low-income family housing in areas outside the urban core were resisted by communities and have continued to be resisted for nearly two decades.[9]

Meeting the shelter needs of the low-income elderly has not been nearly so contentious. Provision of affordable housing for the elderly is a social policy success story. They are society's "worthy" poor, entitled to decent accommodations, respectable living conditions, and rent subsidies.

Single mothers, on the other hand, are a suspicious category, as they appear to be sliding down the "ladder of life," out of synchronization with an assumed upward progression. In this analogy, the "ladder of life" is linked with the life cycle and with housing tenure. For example, people are assumed to move from single status to married status, then to trade up their housing rung by rung. Young households are expected to live initially in rental apartments, then trade up to condominium ownership, and finally to the pinnacle of the ladder—ownership of a single-family house.[10] Single mothers may be shifting from married to single status, then trading down their housing from single-family homes to rental apartments, and then from large apartments to smaller ones, often in less desirable neighborhoods. These characteristics create another "mixed" category to be feared, which in turn, serves to strengthen local exclusionary rental practices which deny single mothers stable housing opportunities and valuable community resources.

Community resistance to affordable housing may stem from the leap-frog effect that housing subsidies provide. That is, the subsidy enables low-income families to jump up and over a rung or two on the ladder of life, improving the household's living conditions sooner than those without a subsidy, who must wait and save to make a similar move on their own. What home owners appear to forget is that ownership opportunities were made possible through government subsidies to the middle class through tax incentives, to builders through low-interest loans, and to investors through tax losses in depreciation. Community resisters may need to be reminded that they may have been beneficiaries of fiscal welfare for home ownership. Affordable rental and home ownership programs give low- and moderate-income families the opportunity to climb back up the ladder of life, not down. This redirection in mobility is the cornerstone on which access to improved community conditions is based. Moreover, it is a moral imperative for those who decry the feminization of poverty, and the deteriorating central city conditions under which the majority of poor children live.

The social environment of community resistance makes implementation of laissez-faire approaches to affordable housing very difficult approaches to use, as discussed in Chapters 6 and 9. The Reagan administration's New Federalism has put the burden of sheltering the poor on the shoulders of states and localities. This shift in intergovernmental relations has given recalcitrant communities more comfort and support in their efforts to roll back the limited progress which was made during the past two decades through zoning changes, state court action, fair housing laws, and federal and state regional allocation plans that supported fair share of affordable housing.[11] A "macro" problem-solving model is needed that will allocate housing as one element of an overarching land use approach, while still retaining some local control. A regional land use consortium of localities is recommended and will be discussed next.

Regional Land Use Consortium

A regional land use consortium is based on the regional allocation idea but is a departure from the model used by government in the 1970s in several ways. First, one drawback to implementing government-sponsored regional allocation plans (called Areawide Housing Opportunity Plans) was that localities did not like state or federal governments dictating local housing solutions to them. With the regional land use consortium idea, the mandate does not come from the state or federal levels but from the regional self-interest of communities that are already convened to examine and find collaborative solutions to common problems, such as deteriorating air and water quality, and encroaching, haphazard urban growth and development. (Such a model was created to locally implement provisions of the federal Clean Water and Clean Air Acts in the mid- to late 1970s.) Second, the goal of the early regional allocation plans was to oversee a fair share distribution of affordable housing. This model expands the concept by including a fair share distribution of *all* housing—luxury, low income, elderly, as well as low-income family. Third, it brings housing decisions into a framework that requires meshing of regional and local housing needs with all other regional and local needs, such as patterns of economic development, diminishing natural resources, and public services required for the growing work force.

Community resistance can remain intransigent as long as land use decisions stay decentralized. A regional land use consortium would tend to dissipate this resistance. It would be created from membership of contiguous communities that have a vested interest in common land use issues. For example, economic development often occurs along identifiable transportation routes that intersect several communities. Yet these communities have uneven technical capacity to negotiate sophisticated development packages such growth brings. Furthermore, many do not have updated land use plans which delineate community-based criteria with which to measure zoning changes requested by new development. The result is piecemeal decision-making that has had the power to change the character of whole neighborhoods and communities— change which may ultimately not be in the public interest.

Implementation of a regional land use consortium would require technically complex public/private partnerships and public/public partnerships. There would be resistance to intervention in the dynamics of the housing market. But it is not an unfettered market anyway, especially in states like California, New Jersey, and Massachusetts, which have taken an active role in combining technical analysis with local government requirements for fair share hous-ing.[12] Also, some critics will object to its "selective" rather than "universal" scope. While a universal scope is more desirable to meet national equity goals, this regional approach will target community resistance without a federal mandate. Some general guiding principles could be followed:

- A regional land use consortium would centralize policy-making at the regional level. The impacts of increased urban growth and development on water, air, transportation patterns, schools, public facilities, and open space would be assessed locally and regionally. Housing would be one of the elements assessed.
- All environmental impact statements would require evaluation of *social* as well as physical impacts.
- Housing needs assessments would be conducted regionally. One factor used to determine need for affordable housing would be the *projected* income levels of the region's growing work force. Another factor would be household size.
- One consortium goal would be the commitment to provide rental and home ownership opportunities for the region's workers in low-, moderate-, and high-income brackets.
- The self-interest of the region would be served because re-gional growth would now be managed. Moreover, attention to meeting the housing needs of all the area's work force would motivate corporations to relocate there.
- The self-interest of communities would be served in two ways. First, all communities would receive technical assistance from the consortium staff to help negotiate mutually beneficial partnerships between the developers and the local commu-nity. Second, the consortium would act as a clearing house. All developers' applications for building permits would be made to the consortium where they would be evaluated for their local and regional impacts. No single neighborhood or community would be allocated all of the permits for luxury housing nor all of the permits for affordable housing. The allocation would be based in part on work force needs, and on community capacity to sustain new development relative to open space, tax base, public facilities, natural resources, and school enrollment figures. Local control would be retained in matters of siting and density.
- Developers would receive "points" of financial value if they built housing projects where the regional need for a certain housing type was determined to be the greatest.

- Low-income workers, including single mothers, would benefit by having access to a greater supply of mixed-income family housing in communities that bring them closest to employment that pays a "family wage."

State and Regional Policy Planning

Major benefits are to be derived from the development of a comprehensive state and regional policy-planning apparatus that focuses on social programs.[13] Many social programs have not worked very well. There has been inadequate attention to the management of delivery systems. Federal program managers say that programs can be effectively and efficiently implemented at the local level; local program managers complain of bureaucratically complex, difficult-to-administer programs. Relationships between public and voluntary social agencies increase, blurring the distinction between what is in the public domain and what is in the private. Lost in this morass is the equity question: Who is to be served? and How effectively are programs serving the needs of the intended beneficiaries?

For example, the nation is shocked daily by reports of increasing homelessness in our metropolitan areas. Researchers are demonstrating the relationship between the diminished supply of affordable housing and homelessness, especially among single-parent families.[14] The long-term costs of homelessness to the families and to society are difficult to measure. Fiscal pressure is on state budgets to house the homeless in shelters, hotels, and motels; to pay increased costs of medical care for their illnesses; to meet increased demand for services through departments of public welfare, social services, public health, mental health, and their private contractors; and to increase AFDC budgets so families will not be evicted from private rental housing in the first place.

One solution being tried to secure permanent, nontransient housing for the homeless is to provide them with Section 8 Rental Assistance certificates and vouchers (a variation of the certificate but without the fair market rent ceiling). This suggests that policymakers expect the homeless to succeed as program participants. Yet with accessibility as difficult as it has been demonstrated to be here, success rates among the homeless are doubtful, unless significant changes are made. Implementation needs to be improved so multiple human service agencies can work more cooperatively with each other. This will require less bureaucratic rigidity. What is needed is a policy planning approach that would look broadly at implementation in order to evaluate (1) the cross-cutting implications of multiple human service agencies' policies and regulations at the state and regional levels; (2) the interactive effects of their programs on direct service agencies at the local level; (3) collaborative strategies to conserve scarce financial resources more efficiently and to serve clients more cooperatively.

Portable Benefits for Regional Mobility

While solutions are encouraged at the state and regional levels, limiting recommendations to these levels alone will not change the dilemma of state and regional disparity and bureaucratic gridlock that have plagued recipients of AFDC and public or subsidized housing when making mobility decisions. If independence from government programs, not dependence, is indeed a goal of some policymakers, federal responsibility should be assumed to guide a national program of "portable" benefits.

Analyses by contributors to this volume suggest that existing policies in a wide range of areas and exigencies of the marketplace can restrict families economically, socially, and physically, and in effect, leave them stuck. Benefits that can be easily transported among local jurisdictions and across state lines will give single mothers the mechanism to transition out of deteriorating central city neighborhoods to stronger economies in suburbs and the Sunbelt where firms with better paying jobs have relocated.[15] Regulatory change that would permit the transfer of housing subsidies across state lines would, in effect, create freedom of choice in employment and in making locational decisions which, in turn, become vehicles for independent living.

The Court's Role in Transition Planning

A final recommendation calls for greater responsiveness from the court system. Family courts are an institution that could better assist mothers in coping with their housing problems after separation and divorce by requiring a Five-Year Housing Transition Plan as part of the court record. Marital dissolution and child support orders bring thousands of middle-income and marginally poor families before the courts every year, but housing arrangements for children in these families are not usually a matter of the court's concern unless there is a home in the property settlement. The high level of residential mobility and insecurity exhibited after separation and divorce are contributing to the role burden syndrome, as new responsibilities for household headship are thrust upon mothers who have inadequate resources.

The courts could intercede in reducing the incidence of role burden by demonstrating more sensitivity to the housing element in separating families' lives. Family courts should hear findings on a Five-Year Housing Transition Plan as a matter of record. The plan would set forth the children's living arrangements for a five-year period following separation or divorce. It would require stipulation of which public or private housing resources were going to be used, and would document how the mother, father, lawyer, or social worker had assessed these systems on behalf of the children. The plan should be evaluated every five years to reassess shelter suitability and stability.

In order to evaluate these findings, the court would have to become knowledgeable on length of public housing waiting lists, availability of mixed income housing in the private sector, availability of rent subsidy programs, and all other affordable housing resources that meet the needs of poor families before the court. In turn, with its heightened awareness level the court could set child support orders for fathers with the ability to pay in amounts that reflect actual market rents charged to shelter children, or amounts of the family's share of a subsidized rent. The court could require speedy access to housing programs for families where fathers do not have the ability to pay. The intent of this judicial intervention is to *plan* for family residential stability over time. The cycle of residential mobility and insecurity that disrupts poor families after separation and divorce that is so debilitating to single-parent families would be substantially reduced.

Conclusion

Our purpose has been to investigate the realities of family life for single-parent mothers in the context of their social environment. We conclude by recognizing that gender inequality exists, and that it is perpetuated through institutional mechanisms that ration access to resources in order to maintain social control. Those who cling fervently to the old myths do not understand the complex reality faced by families headed by mothers, who now comprise the new American poverty. Moreover, such persons are ignoring the deleterious economic, social, and political consequences of failure to value and invest in all families in American society. Individual chapters in this book have shown the need for changes in national, state, and local policies to diminish the current economic consequences of marital dissolution and thereby blunt the cutting edges of poverty and despair. It will be a hard fight to reach these ends—and with questionable success—until profound changes occur in gender equality in social relationships.

An agenda that addresses gender equality in social relationships calls for a five-pronged approach. First, unwavering attention should be paid to local community development, where civic leaders and developers play out the zoning game in urban and suburban neighborhoods. Since land use regulations and local politics influence the determination of settlement patterns in the metropolitan landscape, participation in local decision-making should be broadened to include single mothers so that their shelter/service needs can be articulated, understood, and met.

Second, advocacy for social change should continue at the state level. Some legislatures and state courts have been responsive to a family agenda, specifically on issues of pay equity, employer-supported health care benefits, child care, welfare reform, and housing rights. These victories can be significant, as analyzed in Chapters 7 and 9.

Third, federal responsibility must be assumed for family policy. This will require supportive executive and legislative branches of government. Transformation of the American family is a national phenomenon, and transformation of the economy is global. Therefore, social policy should derive from national compassion, commitment, and resources. The allocation of federal resources must be at a level that will strengthen single-parent families, not serve to keep them impoverished below the poverty line.

Fourth, social action by women alone, especially poor women, will not achieve systemic gender equality. Achievement of this goal will require mobilization of a social movement of women and men, working in coalitions and with systematic effort outside the bureaucratic structures they want to change. The social movement needs to incorporate a variety of change strategies appropriate for different issues. For example, when the goal is to eliminate the gender bias of judges, education and persuasion are being used. When the goals of groups are in opposition, such as legislators and welfare mothers, a litigation strategy may be required.

Fifth, it is a moral imperative that equal rights for women be guaranteed in the U.S. Constitution through passage of the Equal Rights Amendment. Equal political rights signify equal access to valued relationships. When the equal rights of women are guaranteed in the Constitution, the power content of other relationships should change, bringing a higher valuation of women's social and economic worth to their endeavors in the home and in the workplace.

Michael Harrington suggests, "The structures of misery were

created by men and women; they can be changed by men and women. That, we shall see, is easier said than done—but it can be done."[16] This vision is achievable if the fundamental goal of reform would seek freedom and independence for the poor. In the end, however, values and attitudes continue to shape social policy and family welfare. If we are willing to transform institutions to serve as social infrastructure instead of barriers, future generations of children who live in single-parent families and their mothers will finally have enabling structures to help them meet their basic human needs.

Endnotes

1. See, for example, Rosanna Hertz, *More Equal Than Others: Women and Men in Dual Career Marriages* (Berkeley: University of California Press, 1986).
2. For an example of working mothers, conflicts of child care, and moral sanctions, see Greer Litton Fox and Jan Allen, "Child Care," in *The Trapped Woman*, ed. Josefina Figueira-McDonough and Rosemary Sarri (Newbury Park, Calif.: Sage Publications, 1987).
3. *Paul E. Johnson* v. *Transportation Agency, Santa Clara Co., Calif.*, 107 S.Ct. 1442, 94 L.Ed. 2d 615 (1987). Diane Joyce was a single mother with four children who worked her way from the low-paying clerical pool to the blue-collar ranks in California's Santa Clara County Transportation Agency's road maintenance crew. Throughout her road crew employment, she was harassed, and demeaned. From 1974 to 1980 she sought promotion to the dispatcher position because it paid more than the road crew. In spite of performing well in candidate tests and interviews, she never got the dispatcher's job. Finally she appealed to an affirmative action officer, and eventually the director of the Transportation Agency overturned the decision and Ms. Joyce got the dispatcher's position. She became the first woman to fill one of the Transportation Agency's skilled crafts jobs. In 1980, Paul Johnson, the man who was the original candidate of choice, filed a reverse discrimination lawsuit. After seven years of litigation the U.S. Supreme Court ruled in March 1987 that Joyce could keep her job. The landmark decision was a renouncement of the Reagan administration's position on affirmative action. The Court ruled that employers could offer a preference to women to erase a "manifest imbalance in traditionally segregated job categories."
4. See, for example, Daniel Golden, "What Makes Mommy Run?" *The Boston Globe Magazine*, April 24, 1988, p. 14, and Shiela Weller, "Middle Class Murder," *Ms. Magazine*, May 1988, p. 56.
5. Wilbur Cohen, "The Social Security Act of 1935: Reflections Fifty Years Later," in *The Report of the Committee on Economic Security of 1935*, (1985), pp. 3–14.
6. This discussion relies on Bruce Jansson, *The Reluctant Welfare State* (Belmont, Calif.: Wadsworth, 1988).

7. Jansson, *The Reluctant Welfare State*, p. 254.

8. See, for example, Anthony Downs, *Opening Up the Suburbs* (New Haven: Yale University Press, 1973); Chester Hartman, "The Politics of Housing," in *Housing Urban America*, ed. Jon Pynoos et al. (New York: Aldine, 1980); and Alexander Polikoff, *Housing the Poor: The Case for Heroism* (Cambridge, Mass: Ballinger, 1978).

9. Nina Gruen and Claude Gruen, *Low and Moderate Income Housing in the Suburbs* (New York: Praeger, 1972).

10. For a full discussion of the ladder-of-life metaphor, see Constance Perin, *Everything in It's Place: Social Order and Land Use in America* (Princeton, N.J.: Princeton University Press, 1977).

11. For an interesting historical discussion of local and regional fair share plans see William C. Baer, "The Evolution of Local and Regional Housing Studies," *Journal of the American Planning Association* 52, no. 2 (Spring 1986): 172–84.

12. See, for example, Robert W. Burchell et al., *Mount Laurel II: Challenge and Delivery of Low-Cost Housing* (New Brunswick, N.J.: Center for Urban Policy Research, Rutgers University, 1983).

13. See Walter D. Broadnax, "Policy Planning and the Poor," in *The State and the Poor in the 1980s*, ed. Manuel Carballo and Mary Jo Bane (Dover, Mass: Auburn House, 1984).

14. See, for example, James Wright and Julie Lamm, "Homelessness and the Low-Income Housing Supply," *Social Policy* 17, no. 4 (Spring 1987): 48–53; and Chapter 7, this volume.

15. For a discussion of the impacts of regional shifts in employment and recommendations of portable benefits to assist low-income households, see Franklin James and John Blair, "The Role of Labor Mobility in a National Urban Policy," *Journal of the American Planning Association* 49, no. 3 (Summer 1983): 307–15.

16. Michael Harrington, *The New American Poverty* (New York: Penguin Books, 1984), p. 12.

BIBLIOGRAPHY

ABRAHAMOVITZ, MIMI. *Regulating the Lives of Women*. Edison, N.J.: South End Press, 1988.

ACHTENBERG, EMILY. *Preserving Affordable Housing in Boston*. Report prepared for the Boston Rent Equity Board and the Mayor's Housing Advisor, 1984.

AHRONS, CONSTANCE R. "Redefining the Divorced Family: A Conceptual Framework," *Social Work* 25 (November 1980): 437–41.

AMOTT, TERESA. "Put Responsibility Where It Belongs," *Dollars and Sense* (October 1987).

AMOTT, TERESA, and JULIE MATTHAEI. "Comparable Work, Incomparable Pay," *Radical America* (September-October 1984).

ANDERSON-KHLIEF, SUSAN. *Income Packaging and Life Style in Welfare Families*. Family Policy Note 7. Cambridge, Mass.: Joint Center for Urban Studies, 1978.

———. "Housing Needs of Single Parent Mothers." In *Building for Women*, ed. Suzanne Keller. Lexington, Mass.: Lexington Books, 1981.

———. *Divorced But Not Disastrous*. Englewood Cliffs, N.J.: Prentice Hall, 1982.

ATKINS, RICHARD N. "Single Mothers and Joint Custody: Common Ground." In *In Support of Families*, ed. Michael W. Yogman and T. Berry Brazelton. Cambridge, Mass.: Harvard University Press, 1986.

AVNER, JUDITH, and SUSAN HERMAN. *Divorce Mediation: A Guide for Women*. New York: NOW Legal Defense and Education Fund, 1984.

AXINN, JUNE, and HERMAN LEVIN. *Social Welfare: A History of the American Response to Need*. White Plains, N.Y.: Longman, 1982.

BAER, WILLIAM C. "The Evolution of Local and Regional Housing Studies." *Journal of the American Planning Association* 52, no. 2 (Spring 1986): 172–84.

BANE, MARY JO, and DAVID ELLWOOD. *Single Mothers and Their Living Arrangements*. Report prepared for the Department of Health and Human Services. Cambridge, Mass.: Harvard University, 1984, mimeo.

BANE, MARY JO, and ROBERT WEISS. "Alone Together: The World of Single-Parent Families." *American Demographics* (May 1980).

BARTLETT, SUSAN. *Residential Mobility and Housing Choices of Single-Parent Mothers*. Cambridge, Mass.: Joint Center for Urban Studies, 1980, mimeo.

BEAL, EDWARD W. "Separation, Divorce and Single-Parent Families." In *The*

Family Life Cycle: A Framework for Family Therapy, ed. Elizabeth A. Carter and Monica McGoldrick. New York: Gardner Press, 1980.

BERGER, VIVIAN. "Man's Trial, Woman's Tribulation: Rape Trials in the Courtroom." *Columbia Law Review* 77 (1977): 1–100.

BILLINGSLEY, ANDREW, and JEANNE M. GIOVANNONI. "Family, One Parent." In *Encyclopedia of Social Work*, Vol. I, 16th ed. Washington, D.C.: National Association of Social Workers, 1973, pp. 362–73.

BIRCH, EUGENIE. "The Unsheltered Woman: Definitions and Needs." In *The Unsheltered Woman: Women and Housing in the 1980s*, ed. Eugenie Birch. New Brunswick, N.J.: Center for Urban Policy Research, 1985.

BLAU, FRANCINE, and MARIANNE FERBER, *The Economics of Men, Women, and Work*. Englewood Cliffs, NJ: Prentice-Hall, 1986.

BLOCK, FRED, RICHARD CLOWARD, BARBARA EHRENREICH, and FRANCES FOX PIVEN. *The Mean Season: The Attack on the Welfare State*. New York: Pantheon Books, 1987.

BLUESTONE, BARRY, and BENNETT HARRISON. "The Great American Job Machine." Study prepared for the Joint Economic Committee, U.S. Congress, Washington, D.C., 1986, mimeo.

BROADNAX, WILLIAM. "Policy Planning and the Poor." In *The State and the Poor in the 1980s*, ed. Manuel Carballo and Mary Jo Bane. Dover, Mass: Auburn House, 1984.

BRODKIA, E. Z. *The False Promise of Administrative Reform: Implementing Quality Control in Welfare*. Philadelphia: Temple University Press, 1986.

BURCHELL, ROBERT W. et al. *Mount Laurell II: Challenge and Delivery of Low-Cost Housing*. New Brunswick, N.J.: Center for Urban Policy Research, Rutgers University, 1983.

BURTLESS, GARY. "Public Spending for the Poor: Trends, Prospects and Economic Limits." In *Fighting Poverty: What Works and What Doesn't*, ed. Sheldon Danziger and Daniel Weinberg. Cambridge: Harvard University Press, 1986.

CAMARA, KATHLEEN A. "Family Adaptation to Divorce." In *In Support of Families*, ed. Michael W. Yogman and T. Berry Brazelton. Cambridge, Mass.: Harvard University Press, 1986.

CHAMBERS, DAVID L. *Making Fathers Pay: The Enforcement of Child Support*. Chicago: University of Chicago Press, 1979.

CHESLER, PHYLLIS. *Mothers on Trial*. New York: McGraw-Hill, 1986.

Children's Defense Fund. *A Children's Defense Budget FY 1988: An Analysis of Our Nation's Investment in Children*. (Washington, D.C., 1987).

COHEN, WILBUR J. "The Social Security Act of 1935: Reflections Fifty Years Later." *The Report of the Committee on Economic Security of 1935*. 1985, pp. 3–14.

Commonwealth of Massachusetts, Department of Public Welfare. "An Analysis of the First 25,000 ET Placements," Boston, 1986, mimeo.

CRITES, LAURA. "Judicial Guide to Understanding Wife Abuse." *The Judges' Journal* 24 (Summer 1985): 5–9, 50.

CRITES, LAURA L., and WINIFRED L. HEPPERLE, eds. *Women, the Courts and Equality*. Beverly Hills: Sage Publications, 1987.

DOERINGER, PETER, and MICHAEL PIORE. *Internal Labor Markets and Manpower Analysis*. Lexington, Mass.: D.C. Heath, 1972.

DOWNS, ANTHONY. *Opening Up the Suburbs*. New Haven: Yale University Press, 1973.

DREIER, PETER. "Community-Based Housing: A Progressive Approach to a New Federal Policy." *Social Policy* Fall, 1987, vol. 18, no. 2.

DUNCAN, GREG J., and SAUL D. HOFFMAN. "Welfare Dynamics and the Nature of Need." Institute for Social Research, University of Michigan, Ann Arbor, 1986, mimeo.

DUNCAN, GREG J., and JAMES MORGAN. "Persistence and Change in Economic Status and the Role of Changing Family Composition." In *Five Thousand American Families—Patterns of Economic Progress*, vol. IX. Ann Arbor: Institute for Social Research, University of Michigan, 1981.

EARL, LOVELENE, and NANCY LOHMANN. "Absent Fathers and Black Male Children." *Social Work* 23 (September 1978): 413–15.

EBERLE, NANCY. "I Was a Better Mother When I Was a Single Mother." *Redbook* 162 (November 1983), pp. 90–91.

ELLWOOD, DAVID, and MARY JO BANE. *Family Structure and Living Arrangements Research, Summary of Findings*. Report prepared for the Department of Health and Human Services. Cambridge, Mass.: Harvard University, 1984.

FOX, GREER LITTON, and JAN ALLEN. "Child Care." In *The Trapped Woman*, ed. Josefina Figueira-McDonough and Rosemary Sarri. Newbury Park, Calif.: Sage Publications, 1987.

GANS, HERBERT. *The Urban Villagers: Group and Class in the Life of Italian Americans*. New York: Free Press, 1962.

GARFINKEL, IRWIN, and SARA MCLANAHAN. *Single Mothers and Their Children*. Washington, D.C.: Urban Institute Press, 1986.

GELMAN, DAVID, et al. "The Single Parent: Family Albums." *Newsweek*, July 15, 1985, pp. 45–50.

GOLDEN, DANIEL, "What Makes Mommy Run?" *The Boston Globe Magazine*, April 24, 1988, p. 14.

GOLDFARB, SALLY F. "Child Support Guideline: A Model for Fair Allocation of Child Care, Medical and Educational Expenses." *Family Law Quarterly* 21 (Fall 1987): 325–50.

GOLDFARB, SALLY F. "Rehabilitative Alimony, 'The Alimony Drone' and the Marital Partnership." *National Symposium on Alimony and Child Support: American Bar Association Family Law Section and State Bar of Texas*, 1987.

GOLDFARB, SALLY F. "What Every Lawyer Should Know About Child Support Guidelines." *The Family Law Reporter* 13 (September 29, 1987): 3031–37.

GRIGSBY, WILLIAM et al. *Rethinking Housing and Community Development Policy*. Philadelphia: University of Pennsylvania, 1977.

GRUEN, NINA, and CLAUDE GRUEN. *Low and Moderate Income Housing in the Suburbs*. New York: Praeger, 1972.

HANDLER, JOEL. "Continuing Relationships and the Administrative Process: Social Welfare." *Wisconsin Law Review* (1985): 687–706.

———. *Social Movements and the Legal System: A Theory of Law Reform and Social Change*. N.Y.: Academic Press, 1978.

HANDLER, JOEL, and MICHAEL SOSIN. *Last Resorts: Emergency Assistance and Special Needs Programs in Public Welfare*. New York: Academic Press, 1983.

HARRINGTON, MICHAEL. *The New American Poverty*. New York: Penguin Books, 1984.

"Help Wanted." *Business Week*, August 10, 1987, pp. 48–53.

HERTZ, ROSANNA. *More Equal Than Others: Women and Men in Dual Career Marriages*. Berkeley: University of California Press, 1986.

HILL, MARTHA. "Female Household Headship and the Poverty of Children." *Five Thousand American Families—Patterns of Economic Progress*, vol. X. Ann Arbor: Institute for Social Research, University of Michigan, 1983.

HOGAN, M. JANICE, CHERYL BUEHLER, and BEATRICE ROBINSON. "Single Parenting: Transitioning Alone." In *Stress and the Family*, Vol. 1: *Coping with Normative Transitions*, ed. Hamilton I. McCubbin and Charles R. Figley. New York: Brunner/Mazel, 1983.

HORNER, CATHERINE TOWNSEND. *The Single-Parent Family in Children's Books*. Metuchen, N.J.: The Scarecrow Press, 1978.

JAMES, FRANKLIN, and JOHN BLAIR, "The Role of Labor Mobility in a National Urban Policy." *Journal of the American Planning Association*, vol. 49, n. 3 (Summer 1983): 307–15.

JANSSON, BRUCE. *The Reluctant Welfare State*. Belmont, Calif.: Wadsworth, 1988.

Johnson v. Transportation Agency, Santa Clara Co., Calif., 107 S.Ct. 1442, 94 L.Ed.2d 615 (1987).

JOHNSTON, JOHN D. JR. and CHARLES L. KNAPP. "Sex Discrimination by Law: A Study in Judicial Perspective." *New York University Law Review* 46 (October 1971): 675–747.

KAHN, ALFRED J. *Social Policy and Social Services*. New York: Random House, 1979.

KAMERMAN, SHEILA B. *Parenting in an Unresponsive Society: Managing Work and Family Life*. New York: The Free Press, 1980.

KANTROWITZ, BARBARA and ASSOCIATES. "Mothers On Their Own." *Newsweek*, December 23, 1985, pp. 66–67.

KEENAN, LINDA. "Domestic Violence and Custody Litigation: The Need for Statutory Reform." *Hofstra Law Review* 13 (Winter 1985): 407–41.

KESSLER-HARRIS, ALICE. *Out to Work*. New York: Oxford University Press, 1982.

KOTZ, NICK, and MARY LYNN KOTZ. *A Passion for Equality: George A. Wiley and the Movement*. New York: W. W. Norton & Co., 1977.

KUTTNER, ROBERT. *The Economic Illusion: False Choices Between Prosperity and Social Justice*. Boston: Houghton Mifflin Company, 1982.

LAW, SYLVIA. "Women, Work, Welfare, and Preservation of Patriarchy" 131 *University of Pennsylvania Law Review* (1983): 1249, 1268.

LEAVITT, JACQUELINE. "Aunt Mary and the Shelter-Service Crisis Facing Single Parents." In *The Unsheltered Woman: Women and Housing in the 80s*, ed. Eugenie Birch. Piscataway, N.J.: Center for Urban Policy Research, 1985.

MASNICK, GEORGE, and MARY JO BANE. *The Nation's Families: 1960–1990*. Dover, Mass.: Auburn House, 1980.

MAY, MARTHA. "Bread Before Roses: American Workingmen, Labor Unions, and the Family Wage." In *Women, Work and Protest: A Century of U.S. Women's Labor History,* ed. Ruth Milkman. Boston: Routledge and Kegan Paul, 1985.

MCADOO, HARRIET, and DIANA PEARCE. "Women and Children: Alone and in Poverty." Washington, D.C.: National Advisory Council on Economic Opportunity, 1981.

MCGOLDRICK, MONICA. "Ethnicity and Family Therapy: An Overview." In *Ethnicity and Family Therapy,* ed. Monica McGoldrick, John K. Pearce, and Joseph Giordano. New York: The Guilford Press, 1982.

MCLANAHAN, SARA S. "Family Structure and Stress: A Longitudinal Comparison of Two-Parent and Female-Headed Families." *Journal of Marriage and the Family* 45 (May 1983): 347–57.

MEINDL, NOMSA VANDA, and CATHLEEN GETTY. "Life Styles of Black Families Headed by Women." In *Understanding the Family: Stress and Change in American Family Life,* ed. Cathleen Getty and Winnifred Humphreys. New York: Appleton-Century-Crofts, 1981.

MENDES, HELEN A. "Single-Parent Families: A Typology of Life-Styles." *Social Work* 24 (May 1979): 193–200.

MINUCHIN, SALVADOR. *Families and Family Therapy.* Cambridge, Mass.: Harvard University Press, 1974.

MORRIS, ROBERT. *Social Policy and the American Welfare State.* New York: Harper & Row, 1979.

MULROY, ELIZABETH. "The Housing Plight of Low-Income Single-Parent Mothers: A Study of Housing Search and Housing Choice in the Section 8 Rental Assistance Program." Ph.D. dissertation, University of Southern California, 1986.

MURRAY, CHARLES. *Losing Ground.* New York: Basic Books, 1984.

MYERS, HECTOR F. "Research on the Afro-American Family: A Critical Review." In *The Afro-American Family: Assessment, Treatment and Research Issues,* ed. Barbara Ann Bass, Gail Elizabeth Wyatt, and Gloris Johnson Powell. New York: Grune & Stratton, 1982.

National Association of Working Women. "Working at the Margins: Part-Time and Temporary Workers in the U.S." Cleveland, September 1986.

National Commission on Working Women. "Fact Sheet on Women in the Workforce" and "Fact Sheet on Child Care," Washington, D.C., 1987.

NETTER, EDITH, and RUTH PRICE. "Zoning and the Nouveau Poor." *Journal of the American Planning Association,* Spring 1983.

New Jersey Supreme Court Task Force on Women in the Courts. Report of the First Year. Administrative Office of the Courts. Trenton, N.J.: *Women's Rights Law Reporter* 9 (Spring 1986): 129–77.

"Notes—The Cost of Divorce." *American Demographics* (May 1980).

NOW Legal Defense and Education Fund and Renee Cherow O'Leary. *The State-by-State Guide to Women's Legal Rights.* New York: McGraw-Hill, 1987.

O'HARE, WILLIAM P. *America's Welfare Population: Who Gets What?* Washington, D.C.: Population Reference Bureau Inc., 1987.

OLIVER, STEPHANIE STOKES. "The New Choice: Single Motherhood After 30." *Essence,* October, 1983, pp. 131–34.

PAYTON, ISABELLE S. "Single-Parent Households: An Alternative Approach." *Family Economics Review* (Winter 1982): 11–16.

PEARCE, DIANA. "On the Edge: Marginal Women Workers and Employment Policy." In *Ingredients for Women's Employment,* ed. Christine Bose and Glenna Spitz. Albany: State University of New York Press, 1987.

PERIN, CONSTANCE. *Everything in Its Place: Social Order and Land Use in America.* Princeton, N.J.: Princeton University Press, 1977.

PIVEN, FRANCES FOX, and RICHARD A. CLOWARD. *Regulating the Poor.* New York: Pantheon Books, 1971.

——. *Poor People's Movements: Why They Succeed, How They Fail.* New York: Pantheon Books, 1977.

——. "The Contemporary Relief Debate," In *The Mean Season,* ed. Fred Block et al. New York: Pantheon, 1987.

"Playing Both Mother and Father." *Newsweek,* July 15, 1985, pp. 42–43.

POLIKOFF, ALEXANDER. *Housing the Poor: The Case for Heroism.* Cambridge, Mass.: Balinger Press, 1978.

POLIKOFF, NANCY D. "Why Are Mothers Losing: A Brief Analysis of Criteria Used in Child Custody Determinations." *Women's Rights Law Reporter* 7 (Spring 1982): 235–43.

PRICE, FRANCINE. *The Adequacy of the Section 8 Fair Market Rents for the City of Boston.* Report prepared for the Boston Housing Authority, Boston, 1986.

RAINWATER, LEE. *Welfare and Working Mothers.* Family Policy Note 6. Cambridge, Mass.: Joint Center for Urban Studies, 1977.

REICH, CHARLES. "Individual Rights and Social Welfare: The Emerging Legal Issues." *Yale Law Journal* 74 (1965).

REIN, MARTIN, et al. "The Impact of Family Change on Housing Careers." Report prepared for the Department of Housing and Urban Development. Cambridge, Mass.: Joint Center for Urban Studies, 1980.

Report of the New York Task Force on Women in the Courts. Office of Court Administration, New York. *Fordham Urban Law Journal* 15 (1986–1987): 11–198.

ROTHBLUM, ESTHER, and VIOLET FRANKS. "Custom-Fitted Straightjackets: Perspectives on Women's Mental Health." In *The Trapped Woman,* eds. Josefina Figueira-McDonough and Rosemary Sarri. Newbury Park, CA: Sage, 1987.

SACHS, ALBIE, and JOAN HOFF WILSON. *Sexism and the Law: Male Beliefs and Legal Bias.* New York: The Free Press, 1978.

SCHAFRAN, LYNN HECHT. "Documenting Gender Bias in the Courts: The Task Force Approach." *Judicature* 70 (Feb-Mar 1987): 280–90.

SCHAFRAN, LYNN HECHT. "Eve, Mary, Superwoman: How Stereotypes About Women Influence Judges." *Judges' Journal* 24 (Winter 1985): 12–17, 48–53.

SCHARF, LOIS. *To Work and to Wed: Female Employment, Feminism, and the Great Depression.* Westport, Conn.: Greenwood Press, 1980.

SCHULTZ-BROOKS, TERRI. "Single Mothers." *Redbook,* November 1983, p. 87.

SIDEL, RUTH. *Women and Children Last,* New York: Viking Penguin, 1986.

SIMON, WILLIAM H. "Legality, Bureaucracy and Class in the Welfare System." *Yale Law Journal* 92 (1983).

SOSIN, MICHAEL. "Legal Rights and Welfare Change." In *Fighting Poverty: What Works and What Doesn't,* ed. Sheldon Danziger and Daniel Weinberg. Cambridge: Harvard University Press, 1986.

SPARER, EDWARD. "Fundamental Human Rights, Legal Entitlements, and the

Social Struggle: A Friendly Critique of the Critical Legal Studies Movement." *Stanford Law Review* 36 (1984).

―――. "Social Welfare Law Testing." *The Practical Lawyer,* vol. 12, no. 4 (April 1966).

STEGMAN, MICHAEL. "Financing Housing Programs." In *The Unsheltered Woman: Women and Housing in the '80's,* ed. Eugenie Ladner Birch. Piscataway, N.J.: Center for Urban Policy Research, 1985.

STONE, MICHAEL E. "Housing and the Dynamics of U.S. Capitalism." In *Critical Perspectives on Housing,* ed. Rachel Bratt and Chester Hartman. Philadelphia: Temple University Press: 1986.

―――. "Shelter Poverty in Boston: Problem and Program." In *Housing Policies in the Eighties: Choices and Outcomes,* ed. Chester Hartman and Sara Rosenberry. New York: Praeger, 1987.

"Symposium: Judicial Review of Administrative Action in a Conservative Era." *Administrative Law Journal* (Summer 1987).

TAKAS, MARIANNE. *Child Support: A Complete, Up-to-Date Authoritative Guide to Collecting Child Support.* New York: Harper & Row, 1985.

TEN BROEK, JACOBUS. *California's Dual System of Family Law: It's Origin, Development, and Present Status.* Berkeley: University of California, Dept. of Political Science, 1985 (reprint series no. 23).

THOMPSON, EDWARD H. JR., and PATRICIA A. GONGLA. "Single-Parent Families: In the Mainstream of American Society." In *Contemporary Families and Alternative Lifestyles,* ed. Eleanor D. Macklin and Roger H. Rubin. Beverly Hills, Calif.: Sage Publications, 1983.

U.S. Bureau of the Census. "Household After Tax Income: 1985," *Current Population Reports,* series P-23, no. 151. Washington, D.C.: U.S. Government Printing Office, 1987.

―――. "Money Income and Poverty Status of Families and Persons in the United States: 1985," *Current Population Reports,* series P-60, no. 154. Washington, D.C.: U.S. Government Printing Office, 1986.

―――. *Statistical Abstract of the United States.* Washington, D.C.: U.S. Government Printing Office, 1986.

U.S. Catholic Bishops. *Catholic Social Teaching and the U.S. Economy,* 2nd Draft, October 1985.

U.S. Conference of Mayors. *A 29-City Survey: A Status Report on Homeless Families in American Cities.* Washington, D.C., 1987.

U.S. Congress. House. Committee on Ways and Means. *Background Material and Data on Programs Within the Jurisdiction of the Committee on Ways and Means, 1986 Edition.* 99th Cong., 2nd sess., 1986, Committee Print 14.

―――. Committee on Ways and Means. Background Material on Poverty. 98th Cong., 1st sess., 1985, Committee Print 15.

U.S. Congress. Senate. Committee on Finance. *Data and Materials Related to Welfare Programs for Families with Children.* 100th Cong., 1st sess., 1987, Committee Print 20.

U.S. Congressional Budget Office, *The Growth in Poverty: 1979–1985: Economic and Demographic Factors* (Washington, D.C., 1986).

U.S. Department of Commerce, Bureau of the Census. "Economic Characteristics of Households in the United States: Third Quarter, 1983," Average Monthly

Data from the Survey of Income and Program Participation, *Current Population Reports,* series P-70 no. 1 (Washington, D.C.: U.S. Government Printing Office, 1984).

————. "Families Maintained By Female Householders, 1970-79." *Special Studies,* series P-23, no. 107. (Washington, D.C.: U.S. Government Printing Office, 1983).

U.S. News and World Report, "One-Parent Family: The Troubles—and the Joys," November 28, 1983, pp. 57–58.

WALLERSTEIN, JUDITH S., and JOAN BERLIN KELLY. *Surviving the Breakup: How Children and Parents Cope with Divorce.* New York: Basic Books, 1980.

WALSH, FROMA. "Conceptualizations of Normal Family Functioning." In *Normal Family Processes,* ed. Froma Walsh. New York: The Guilford Press, 1982.

WATTENBERG, ESTHER. "Family: One Parent." In *Encyclopedia of Social Work, Volume I,* 18th ed. Silver Spring, Md.: National Association of Social Workers, 1987.

WEISS, ROBERT S. "Growing Up a Little Faster: The Experience of Growing Up in a Single-Parent Household." *Journal of Social Issues* 35 (Fall 1979): 97–111.

————. "The Impacts of Marital Dissolution on Income and Consumption in Single Parent Households." *Journal of Marriage and the Family* (February 1984).

WEITZMAN, LENORE J. *The Divorce Revolution: The Unexpected Social and Economic Consequences for Women and Children in America.* New York: The Free Press, 1985.

WELLER, SHEILA. "Middle Class Murder." *Ms. Magazine,* May 1988, p. 56.

White House Domestic Policy Council Working Group on the Family. "The Family: Preserving America's Future" Washington, D.C.: 1987, mimeo.

WIKLER, NORMA J. "The Economics of Divorce." *Judges' Journal* 25 (Summer 1986): 8–11, 47–50.

————. "On the Judicial Agenda for the 80's: Equal Treatment for Men and Women in the Courts." *Judicature* 64 (November 1980): 202–09.

WILSON, WILLIAM JULIUS, and KATHRYN M. NECKERMAN. "Poverty and Family Structure: The Widening Gap Between Evidence and Public Policy Issues." In *Fighting Poverty: What Works and What Doesn't,* ed. Sheldon H. Danziger and Daniel H. Weinberg. Cambridge, Mass.: Harvard University Press, 1986.

YINGER, JOHN. "State Housing Policy and the Poor." In *The State and the Poor in the 1980s,* ed. Manuel Carballo and Mary Jo Bane. Dover, Mass.: Auburn House, 1984.

INDEX

ABC bill (Act for Better Child Care Services), 211
Abortion, and family policy, 224
Achtenberg, Emily, 244
Affordable housing (*See* Housing, affordable)
Aid to Families with Dependent Children (AFDC), 26, 108–109, 167
  and child custody, 58
  and child support, 50, 107, 108
  and Congress, 179, 182
  conservative attack on, 110–111
  discrimination against, 276
  and discussions on single-parent family, xi
  and divorce rate, 26–27
  duration of dependence on, 109
  vs. employment, 115–117
  fair hearings for, 183–184
  goal of, 275
  and housing affordability, 232–233, 235
  increase in caseload of, 113, 171
  and inflation, 115, 189, 198
  legal structure of, 179–181
  and OBRA, 111–113, 120
  organization by recipients of, 275–276
  reform needed for, 119
  and rent subsidy, 162n.16
  as second-tier welfare, 110
  and Section-8 study searchers, 129, 134, 156
  and single mothers in labor force, 99

spending on, 114
stringent eligibility for, 119
and welfare litigation, 168–169, 176, 181–198 (*See also* Welfare litigation)
Alimony, and court system, 47–50
"Alimony drone," 47–48
American Bar Association, 68
Anderson-Khlief, Susan, 22, 24
Antifeminism, 207
  of Reagan administration, 204, 208, 223
Anti-Snob Zoning Law, 251, 252
Arizona, education right in, 249–250
Armey, Richard, 220
Auxiliary parent, 81–82

Bane, Mary Jo, 15–16, 17–18, 27
Battered women (*See* Domestic violence)
Bias
  against children (housing), 138
  gender, 9, 41–42, 45, 54, 61, 65–67, 70, 278, 287
  against single mothers, 134, 271
Billingsley, Andrew, 76
Biotechnology, and assumptions about family form, 6
Birthrates, teen, 111
Black, Charles L., Jr., 240
Black families
  changes in marital status among, 16, 17–18
  income change for, 117
  single-parent, 3, 15–16
  under slavery, 74

299

and right to housing, 258
Section 8 as, 124 (*See also* Section 8
	Rental Assistance Program)
for single mothers, 26, 262
tenants' rights in, 247, 256
Suburban displacement, 31–32
Suburbs, "opening up" of, 280
"Supermom," 5, 81, 90 (*See also* Role
	burden syndrome)
Supplemental Security Income (SSI),
	26, 99, 168
Supreme Court, U.S.
	and AFDC cases, 168–169, 176,
		181–186
	and entitlement, 174–177
	and right to housing, 244–245
	and sex discrimination, 40
Supreme Court of India, on housing,
	245–246
Surrogate motherhood, 6
Sweden, family-allowance policy in,
	118–119

Tax code reform, 210–211, 225n.5
Teen birthrates, 111
Tellis v. *Bombay*, 245
Tenement Act (New York) (1901), 242
Tenement Housing Act (1867), 242
"Thirty and a third" rule, 111, 112
Title VII, Civil Rights Act of *1964,* 205
Title IX, Education Amendments of
	1972, 205, 210
Title XX, 105, 117, 120
Titular parent, 84
Transfer payments, 26–27
Transitional points, in life of family,
	88–90
Transportation
	and housing search, 138
	importance of, 274
	and rural "other court," 63
	and Section 8 searchers, 144, 145,
		148–149
Two-sector labor market (*See* Dual
	labor market)
Two-sector (dual) welfare system, 110

Unemployment

and child support enforcement, 216
of former husbands in Section 8
	study, 129
rates of for single mothers, 104
Unemployment compensation, and
	dual welfare system, 110
Unions, and female workers, 119
Universal Declaration of Human
	Rights, on housing, 238–239
Unrelated substitute parent, 83–84
Up to the Poverty Level campaign,
	188, 189, 192, 197

Vermont study on divorce settlements,
	46, 56
Victim blaming, for domestic violence,
	60
Violence, domestic (*See* Domestic
	violence)
Visitation interference, and child
	support enforcement, 55

Wagner-Steagall Act (1937), 242–243
Waldorf, Frank, 238
Walsh, Froma, 77
Weiss, Robert S., 19–20, 91
Welfare assistance, public, 108–117,
	167–168 (*See also* Aid to Families
	with Dependent Children)
and divorce, 54
dual system of, 110
and father's leaving, 87
in income support package, 26–27
and labor market, 114–115
real crisis in, 113–117
single mothers' experience of, 95
and single-mother myths, 4
and single mothers in labor force, 99
Welfare litigation, 168, 198–199
case study in (Massachusetts), 187–
	198
and court role as ambivalent, 182–
	185
and entitlement, 172–174, 183
and "fair procedures," 174–175,
	182–185
and "Federalization" of eligibility,
	179–182